Press Gallery

Press Gallery

—

CONGRESS AND THE WASHINGTON CORRESPONDENTS

Donald A. Ritchie

HARVARD UNIVERSITY PRESS
Cambridge, Massachusetts
London, England
1991

This book is printed on acid-free paper, and its binding materials have
been chosen for strength and durability.

Library of Congress Cataloging-in-Publication Data

Ritchie, Donald A., 1945-
    Press gallery: Congress and the Washington correspondents /
Donald A. Ritchie
        p.   cm.
    Includes bibliographical references and index.
    ISBN 0–674–70375–8
    1. Journalists—Washington (D.C.)—History   2. United States.
Congress—Reporters and reporting—History.   3. Press and politics—
Washington (D.C.)—History.   4. Washington (D.C.)—Politics and
government—1878–1967.   I. Title.
PN4899.W3R58   1991
070'.92'273—dc20   90–43676
                    CIP

*For Horace Samuel Merrill
and Marion Galbraith Merrill*

Acknowledgments

IN PURSUING the history of Washington correspondents, I have benefited from almost daily contact with the press at the United States Capitol. Routinely, members of the media contact the Senate Historical Office in search of some precedent, the source of a quote, a statistic, or other historical information. In trying to meet these requests, I became aware of the pressures on reporters' time, their need for quick, useful information, their probing and sometimes leading questions, their impatience with overly qualified responses, and their dependence upon oral rather than written sources. My personal observations of current reporters raised questions about how their predecessors worked, and suggested some answers. Reporters' patterns of behavior, like the press galleries they occupy, are well established and have a long, documentable history.

Through conversations with reporters I have enjoyed a running seminar on congressional reporting. Bob Barr of *U.S. News and World Report,* Neil MacNeil of *Time,* Phil Jones of CBS News, Susan Rasky and the photographer George Tames of the *New York Times,* and countless other journalists have guided me through the idiosyncrasies of Capitol Hill. One reporter pointed out how the House had ejected reporters on the day after it passed the First Amendment, laughing at what this action said about the precarious, contradictory relationship between Congress and the press. On a memorable occasion, I escorted Joseph Alsop on a visit to the Senate Press Gallery, where I heard him lament the working conditions, with desks cramped together, rabbit-warren style, no longer the comfortable quarters he remembered from the 1930s. Suddenly, he burst through the swinging doors into the gallery overlooking the chamber and peered down upon a solitary senator reading a speech. "Who is that?" Alsop said in a voice loud enough to turn heads. When told the senator's name, he replied in astonishment, "I've never heard of him!" Perhaps the most telling commentary on the modern status of the press versus the politicians, came from a college intern at the historical office who positioned herself within a roped-off press area at the Capitol to catch a glimpse of President Jimmy Carter. Had she seen the President of the United States? I asked later. "Oh, yes," she replied. "But I stood next to Roger Mudd!"

Many friends and colleagues offered suggestions, criticism, and support for this book. I owe deep-felt thanks to Richard Allen Baker, whose direction of the Senate Historical Office stimulated and sustained my research, and whose discerning scholarship has enriched my understanding of the legislative branch. Over the years, I have received abundant assistance from the Senate Library, an unparalleled resource collection of materials by and about the U.S. Senate. Roger Haley, Ann Womeldorf, Greg Harness, Thea Koehler, Tom McCray, and everyone else on the library staff helped me uncover a wealth of information on seemingly obscure newspaper correspondents from the past. Significant help also came from the staffs of the Manuscript Division of the Library of Congress and the Center for Legislative Archives at the National Archives.

My thanks go to many individuals who contributed to this project, especially James L. Baughman, Terry L. Birdwhistell, Diane Boyle, G. Cullom Davis, Jean Folkerts, John Fox, Carol J. Frost, Richard Fyffe, Bob Goshen, Sally Griffith, John Hamilton, Gary Hoag, Kathryn A. Jacob, Charles E. Kern II, Samuel Kernell, James R. Ketchum, Harry Liebersohn, Richard L. McCormick, John Odell, Grace Palladino, Beverly Palmer, Karen Paul, Bruce Ragsdale, Dorothee Schneider, Constance Schultz, Diane Skvarla, Raymond Smock, Mark Summers, Barbara Vandergrift, Bill Wears, and David Wigdor. James Free granted me access to the historical records of the Gridiron Club, and Bob Petersen opened the minutes of the Standing Committee of Correspondents. Susan Oulahan Bishop and Courts Oulahan read and commented helpfully on the chapter about their father. Their donation of his memoirs and papers to the Herbert Hoover Library made that chapter possible.

I was fortunate to have had the opportunity to test the themes of this study at several forums. I drew from the manuscript to deliver the fourteenth annual Letitia Woods Brown memorial lecture at the Conference on Washington, D.C., Historical Studies. Maureen Beasley invited me to speak about the evolution of press ethics at a meeting in the National Press Club, where Sarah McClendon offered sharp questioning and commentary. I also read papers at the Smithsonian Institution's Nineteenth Century Seminar, led by Nathan Reingold; at the Center for Anthro-Journalism, headed by Randolph Fillmore; at the George Washington University history seminar, directed by Edward Berkowitz; and at meetings of the Organization of American Historians and the Society for History in the Federal Government. One of these papers was published as " 'The Loyalty of the Senate': Washington Correspondents in the Progressive Era," in the *Historian* (August 1989), and received the James Madison Prize from the Society for History in the Federal Government.

I am especially indebted to James Sayler, of the Congressional Research Service, for sharing insights from his work on a biography of Arthur Krock, and for convening a long-running, freewheeling monthly historical reading group whose members—John Carland, Ronald Gebhardt, Gerald Gewalt, John Haynes, David Kepley, Marvin Kranz, Mark Lowenthal, R. David Myers, and Gene Smith—reviewed various chapters with good humor and good sense.

Support at home from my wife, Anne Ritchie, and my stepdaughters, Jennifer and Andrea Campbell, made my labors all the more tolerable. Encouragement came as always from my parents, Arthur and Jeannette Ritchie. This book is dedicated to Sam and Marion Merrill, who have always cared as much for the well-being of their students as for the history we write.

Contents

Illustrations

In the Press Gallery we sit at the
top of the world and the kingdoms
of earth are at our feet.

—*Louis Ludlow*

Introduction

"CERTAIN RULES OF HYGIENE," Walter Lippmann once commented, require newspaper reporters to maintain their distance in dealing with government officials. "I wouldn't say a wall or a fence," he elaborated, "but an air space, that's very necessary." Journalists generally honor Lippmann's rule in principle while violating it in practice, the air space being too easily deflated. Close personal relationships have long flourished between politicians and the press, tempting reporters to become participants as well as observers. In one celebrated incident, Lippmann himself helped draft the speech in which Senator Arthur Vandenberg announced his conversion to internationalism and then praised the address in his columns. Edward R. Murrow secretly coached Adlai Stevenson on his television campaign appearances; George F. Will similarly prepared Ronald Reagan for a televised presidential debate and then acclaimed the candidate's performance in his own post-debate commentary. At the White House and on Capitol Hill, reporters exchange jobs with press secretaries in a revolving arrangement, while editorial opinion pages devote conspicuous space to the syndicated columns of former officeholders. The list proceeds at such length as to suggest that distance is a false standard.[1]

The historical relationship between press and politicians in Washington has been far more intimate than adversarial. A "symbiotic" partnership has existed, alternately described as a state of mutual benefit or mutual seduction. From one perspective, intimacy runs contrary to objective reporting, because it undermines a journalist's disinterestedness. But the recurrence of intimacy indicates an unavoidable pattern of behavior. Reporting at the high-

1

est levels of government has always required the highest level of sources, and cultivation of those sources has promoted closeness between reporters and their subjects. In American journalism, this pattern is as old as colonial newspapers published "by authority." Its roots were planted in the newspaper patronage that Thomas Jefferson and Alexander Hamilton disbursed in the first cabinet, in the "official organs" of pre–Civil War presidential administrations, and in the abundance of journalists who ran for office or accepted a government sinecure.[2]

Journalism history has generally focused on relations between the press and the presidency. Identified with a single leader, and at least attempting to speak with a single voice, a presidential administration makes a more manageable subject for both reporters and historians. Yet for the press, the White House has presented a more closed and controlled working environment than has the Congress. Capitol Hill has provided a more fairly contested battle-ground, more open, more chaotic, more comfortable for the reporter, and more favorable to close relations between the estates. For a century and a half, Congress rather than the presidency sat at the epicenter of Washington journalism.

In 1932, Washington correspondent Paul Anderson identified the United States Senate as "the choicest assignment of the Washington correspondent," and found the White House "devoid of allurements to all except chess players and gentlemen in need of sleep." In 1987, political columnist David Broder pronounced Congress "the worst-reported part of our government." By then, no matter how avidly senators and representatives courted the press, or how open the legislative process, the Washington press corps fixed its gaze upon the presidency, and ambitious reporters coveted the White House beat. During the half century between those assessments, the emergence of a dramatically expanded executive branch and the predominance of radio and television reporting shifted the center of Washington news from Capitol Hill to the White House. Through sophisticated manipulation, presidential media advisers further tipped the balance. As one press secretary cautioned White House reporters, "You don't tell us how to stage the news, and we won't tell you how to cover it."[3]

Patterns of Washington reporting since 1932 have obscured the earlier era when Congress rather than the president held the advantage in press relations. Throughout the nineteenth century, the White House remained such a poor news source that no newspaper bothered to station reporters there. Reporters simply dropped by at random to collect information as needed or, lacking any official press room inside, stood outside the North Portico to interview presidential visitors. The correspondents could be found instead at the Senate and House press galleries, where they gathered daily to view the proceedings, collect and swap news, and write and telegraph their dispatches to their papers.

This book offers a gallery of press portraits, individuals who represented some significant aspect of Washington reporting during the nineteenth and early twentieth centuries. It follows news-gathering from the era when political editors Joseph Gales and William Seaton produced their quasi-official paper, the *National Intelligencer.* These first congressional journalists acted primarily as reporters of debate, who summarized the floor proceedings and transcribed the more important speeches. Newspapers outside the capital clipped and reprinted their material as it suited their needs. By the 1820s, with the proliferation of both rural weeklies and metropolitan dailies, editors from out-of-town papers appeared in the Capitol to report from the galleries, to buttonhole members in the lobbies, and from time to time to stand for election to Congress themselves. When congressional reporting required full-time attention, editors like Horace Greeley hired letter-writing correspondents ("mercenaries," as more than one senator labeled them) to spend a session in Washington. In steadily growing numbers throughout the 1840s and 1850s, they sat in the galleries to prepare commentary for whatever papers could afford their services.[4]

By the time of the Civil War an identifiable press corps had settled in Washington. Colorful, talented, opinionated, self-styled Bohemians, the Washington correspondents numbered among their ranks crusaders, lobbyists, politicos, and novelists. The almost exclusively white, male, middle-class, college-educated band of correspondents clustered together in the congressional press galleries and in bureaus along Washington's Newspaper Row, where they alternately competed and collaborated with one another. Although seeking to scoop the pack, individual reporters regularly pooled efforts, covered for absent colleagues, and fought political harassment, all of which created a sense of fraternity.

From their collective experiences a Washington press ethic evolved. Among the Civil War era correspondents, Horace White of the *Chicago Tribune* mixed journalism with speculation, while Ben: Perley Poore of the *Boston Journal* depended upon patronage from the politicians he covered. Although better paid than most newspaper reporters, mid-nineteenth-century Washington correspondents collected salaries from their papers only for the months that Congress met. During the extended congressional recesses, sometimes lasting half the year, a skeleton crew of reporters remained in the capital to cover the bureaucracy. The rest returned to their papers to take less desirable assignments or scrambled for other sources of income. Responding to their plight, obliging members of Congress hired the reporters as their secretaries and committee clerks, expecting favorable publicity in return.

More subtle influences were also at work. Washington correspondents were only as good as their sources, the more prominent the better. Inside sources became all the more critical at a time when the federal government conducted so much of its official business in secret. Although its doors stood wider open than at the executive and judicial branches, the legislature was often closed to the press. Throughout the nineteenth century, the Senate routinely debated treaties and nominations in secret. House and Senate committees regularly convened in executive session, beyond public scrutiny. Close relationships with politicians cultivated access to the secrets of closed sessions and other leads that satisfied one's editors. Understanding such needs enabled shrewd politicians, particularly those with a background in journalism like James G. Blaine, to manipulate the press into promoting their careers. Persistent leaks of secret information also strained relations between Congress and the press, leading to periodic investigations and the symbolic dismissal of James Rankin Young, the newspaper correspondent who served as the Senate's executive clerk. On the reverse side of the arrangement, reporters suppressed much news given to them in confidence, in order to maintain close relations with their government sources.

The unregulated behavior of Washington journalists permitted lobbying, the sale of news, and collection of patronage to thrive within their ranks. The involvement of the *Philadelphia Inquirer*'s Washington correspondent Uriah Hunt Painter in nearly every lobbying scandal of the Gilded Age stirred calls for reform. Led by

Henry Van Ness Boynton of the *Cincinnati Gazette,* correspondents struggled to define more carefully the practices they considered illegitimate and to instill a deeper sense of professionalism in the Washington press corps as a whole. Formally, they created the Standing Committee of Correspondents to enforce specific rules for membership in the press galleries, while informal and unwritten rules set further limits on reporters' behavior. Designed to bar lobbyists, the new rules also exiled from the press galleries all women journalists, who like Emily Briggs blended social and political reporting.

Each adjustment to the formal and informal rules advanced better relations with the political establishment but also allowed an intimacy to develop with those politicians who bothered to learn the rules. Reporting the news, however, remained a competitive business, whether between individual journalists or entire forms of news media. Any mutually agreed upon rules of the trade prevailed only until upset by competition from new media entities, a pattern repeated from the telegraph, with which Ben: Perley Poore grappled, to the muckraking magazines that newspaper correspondent David Barry denounced. Richard Oulahan, who spanned the generations from the Bohemians to the modern professionals, in his last years confronted news broadcast over the radio. Meeting these new challenges, and adapting to them, regularly prodded the Washington press corps toward improved professional behavior and ethics and compelled public officials to devise alternative means to shape the news.

Like the public, historians rely upon the press for information without much awareness of who collected it. Scholarly studies have tended to focus on editors and publishers rather than reporters, partly because editors were better-known public figures, and partly because reporters so rarely left personal papers—other than their own press clippings—for research. With few exceptions, nineteenth-century correspondents never signed their names to their articles, leading scholars to cite newspaper sources generically. But anonymity should not be mistaken for neutrality. Correspondents brought countless perspectives to Washington reporting, biased by personal background, ambition, party affiliation, demanding editors, and the exigency of sources. When and how Washington correspondents shifted from overtly partisan to more objective reporting, how their working patterns affected their reporting, what official and unofficial rules they established as a profession, why they developed alliances with public officeholders, how politicians attempted to influence them, and what effect political pressures had in shaping the newspaper accounts that finally reached the public are the themes of these press gallery portraits.

1

Gales and Seaton

THE DAY AFTER the House of Representatives approved the First Amendment to the Constitution, protecting the freedom of the press, it debated barring reporters from the House floor. Angry representatives charged reporters with distorting their arguments, mutilating their words, and "throwing over the whole proceedings a thick veil of misrepresentation and error." Since the targets of their fury were primarily stenographers who recorded the debates of the First Congress for a handful of newspapers, the House considered hiring its own impartial reporters of debate. But Representative James Madison reminded members that official reporting would burden each of them with the ceaseless task of correcting and revising his own remarks. The debate ended unresolved, but the reporters, who had strategically retreated to the galleries, found that House doorkeepers barred their way back to the floor.[1]

Congressional hostility toward press coverage of debates reflected dramatic tensions within the early republic. The representatives of the people accepted the concept of a free press but had trouble distinguishing between press freedom and licentiousness, particularly when press attacks were aimed at themselves. Members of Congress felt torn between their desire for newspaper coverage and their inability to control the substance of the reporting. Newspapers informed constituents of news from Washington and provided Congress with current news from home. Newspapers rallied political parties and kept political names before the voting public. Newspapers established reputations but could also destroy them. The same congressmen who professed to ignore press criticism regularly sought to refute some unpardonable attack in the papers. More than one declared himself the most misrepresented man in public life.[2]

Members of Congress decried newspaper libels on their good names and virtue at the same time they subsidized official party papers, fed information to favorite editors, rewarded journalists financially, and goaded them into attacks on the opposition. Even as they lamented the "demon" of party spirit, congressmen used newspapers to bolster party organization and discipline. It had been from Congress that America's first political party system emerged. Congressional caucuses chose presidential candidates, set party agendas, and anointed the party press with patronage. As parties developed, the federal government embraced the "official organ"—the single newspaper that could speak authoritatively for the incumbent administration and its allies in Congress. This mutual dependency benefited both the politicians and the press during the era from the Federalists to the Jacksonians. The most successful of these official papers, the *National Intelligencer,* developed national influence, served a succession of Republican presidents, and reported the congressional debates, while Congress rewarded its editors, Joseph Gales and William Seaton, by electing them official printers of the Senate and House. The *Intelligencer's* supremacy lasted as long as did the relatively centralized, Washington-based party system.[3]

Congress and the press defined the requirements of their relationship as it unfolded. Simply opening congressional proceedings to the press required conscious political decisions. Having met in secret themselves, the framers of the Constitution imposed no obligation on Congress to conduct their sessions under public scrutiny. The Constitution required only that each house publish a journal. As the sole federal officers directly elected by the people, members of the House of Representatives found it expedient to open their doors and keep their constituents informed. Worried that a divisive press might splinter both public opinion and the nation, Vice President John Adams judged this a risky experiment. "Making the debates public will establish the National Government or break the Confederation," Adams fretted. "I can conceive of no medium between these extremes."[4]

The House at first provided space for a handful of newspaper reporters at the foot of the Speaker's chair, but even from this vantage they had difficulty hearing during boisterous debates. Since shorthand was an inexact process, reporters summarized what they heard, rather than record verbatim. Some proved less than diligent, and at least one had a drinking problem that impaired his faculties. Mistakes appeared in such profusion as to raise suspicions of political motivation.[5]

A more distrustful mood prevailed in the Senate. Senators believed that they could work more effectively away from public scrutiny, without the temptation of addressing a public gallery, and that some legislative foibles "had better be concealed from observation." Secrecy suited the Federalist concept of government by an educated elite, insulated from the sway of the masses. Federalist senators confidently predicted that they could achieve more through private correspondence than through newspapers. Beyond ideology, architecture contributed to the closed doors, since the Senate chambers in neither New York nor Philadelphia were equipped with public galleries.[6]

The Federalist majority in Congress perceived newspapers as instruments of potential social unrest and civil strife, while the Republican minority saw the press as a powerful weapon against the incumbent majority. To Republicans, the preservation of liberty against the central government required that citizens know what their representatives were saying and doing in their name. The Republican press therefore bore special obligation to provide news of congressional debates and other federal activities. Employing newspapers, circular letters, handbills, and any other means of communication within their means, Republicans sought public attention. In the Senate, they led the movement for open sessions. In the House, they defended the rights of reporters and fought restrictions on the press.[7]

Republican newspapers railed against Senate secrecy. "Are you freemen who ought to know the individual conduct of your legislators," editor Philip Freneau challenged readers of the *National Gazette*, "or are you an inferior order of beings incapable of comprehending the sublimity of Senatorial functions, and unworthy to be entrusted with their opinions?" The longer the Senate's doors remained closed the more suspicion they generated. In 1794, when Federalists questioned the credentials of Republican Senator-elect Albert Gallatin, they feared that a secret debate might raise accusations of a Star Chamber proceeding. They agreed to open this one debate to the public, but the doors never completely shut. The Senate ordered construction of a gallery, which it opened in December, 1794—for legislative debates. All treaties and nominations continued to be debated in secret until the twentieth century.[8]

A fickle press showed little interest in the Senate's open sessions. Freneau's *National Gazette* closed down before it could cover the Senate. The *Philadelphia Aurora* sent a reporter to the Senate gallery but found the show too staid. Newspapers admired the dignity of the senators but devoted more space to the rambunctious House. "Henceforth you will read little of me in the Gazettes," one representative advised his wife after his election to the Senate in 1804. "Senators are less exposed to public view than Representatives."[9]

Congressional Federalists compiled a contradictory record in their treatment of the press. They empowered the government to pay selected newspapers to publish the laws and to set lower postal rates for the press, and they permitted publishers to mail free copies of their journals to other newspapers, a practice that enabled small rural papers to reprint news from the metropolitan press. The same Federalists sponsored the Alien and Sedition Acts, making it a crime to criticize either house of Congress or any other branch of government. Benjamin Franklin Bache, grandson of Benjamin Franklin and editor of the *Aurora*, predicted that "to laugh at the cut of a coat of a member of Congress will soon be treason." In truth, almost any provocation sufficed to put Bache and other Republican editors under indictment.[10]

After Bache died in a yellow fever epidemic, William Duane inherited both the editorship of the *Aurora* and its Federalist enemies. It was to Duane that three Republican senators turned in February 1800 to leak the text of a bill to alter the means of deciding disputed presidential electors, a Federalist plan designed to defeat Thomas Jefferson's candidacy. The *Aurora* published the bill along with scathing editorials, a breach of Senate secrecy that triggered the first congressional investigation of the press, the first forcible detention of a journalist by Congress, and the first citation for contempt of Congress.[11]

"Public bodies are public property; and so indeed are public men," protested Republican Senator Charles Pinckney of South Carolina. "Men who engage in public life, or are members of legislative bodies, must expect to be exposed to anonymous, and sometimes avowed, attacks on their principles and opinions." Not so, rebutted the Connecticut Federalist Uriah Tracy, who argued that if the Senate could punish its own members for attacking each other within the chamber, "it follows of course that we are not to be slandered and questioned elsewhere."[12]

Federalists transparently intended the Duane investigation to embarrass Vice President Jefferson. They hauled the editor before the bar of the Senate and directed the vice president, as presiding officer, to question him about who had leaked the bill. On the advice of Republican senators, Duane asked for time to consult with counsel, which Jefferson readily granted. Once free of the Senate chamber, Duane never returned. In his absence, the Senate voted him in contempt, but was otherwise powerless to act. "Very little Exertion was made to discover & arrest him," Senator William Bingham complained, noting that Duane reappeared as soon as the Senate adjourned, to claim the role of "persecuted Patriot & Martyr to the Liberty of the Press."[13]

In the spring of 1800, as government clerks packed their records for the move from Philadelphia to Washington, both Federalists and Republicans made plans to establish official newspapers in the new capital on the Potomac. Anticipation of printing contracts lured an array of editors into the wilderness. That September, a group of Federalist congressmen and Georgetown merchants prompted John Stewart to launch the *Washington Federalist*. On the Republican side, among other editors, William Duane prepared to publish a Washington edition of the *Aurora*. For his past services, the much-persecuted Duane had reason to expect official blessing for his paper, but Thomas Jefferson had in mind a more temperate editor. At his urging, and with the support of leading Republicans in Congress, Philadelphia editor Samuel Harrison Smith ventured to the new capital. Late in October, delayed by the slow arrival of his printing presses, Smith published the first edition of a new triweekly paper, the *National Intelligencer*. This late entry into the crowded field soon eclipsed the rest of the pack.[14]

That fall, voters repudiated the Federalist party. "The newspapers are an overmatch for any government," bemoaned Federalist Representative Fisher Ames. "They will first overawe and then usurp it." Although the Federalists had lost their majorities in both the Senate and House, they retained control for the remaining four months of the lame-duck session, which convened in the unfinished Capitol Building on a snowy November day in 1800.

Samuel Smith of the *Intelligencer* and John Stewart of the *Federalist* were on hand to cover its debates, and the two reporters petitioned for a place on the House floor. Federalist Speaker Theodore Sedgwick cast a tie-breaking vote against them, on the grounds that their presence would destroy the dignity of the chamber and inconvenience its members. When the *Intelligencer* challenged the Speaker's ruling, Sedgwick ordered editor Smith banned from the House lobby and galleries.[15]

The inauguration of Thomas Jefferson, together with new Republican majorities in Congress, vastly improved Samuel Smith's fortunes. The House welcomed him back, and in January 1802 voted forty-seven to twenty-eight to find room on the floor for the reporters. The Senate, which had also relegated reporters to the galleries, followed suit and accepted Smith's petition for a floor seat. Senator Gouvernor Morris, a Pennsylvania Federalist, happened to deliver an attack on Jefferson's judicial policies that day and found himself among the first to have his speech recorded under the new arrangement. In his diary, an unhappy Morris labeled it "the beginning of mischief."[16]

Ownership of the administration's official paper in a new capital city that lacked an established press for competition assured its editor's prosperity. Samuel Smith personally reported the congressional debates, published his paper, printed the public laws, and became a leader of Washington society. Eventually, the pressures of these multiple roles began to weigh upon him, and with Jefferson's second term as president moving toward an end Smith resolved to abandon journalism for a more genteel life. He advertised his willingness to sell the paper "to a person of sound republican principles." More than simply a party loyalist, Smith sought a thoroughly Jeffersonian journalist who would scorn aristocratic tendencies, venerate self-government, and defend legislative supremacy against executive encroachment. Yet this ideology had its inconsistencies. Although Smith and other Republican leaders rejected the Federalist concept of inherent social differences among men, they were hardly commoners. They praised the yeoman farmer while adopting the life of the country gentry. They agonized over, but profited from, human slavery. Such contradictions blended into the pages of the *National Intelligencer.*[17]

Smith's advertisement attracted a proposal from a former associate, Joseph Gales, Sr. In 1797, Gales had sold Smith his weekly newspaper, the *Independent Gazette*, before moving to North Carolina to publish the *Raleigh Register* (to escape Philadelphia's recurring yellow fever epidemics and perhaps also the Alien and Sedition Acts). A decade later, Gales proposed to acquire the *Intelligencer* not for himself but for his son, Joseph, Jr. The boy had been expelled from the state university for a breach of discipline and for being "loose in his manners," and had returned to work at the family paper. The senior Gales worried that too much of the "easy life of home" would cause his son to "fall into inertness" and sent him to Philadelphia as an apprentice printer. Since his son still lacked seasoning, Gales persuaded Smith to hire him on a trial basis, before selling the paper. There began a period of studious grooming of the prospective editor. Smith took him into his office; the father arrived to spend a session of Congress personally training him in stenography; and Smith's wife, Margaret, labored—ineffectually, she feared—to "soften & polish his manners."[18]

Two years later, Samuel Smith retired, having deemed the twenty-four-year old Joseph Gales, Jr., ready to assume the editorship. Young Gales operated the *National Intelligencer* single-handedly until 1812, when in anticipation of converting it from a tri-weekly to a daily he took as a partner his brother-in-law, William W. Seaton. For fifty years the partnership of Gales and Seaton would preserve the Republican principles of their paper's founder. By the time they relinquished the paper's helm in the 1860s, one commentator declared that their careers embraced "the secrets of Cabinets, the scenes and subjects of Congress and of the Supreme Court, the tenants of the White House, the cycles of parties and of public opinions, and all the tones of the social circles since 1800."[19]

Gales and Seaton resembled each other only in their politics. Tall, well-built William Seaton towered over the diminutive Joseph Gales. Like Gales, Seaton had entered journalism as a youth. He had worked for Thomas Ritchie's *Virginia Patriot* at seventeen and later edited the *Petersburg Republican* and *North Carolina Journal*. In 1809, Seaton married Sarah Gales and joined her family's paper in Raleigh. Although a year older than his brother-in-law, Seaton became the junior partner on the *Intelligencer*. With time their friendship and family ties matured into a close bond, a "oneness and identity of all purposes, opinions, and interests." During their half century of partnership, they claimed never to have bickered or to have had an unreconcilable difference of opinion.[20]

Joseph Gales, Jr.

W. W. Seaton

Published by C.H. BRAINARD, Boston 1855

William W. Seaton.

As businessmen, Gales and Seaton started with the advantage of a financially sound paper that already dominated Washington reporting. Like Samuel Smith, they recorded the debates of Congress at their own expense, although the Republican majorities in the Senate and House bestowed on them sufficient public printing to subsidize their reporting. The opposition *Washington Federalist* struggled haplessly without federal support. At times, the *Federalist* lifted speeches directly out of the *National Intelligencer,* partly to cover its inadequacies, and partly to satisfy the wishes of congressmen who preferred the *Intelligencer*'s version. Some Republican members flatly refused to cooperate with an opposition paper, neither providing them with copies of their speeches nor editing their notes. But occasionally party spirit worked in reverse. Republican Representative John Bacon once allowed the *Federalist* to print a speech he withheld from the *Intelligencer.* Its publication might have caused divisions within his own party's ranks, but he saw no harm in the speech appearing in the opposition paper, since "all the readers of that paper were of the same opinion before."[21]

At first, congressmen felt the need to read papers from both political parties for the fullest accounts of their debates. Senators voted themselves free subscriptions to three papers of their choice. Of the thirty-two senators in December 1801, twenty-three requested the *Intelligencer,* twenty the *Federalist,* and thirteen took both. By 1803, as the Republican majority grew, twenty-seven senators read the *Intelligencer,* while Senate subscriptions to the *Federalist* dropped to eight. The next year, the *Federalist* fell into such an embarrassed financial state that its editor determined to sell the paper, sending Federalists in a scramble to find another editor to promote their party.[22]

The *Federalist* offered an alternative source of Washington reporting for the Federalist press outside Washington, which even after 1800 still outnumbered Republican papers. During the raucous national debate over Jefferson's embargo in 1808, the *United States Gazette,* a Philadelphia Federalist paper, denounced the *National Intelligencer*'s Jeffersonian bias and announced that its own reporter would cover the debates in Congress, in order to obtain "*more full and correct information.*" In fact, the *Gazette*'s "correspondent at Washington" was the editor of the *Federalist.* At the same time, the *Philadelphia Freeman's Journal* published letters from a Washington correspondent signed "Ariel," the pen name of Federalist Representative James Elliot. Neither arrangement lasted long. By 1809 the representative had been defeated and the Washington *Federalist* was defunct.[23]

As the Federalist party and press crumbled, the *Intelligencer* firmly established its reputation as the most reliable reporter of congressional debates, accurate source of news from the White House, and faithful exponent of Republican principles. The nation entered an era of one-party rule that centered political authority in Washington, where the *National Intelligencer* held a monopoly on the news. Urban dailies and rural weeklies around the nation clipped congressional proceedings and other federal news from the *Intelligencer*, until the paper could boast that some six hundred papers were reprinting its reports. Despite these statistics, Gales and Seaton expressed dismay over the limited coverage of debates in other papers. "It has given us some pain," they reported, "for more important reasons than that our labors are thrown away, or undervalued, to find, that so small a portion of the debates of Congress find their way into the newspapers dispersed over the country."[24]

Taking pride in their role as recorders of debates, Gales and Seaton reaped more tangible rewards in the form of government contracts. Congress was exceedingly generous to the paper, particularly to compensate for the damages that the *Intelligencer* suffered in 1814, when invading British troops sacked and burned its offices. House Speaker Henry Clay engineered passage of a bill by which Congress would elect official printers at each session. The arrangement favored Gales and Seaton, who from 1819 until 1827 repeatedly won election as printers for both the Senate and House. Freed from having to bid against other local printers, the *Intelligencer* constructed the largest print shop in Washington, employed over a hundred people, and operated a dozen presses around the clock.[25]

Patronage as official printers indirectly reimbursed Gales and Seaton for their coverage of Congress. William Seaton often personally reported debates in the House, while Joseph Gales handled the Senate. Members genuinely liked the two men, and even invited them to dip snuff from the official snuff boxes. Still, while generally approving of the *Intelligencer*'s editors and their reporting, undercurrents of dissatisfaction rippled through Congress. In

1814, one representative led an unsuccessful campaign to require congressional reporters to take an oath. And in 1820, another proposed that reporters swear they would report the debates "without addition, diminution, or alteration."[26]

Despite the *Intelligencer*'s goals of accuracy and impartiality, its hired reporters showed occasional favoritism and incompetence. Once a reporter dozed off during one speech, awoke during another, and recorded both as the same. John Randolph of Virginia frequently tangled with the *Intelligencer*, once complaining that its reporter had substituted the word "Irish" for "slave" in his speech, and demanding revision of House rules to prevent further distortions. Gales and Seaton snapped back that Randolph had himself to blame for not correcting and returning the reporter's notes. Other journalists in the gallery cited Randolph's convoluted speaking style. "His remarks are filled with parentheses and inversions," wrote a visiting editor, "while the abruptness with which he flies off from one subject to another, renders the difficulty in following him very great." Members of the House rallied behind Gales and Seaton, who "corrected more errors than they made blunders." Because Randolph spoke extemporaneously, he became carried along by the passion of the moment and could not restrain his tongue. "The truth is, that after the occasion passes away, I can seldom recall what I said until I am put in mind, by what I did not say," Randolph privately admitted. He convinced himself that he could not have uttered such nonsense and denied the accuracy of press reports of his speeches. His criticism stung Joseph Gales, while Mrs. Seaton privately labeled congressional reporting a thankless task and doubted whether printing the debates was worth the "querulous carping and fault-finding from dissatisfied members."[27]

Far greater challenges faced Gales and Seaton during the 1820s, as the old Jeffersonian political coalition that had employed them for so long began to collapse. The centrifugal forces of sectionalism, economics, religion, and technology fragmented national politics. No longer would congressional caucuses select presidential candidates. On the state level emerged new party organizations, rallying less around Republican principle than patronage, and appealing as much to voters' religious and cultural impulses as to national issues debated in Congress. Party conventions outside the capital would nominate strong regional presidential candidates and expand political leadership well beyond any elite band of Republican gentry.[28]

The same forces that dethroned "King Caucus" toppled Gales and Seaton. For years the editors had been linked intimately with the Republican establishment that ruled national politics. They figured prominently in Washington's small permanent social elite, operating in close proximity with the city's transient political population, whether at the Senate and House chambers, at evening receptions, or at Sunday sermons. In 1821, Gales and Seaton were recorded among the charter members of Washington's First Unitarian Church, along with Secretary of State John Quincy Adams and Secretary of War John C. Calhoun, but as the decade progressed the congregants went their separate political ways. As presidential hopefuls, each considered it essential to have his own official paper in the capital. Calhoun counted on the *Washington Republic*, while the *National Journal* promoted Adams. Having served as the organ of the Jefferson, Madison, and Monroe administrations, the *Intelligencer* reserved its endorsement for the congressional caucus's candidate, Treasury Secretary William H. Crawford—until severe illness debilitated Crawford and undermined his candidacy.[29]

For Gales and Seaton the new presidential politics inverted the Republican system. It elevated the presidency—"the Third power in the government"—and subordinated Congress and the judiciary. "We cannot conceive, under our government, an evil more to be deprecated than this." The editors eventually made their peace with the victor, John Quincy Adams, although his administration deprived them of its public printing.[30]

The *National Intelligencer* faced an even greater threat in Adams's rival, Andrew Jackson. The editors perceived General Jackson as far too impetuous, arbitrary, and military-minded to be president, and saw the mass political party emerging around him as the death knell of the Republican coalition. They identified New York's Senator Martin Van Buren as the "arch intriguer" behind this party building. Although General Jackson had no official paper in Washington, Van Buren was orchestrating press support for his candidacy. Most unsubtly in 1827, Van Buren proposed reforming the allotment of public printing. Alarmed, the *Intelligencer*'s editors denounced the proposal as an effort to "control the press here by means of the printing of the Senate."[31]

Jackson's victory in 1828 realized the editors' worst fears. Gales and Seaton watched the capital fill with editors hungry for the spoils. ("The *Typographical* Corps is assembled with great force," Senator Daniel Webster commented dryly.) President Jackson wanted no part of the *National Intelligencer* as an official organ, settling instead on Duff Green's *United States Telegraph* and later on Francis P. Blair and John C. Rives's *Washington Globe*. Jacksonian Democrats in Congress threw their support behind Green, Blair, and Rives to replace Gales and Seaton as official printers of the House and Senate.[32]

Buffeted by Jacksonian editors, Gales and Seaton faced further encroachment from a growing band of letter writers in Washington. The same sectional issues that dismantled the Republican coalition had spurred newspapers outside the capital to send their own editors and correspondents to cover Congress. Rather than competing with the *National Intelligencer*'s summaries of the debates, these papers published special commentaries on public men and events. When Congress convened in December 1822, editor Nathaniel Carter of the *Albany Statesman and Evening Advertiser* sat in the gallery to write the first-person letters that would appear in his paper under the heading "Washington Correspondence." Two years later, Eliab Kingman, an amiable, lanky clerk in the House of Representatives, bolstered his income by sending commentary to out-of-town papers. After a brief fling as publisher of a Boston business paper, Kingman conceded that his talents lay more with reporting than editing and returned to Washington, where he became the first year-round correspondent in the capital, supporting himself by letter writing and real estate speculation. Samuel Knapp, another of the early correspondents, wrote for the *Boston Gazette, Charleston Courier,* and *New York Advertiser,* while on the side "concocting speeches for members who had more money than brains."[33]

Tariff legislation aroused the most intense sectional interest, drawing letter writers from protectionist and free-trade papers. In December 1827, wealthy Bostonians underwrote the sarcastic editor of the *Boston Courier,* Joseph Buckingham, to cover that session of Congress for New England's high-tariff advocates. "By their persuasion," Buckingham later recalled, "I was induced to spend the winter in Washington, in order to keep our friends at home informed of whatever might be done or contemplated for the accomplishment of their purposes." Some fifty of his letters filled the better part of the *Courier* that season.[34]

The Twentieth Congress also marked the arrival of James Gordon Bennett, the *New York Enquirer* correspondent who would originate a style sharply different from Gales and Seaton's staid and predictable narratives. The young and ambitious Bennett quickly grew bored with dry retelling of floor proceedings. Inspired by a volume of Horace Walpole's witty letters on the intrigues of the British court, which he found in the Library of Congress, he attempted a similar approach with his Washington correspondence, "describing, eulogizing, or satirizing the court of John Quincy Adams." His mixture of hard political news and light commentary on fashionable doings won renown in the *Enquirer* and a host of other papers that reprinted his letters. Although his work was unsigned at the time, Bennett later took proud credit for having changed the "tone, temper, and style of Washington corresponding."[35]

In 1831, after his paper broke with Andrew Jackson, Bennett quit as Washington correspondent, to be replaced by the "Spy in Washington." Anonymity protected correspondents like Bennett and the Spy, helping them avoid personal retaliation in an era of canings and duels. But politically knowledgeable people in Washington—nearly everyone who passed through the city—identified the Spy as Matthew L. Davis. The sixty-year-old Davis was a tireless gatherer of news and collector of political intelligence. "His correspondence was the best ever sent from the national capital," journalist Ben: Perley Poore later wrote, "and it was distinguished for its impartiality, sound judgment, accuracy, and concise style."[36]

The Spy raised hackles in 1838, when he reported on an applicant for government funds who had tried to argue his case on its merits. "Merit?" he quoted an unidentified congressman, "Why things do not go here by merit, but by pulling the right strings. Make it in my interest, and I will pull the strings for you." When published, the Spy's letter touched off a five-hour debate in the House of Representatives, directed chiefly at himself and other correspondents in the galleries. "Is it not known that there is a set of hirelings sent here from year to year from your large cities, which are under the influence of banking corporations, to hold a rod over the heads of your members of Congress?" thundered one solon. "Well, who are your 'Spies in Washington'. . . ? Why, sir, they are a set of individuals which would disgrace any man who comes in contact with them. They are a set of men who batten and fatten upon the slang and slander of bar-rooms and tippling shops, and no honorable and honest man can come in contact with them." Another member doubted that the sun had risen a single day that session without some newspaper attack on the legislative branch by the "base, corrupt, and penniless scoundrels who beset your Capitol in hungry swarms."[37]

The Sergeant at Arms brought Matthew Davis before the Speaker. He refused to acknowledge himself as the "Spy in Washington," admitting only, "I know the author, and I know the member to whom the Spy alludes." Was that person a member of the House? "He is not," Davis replied, bringing the proceedings to an abrupt halt. Suspicion next fell upon the chairman of the Senate Patents Committee, John Ruggles, but a Senate investigating committee exonerated Ruggles without calling Davis to testify. The sole casualty of the affair was a hotheaded congressman from Maine, Jonathan Cilley, who died in a duel fought over the Spy's accusations.[38]

The arrival of letter writers like Matt Davis disturbed the understandings that Washington newspapers had fashioned with Congress. The *National Intelligencer* reported what congressmen said and permitted them to edit their remarks. The letter writers dared to critique, and often ridicule what members said, offering them no chance to correct the record. In 1839, a request from letter writers in the public gallery for seats on the floor, along side reporters from the *Intelligencer* and other Washington papers, led to a tirade from Senator John Niles. Himself a newspaper editor, but often the butt of the letter writers' attacks, Niles denounced congressional reporters as "miserable slanderers—hirelings, hanging on to the skirts of literature, earning a miserable subsistence from their vile and dirty misrepresentations of the proceedings here, and many of them writing for both sides." Soon to retire from the Senate, Niles felt no hesitation in speaking his mind about these "venal and profligate scribblers." Senator James Buchanan, who still harbored political ambitions, suggested that senators should draw a distinction between the reporters for Washington papers, "who gave a faithful historical account of the proceedings of this body," and the letter writers who gave only "partial and piquant accounts of such proceedings and debates as struck their fancy." The Senate voted to keep the letter writers off the floor and let them vie for seats in the public gallery. Only his belief in a free press, grumbled Niles, kept him from moving to bar reporters from the chamber altogether.[39]

Outside Washington, the political fervor of Jacksonian America stimulated the spread of the newspaper press. During the expansionist decades between 1830 and 1860 the number of U.S. newspapers more than doubled, rural weeklies accounting for the greatest number. Every crossroads town claimed a Jacksonian paper and opposition Whig sheet. In the cities one-cent dailies now competed against the regular six-cent papers, with James Gordon Bennett's *New York Herald* among the earliest in 1835. Cheaply printed, sensationalist in style, aimed at a wide popular audience, the "penny press" depended on neither sound Republican principles nor political subsidy, but on mass circulation and high advertising revenue. Less susceptible to patronage, the penny press was harder for politicians to control. Their editors boasted of the more independent line that they could afford to take and showed more interest in giving marching orders than in taking them. Gradually, independent editors came to consider more balanced or objective reporting as their goal rather than ideology and partisanship.[40]

Ignoring such trends, Washington newspapers remained creatures of political parties. The *Washington Globe* spoke for Jackson's Democrats, while the *National Intelligencer* became the voice of the opposition Whig party. Gales and Seaton embraced Henry Clay's "American System," with its increased role for the federal government, but never believed they had strayed from their original republican principles. It was the Jacksonians whom they accused of having turned Republicanism upside down, by asserting executive power against the legislature.[41]

In the newly charged partisan atmosphere of Washington, a paper-thin line separated press reporting from promotion. As the Whig organ, the *Intelligencer* boosted Senator Daniel Webster's national reputation by its handling of his celebrated reply to South Carolina Senator Robert Y. Hayne in 1830. Webster had personally invited Joseph Gales to report his speech, but the senator found Gales's transcript devoid of emotional appeal. Since Webster had spoken only from notes, no other newspaper had published more than a brief summary of the speech. All waited for the *Intelligencer*'s account. But Gales and Seaton delayed publication for an entire month while Webster revised his remarks. The famous reply to Hayne appeared in a form so heavily edited and rewritten that it bore little resemblance to the words Webster spoke in the Senate chamber. Reprinted extensively, the polished version became one of the most widely read speeches in congressional history, forever enshrining Daniel Webster as the Union's most eloquent defender.[42]

Webster diligently edited his speeches. The majesty of his voice and the strength of his arguments swayed his audiences, but they often heard him groping for the right word, trying out one synonym after another until he obtained the desired effect. One listener recalled Webster saying: "Why is it, Mr. Chairman, that there has gathered, congregated, this great number of inhabitants, dwellers, here; that these roads, avenues, routes of travel, highways, converge, meet, come together, here? Is it not because we have a sufficient, ample, safe, secure, convenient, commodious port, harbor, haven?" The senator removed all but the best before his words appeared in print.[43]

Congressmen with national ambitions took care to correct their words before they appeared in the *Intelligencer* or the *Globe*. A Senate page recalled regularly accompanying Senator Lewis Cass to the *Globe* offices at night with the corrected manuscript of his speeches. Evenings after a session saw Henry Clay, John C. Calhoun, Thomas Hart Benton, and other legislative giants dutifully strolling to one of the newspaper offices for a few hours of editing. "It is such a wearisome drudgery to prepare a speech, to wait with feverish anxiety for an opportunity to deliver it, and then to prepare it for the press, and superintend its publication," a North Carolina representative complained to his wife. "I was kept up last night 'til near midnight waiting for the proof sheets. I waited for them with great impatience, and then went to the office through the rain to correct them. After all there are several errors."[44]

Mistakes in the record became even more intolerable when made by editors on government patronage. Minority members in Congress bitterly resented biased accounts that appeared in the papers of the official printers. Whigs complained of never being reported correctly in the *Globe*; Democrats protested that the *National Intelligencer* reported only the speeches of its favorites; while each side accused the other's papers of not making requested changes. The Democratic majorities who elected Blair and Rives as official printers expressed satisfaction with the *Globe's* congressional coverage. "The *Globe* paper was a powerful assistant," noted

Senator Benton, "both as an ally working in its own columns, and as a vehicle of communication for our daily debates." Whig Senator John W. Davis charged: "We have little reason for placing reliance on the *Globe*."[45]

Whigs denounced the *Globe*'s reporters as "hired libelers, who are not reporters of our proceedings, but falsifiers of our proceedings." Whig Representative William Bond never expected to be "truly represented" in the *Globe*. The *Globe*'s chief reporter, Lund Washington, admitted that he could not give a word-for-word rendition of every speech, even if he "had as many hands as Belarious," but insisted that neither Congress nor the public would be served "by setting down, word for word, every political skirmish that takes place."[46]

Out of these stenographic limitations evolved a mutually acceptable system: speeches that members wrote out or edited themselves appeared in the first person; speeches that reporters summarized appeared in the second person, past tense. Since the latter predominated, it became custom that members not be held entirely responsible for remarks that appeared in the second person. Nevertheless, some members chafed at the summaries and their inferences. Reporters should give only "a statement of *facts*, and not their *construction* or *inference*," said Senator Clement C. Clay. "We are sufficiently *libeled* and *slandered by letter writers*. I am at least unwilling to tolerate it in Reporters." But Senator Henry Clay defended the reporters' right to draw inferences and to expose measures they considered damaging to the public good. It was "one of the inestimable privileges of a free press."[47]

Similar etiquette developed around edited remarks. Once, after clashing with John C. Calhoun on the Senate floor, Henry Clay discreetly deleted some rash statements from the public record. The South Carolinian insisted upon responding to Clay's original, unexpurgated words. Clay explained that the speech had been printed under his supervision, suggesting that he had sanctioned the omissions as an apology. Senator Thomas Hart Benton accepted Clay's rationale, "for that which is severe enough in speaking becomes more so in writing; and its omission or softening is a tacit retraction, and honorable to the cool reflections which condemns what passion, or heat, had promoted."[48]

Campaigning for "Tippecanoe and Tyler Too" in 1840, the Whigs elected a president, swept into the majority in Congress, and restored the *National Intelligencer* to at least some of its former influence. Gales and Seaton won reelection as printers of the House, while Thomas Allen, editor of the *Madisonian*, became Senate printer. But the era in which the Washington press could monopolize congressional reporting was fast passing. The rise of the penny press helped stimulate an intense hunger for news, which Congress possessed in abundance. James Gordon Bennett hired his own corps of stenographic reporters for the *New York Herald* and campaigned to win them a place on the Senate floor. With the Whigs in the majority, Senate President Pro Tempore Samuel Southard saw no reason to reward reporters from the Democratic *Herald*. Editor Bennett denounced the rejection as "one of the most outrageous, high-handed, unconstitutional acts ever perpetrated by any legislative assembly in a free land," and carried his case to the more accommodating Henry Clay. On 8 July 1841, the Whig majority placated the fiery editor by creating the Senate's first "Reporters' Gallery," reserving the narrow front row of the eastern gallery, above the vice president's chair, for representatives of the press. Washington dailies would have two desks apiece, and one desk would be assigned to each out-of-town paper that applied. Doubting that many newspapers could afford to hire their own reporters, the Senate provided only ten desks in all. Bennett sent his team, headed by Richard Sutton, who had once reported in the British House of Commons beside Charles Dickens. As expected, Sutton's reports added prestige to the *Herald*.[49]

Five years later, as the Senate tried to cope with the swelling crowds of visitors to its public galleries, a committee proposed replacing the reporters' gallery with a ladies' gallery. More limited press gallery space would be set aside for the half dozen regular reporters of debate, while "mere letter writers" would be relegated to the public galleries. This brought the influential North Carolina Senator Willie Mangum to his feet in defense of the letter writers, who, he argued, "diffused more information amongst the masses of the people than the reporters for the city papers, who made the extended and elaborate reports." The Architect of the Capitol promptly responded with plans to rebuild the press gallery to make space for thirty to forty desks. But the senators rejected this plan out of fear that a high-tiered gallery would block the light and impair the chamber's architectural beauty. In any event, the Senate as a whole was so rapidly outgrowing its quarters that it would soon need a much larger hall, with more spacious galleries for the public and the press.[50]

Even as the letter writers were winning support on the Senate floor, a succession of editors still vied for more traditional sources of political patronage. Gales and Seaton's patronage quest had never lacked risk, and those editors seeking to replace them as congressional printers and administration spokesmen encountered similar cycles of acceptance and rejection. The luckless Jesse Dow regularly lost his bids for government printing. He had purchased the *Madisonian*, which had been President John Tyler's official paper, but President James K. Polk had passed it over in favor of Thomas Ritchie's *Washington Union*. The Senate and House gave Ritchie a clean sweep of the printing patronage by electing him as their official printer. In a desperate effort to salvage his investment, Jesse Dow renamed his paper the *Washington Daily Times* and hired Hiram H. Robinson as his editor. "We intend to be governed wholly by the *principles* of the *Democratic creed*," Robinson proclaimed in his first issue on 2 February 1846. "We will know no interest, section, faction, or individual of our own or any party at the expense of this creed"—an easy pledge considering the paper's complete lack of patronage. To make the *Times* better known in Washington's crowded field, Robinson sent free copies to every member of Congress and adopted a combative editorial style.[51]

The *Times* made American expansionism its chief issue and devoted long columns to the Oregon territory dispute with Great Britain. In March 1846 it printed sensational allegations that a cabal of Whigs and anti-administration Democrats were plotting a deal over Oregon with the British minister. Charges of treason stirred tempers, and a Senate investigation ensued.[52]

In a foolhardy move, Dow and Robinson divulged the sources of their story, not calculating that these sources—a naval officer, a Senate doorkeeper, lobbyists, and other journalists—had everything to lose and nothing to gain by corroborating their account. Under oath, every witness denied knowledge of a plot. The investigating committee branded the paper's accusation "utterly and entirely false"; the Senate banished Dow and Robinson from its galleries; and the *Washington Daily Times* ceased publication. Future editors and reporters would resist congressional demands to name their sources.[53]

Festering issues of slavery and sectionalism in the 1840s caused a distrustful Congress habitually to vent its anger against the press. Within a year after the expulsion of Jesse Dow, the Senate turned on its own printer, Thomas Ritchie. The "kindest and most genteel old fogy," Ritchie had edited a political paper in Richmond since the days of Thomas Jefferson. But he had grown too old by the time he was called into the Washington arena and could only blunder about as editor of Polk's official organ. In February 1847, during the Mexican War, Ritchie's *Washington Union* blasted senators who had opposed the president's military bill for handing a victory to the Mexicans. Since the editorial appeared only hours after John C. Calhoun had spoken out against Mexican policies, the attack appeared directed against him personally. Calhoun's allies moved to bar Ritchie from the Senate floor.

Administration Democrats rallied behind their printer and freedom of the press. Cried Senator William Allen: "If we were to punish a press in Washington, what was to prevent us from punishing an editor in Baltimore next, then in Philadelphia, then in New York, then in Boston, and so on through the whole country, until the word free press would become a nickname?" Virginia Senator James Mason warned that exclusion from the floor would obstruct Ritchie's work as Senate printer. When the vote came, Calhoun's Democratic supporters sided with the Whigs and by a vote of twenty-seven to twenty-one the Senate barred its doors to its own printer.[54]

Leaks of secret documents triggered even louder outbursts. In 1844, the Senate censured one of its own members, Ohio abolitionist Benjamin Tappan, for supplying the press with confidential documents about a treaty to annex Texas. Two years later, the Senate investigated the Washington correspondents of the *New York Tribune* and *Philadelphia North American* for unauthorized publication of the Oregon boundary settlement. By 1848, emotions reached fever pitch when the Senate imprisoned a *New York Herald* reporter for publishing the still secret treaty of Guadalupe-Hidalgo, which ended the Mexican War.

Publication may not have affected the treaty's passage, but it did raise serious questions about the government's ability to keep secrets. President Polk dismissed rumors that cast his secretary of state, James Buchanan, in the role of leaker. Polk was convinced that some senator must have passed a copy of the treaty "to some of the unprincipled letter-writers who are stationed at Washington to collect news." The president's suspicions were reinforced when John Nugent, the *Herald*'s "Galviensis," taunted that "those Senators who most strenuously advocate the system of closed doors, are always the least economical of the Senate secrets." The *Herald* compounded the injury when it published the president's confidential messages to the Senate and promised to print more as space permitted.[55]

This time, when the Senate investigated, John Nugent did not repeat Jesse Dow's error. Nugent refused to name his source, saying only that it had been neither a senator nor Senate officer. The investigating committee thereupon ordered him confined in a committee room until he talked. The Capitol Building was no Bastille, and John Nugent passed his captivity in comfort. His paper published his "Galviensis" letters under the dateline "Custody of the Sergeant-at-Arms" and doubled his salary during his imprisonment. When the Senate awoke to the futility of the situation, it released Nugent on the face-saving grounds of protecting his health.[56]

James Gordon Bennett condemned the Senate's "mean and contemptible" actions toward his correspondent and he demonstrated its hypocrisy by publishing a list of senators who regularly slipped secrets to the Washington letter writers. The *Herald* claimed that Daniel Webster divulged the secret sessions to Charles W. March of the *New York Tribune;* Senator John M. Clayton leaked to James E. Harvey of the *Philadelphia North American;* and Senator Lewis Cass kept Felix Grund of the *Philadelphia Public Ledger* well informed. The Democratic *Herald* commended the Whig *North American* for printing "the best reports of those secret debates" and proclaimed Whig senators as "the most comprehensive leakers." The *Herald* had thus exposed—for a fleeting moment—the mutually beneficial relationship between congressional leaders and the press.[57]

The Senate's imprisonment of John Nugent occurred during a period of momentous changes in congressional reporting. In 1848 the Senate finally voted to hire impartial reporters of debate—a half century after the First Congress had rejected the notion. A committee report prepared by Thomas Hart Benton found that private printing of the debates was too expensive for the Washington newspapers, that such reporting had been "imperfect," and that the system had denied Congress "the proper control and supervision of its own proceedings." The Senate put on its payroll the *Washington Union*'s reporters, headed by the Irish-born physician Dr. James Houston. The almost simultaneous adoption of the Pitman system of stenography permitted these reporters quicker and more accurate transcription of all floor speeches. The Washington correspondent of the *New York Tribune* reported the universal amazement when Dr. Houston recorded one of Daniel Webster's speeches verbatim. "He took it down word for word as it issued from the lips of Mr. Webster and has given it at this early hour to the world," the *Tribune* marveled. To protect themselves from too much accuracy, senators added a provision to the rules that permitted them to correct and rewrite their remarks before publication. The House adopted this procedure two years later. By 1851, the *Congressional Globe* had taken full charge of all House and Senate reporting from the *National Intelligencer* and other Washington papers. Carrying on the tradition that the *Intelligencer* had begun, the *Globe* provided nonpartisan, noneditorialized accounts of the proceedings, until it was replaced by the *Congressional Record* in 1873.[58]

An even greater change in Washington reporting resulted from an invention first tested inside the Capitol Building. A $30,000 congressional appropriation enabled Samuel F. B. Morse to run wires between Washington and Baltimore for a long-distance test of his telegraph. On 24 May 1844, senators and representatives gathered as Morse sent the first ceremonial message: "What hath God wrought?" Back from Baltimore came a more secular question: "What is the news in Washington?" Of special interest to members of Congress were telegraphic reports from the Democratic national convention, then meeting in Baltimore. When the telegraph announced the nomination of New York Senator Silas Wright for vice president, Wright declined the honor, also via telegraph, and did so repeatedly until the convention accepted the new machine's message. This exchange demonstrated the telegraph's validity and demolished forever the Washington papers' monopoly on Washington reporting.[59]

As news came over the wires, Morse gathered up messages and posted them in the Capitol Rotunda, foreshadowing the wire services that would soon become the mainstay of congressional journalism. Newspaper publishers quickly recognized the potential for

instant news transmittal. In 1844, the *Baltimore Patriot* published
the first telegraphic news dispatch about a House vote on the Oregon territory. Soon after, the *Baltimore American* began paying
Professor Morse a penny a word for his reports on the proceedings
of Congress. "Space is . . . annihilated," declared the Baltimore
weekly *Niles' National Register.* "By the time the result of the vote
of congress is announced by the speaker, in the capitol, it is known
at the Pratt street depot, in the city of Baltimore!" The following
year, Morse sold a franchise to the New York, Albany, and Buffalo
Telegraph Company, which stimulated upstate New York papers to
pool their resources to buy telegraphed news dispatches. William
H. Seward's *Utica Gazette* took the lead in organizing the nation's
first wire service among upstate New York papers. Sharing expenses, they hired a correspondent to compile daily telegraphic
news of the legislature at Albany.[60]

Instant news transmittal over the telegraph deprived Washington letters of their "starch of novelty." The letter writers would
have switched all their reporting to telegraph except for the high
tolls, which limited the telegraph's initial use to news bulletins.
When rumors of peace with Mexico circulated in Washington in
1848, editor Horace Greeley instructed the *New York Tribune*'s
Washington correspondent not to hesitate to telegraph "whenever
you have anything of interest." It was late on a Friday night, after
a secret session of the Senate adjourned, when departing senators
told their favorite correspondents that they had ratified the treaty
of Guadalupe-Hidalgo, and the Mexican War was officially over.
John Nugent of the *Herald* and William Robinson of the *Tribune*
hailed cabs and galloped madly down Pennsylvania Avenue to the
Morse Magnetic Telegraph Company. Although they arrived before the posted closing hour, the office was locked tight. After a
frenzied search through nearby taverns, the correspondents found
the operator in no shape to telegraph their messages. Cursing their
fate, they mailed the story to their papers. The news had to wait
for the Monday morning editions.[61]

In New York, Horace Greeley was stunned to learn that the
Washington telegraph office would close with such important news
pending. "There is just one remedy for the ills that journals are
heir to," Greeley threatened, "*telegraphic competition.* I mean to
have it." Similar reactions among New York editors helped forge an
extraordinary alliance among old rivals. In May 1848, Greeley,

Bennett, and other New York editors met to form the New York Associated Press. The news cooperative would allow their papers to reduce telegraphic costs and ensure a steady and reliable stream of telegraphic reporting, free from the uncertain services of the Morse Company.[62]

Telegraphic wire services completed the New York papers' crusade to break the hold of the *Union*, the *Globe*, and the *National Intelligencer* on congressional reporting. "By means of the electric telegraph the local advantages of the Washington papers are transferred to this metropolis," James Gordon Bennett gloated in 1849, "and the superior enterprise and pecuniary means of the journals here will enable them to turn these advantages to the best account." Bennett pledged that the *Herald* would "give telegraphic reports of congressional debates and proceedings which will defy competition, and fully satisfy the country." Nor would his reporters need to accept the "wages of corruption from Congress," in the form of patronage, like that "superannuated pensioner of the Whig party, the *Intelligencer.*" But in fact, Associated Press summaries of the debates soon made the *Herald's* service as obsolete as the *Intelligencer's.*[63]

The new technology also disrupted the informal rules that politicians had established with the press. More senior members of Congress felt especially uncomfortable with the new style and speed of reporting. They thought in terms of the party press, whose chief duties were to publish their speeches, defend their policies, and promote their candidacies. Everyone knew where such papers stood and how their reporters were inclined. But the wire services adopted an impartial style of reporting so they could sell news to customers of all political hues. "I distrust all telegraphic reports," John C. Calhoun commented in the Senate, shortly before his death in 1850. Henry Clay showed similar difficulty in adjusting to the new media. When Clay delivered his last stump speech in Lexington, Kentucky, he refused to talk so long as an Associated Press reporter took notes in the audience. The reporter left but then pieced together the speech by interviewing those who heard it. Swearing profusely, Senator Clay expressed his outrage that a writer for unknown papers would presume to report what he had said to his own constituents without first obtaining his consent. The rules of the game as Clay had so long played it, had passed away.[64]

By the 1850s, the venerable editors of the once dominant *National Intelligencer* had similarly fallen out of step with their times. While remaining consistent to their principles, Gales and Seaton had aged from Republicans into "Old Line Whigs." When the Whig party collapsed, they found themselves editors of a party paper without a party; moreover, two-thirds of their subscriptions came from states threatening to secede from the Union. Neither were they prepared to adjust to the dramatic changes taking place in journalism. Gales and Seaton preferred to write deliberative—some said ponderous—essays and blamed the political ferment of the 1850s on the exaggerated importance of telegraphed news. They likewise accused the correspondents steadily flowing into Washington of sacrificing accuracy and circulating rumors merely to draw attention to their letters. Younger correspondents dismissed Gales and Seaton as relics of an earlier age, elderly editors who refused to show any sense of urgency in printing the news. The *Intelligencer* had become, said Mark Twain, a staid old journal "that regularly comes out in the most sensational and aggressive manner, every morning, with news it ought to have printed the day before."[65]

Society reporter Mary Jane Windle visited the *National Intelligencer*'s "ancient and dingy" offices in 1857. Upstairs, she found Joseph Gales, crippled by a stroke, bent over piles of papers, pamphlets, and manuscripts covering his desk. Gales assured his visitor that he felt neither discouraged nor dismayed over the political defeats his paper had suffered or over the dangers that threatened the Union. He simply carried on as always. Mrs. Windle also claimed that the *Intelligencer*'s old dog could distinguish between Whigs and Democrats and "glare upon the latter."[66]

In declining health for several years, Joseph Gales went "very gradually, down to the tomb." He died in August 1860, after forty-eight years as editor of the *National Intelligencer*. A generous man throughout his life, Gales had long since exhausted the profits of government patronage. "It is doubtful whether has has left a dollar," one of his friends observed. William Seaton carried on until his retirement in December 1864. The once dominant *Intelligencer* survived its editors by only four years. Fellow journalists paid tribute to the last of the old order, "always faithful to principle, never strongly partisan, but always manly and independent." At a time when popular passions ran wild, Gales and Seaton had maintained a perpetual moderation, the *Atlantic Monthly* saluted; "amidst incessant variations of doctrine, they . . . preserved a memory and a conscience."[67]

Despite these accolades, Gales and Seaton advanced American journalism more by their failure than their success. No matter how fair and temperate its style, the *Intelligencer*'s dependent position as an official newspaper ran contrary to the evolving notion of adversarial journalism and gave the federal government far more control over the flow of news than would later seem tolerable. Neither American political nor commercial competitiveness would long permit a government-sponsored monopoly on communications. Politics, principle, and profit irrepressibly combined to open Washington reporting to more dynamic forces in journalism than Joseph Gales and William Seaton could fathom.

2

Horace Greeley's Washington Correspondents

"YOU WON'T SEE ME IN WASHINGTON till the session opens," wrote Horace Greeley in 1850, "and then you can't help it." The New York editor advertised himself prominently whenever he came to Washington, shambling about Capitol Hill in oversized boots, rumpled trousers, battered hat, and white overcoat, pockets bulging with papers. "Uncle Horace" appeared at some time during every session of Congress during the 1840s and 1850s, to watch the scene from the galleries. While his politics often matched his eccentric dress, he published an influential newspaper that required legislators to take note of his views. His *New York Tribune* developed a strong circulation in Washington, as correspondent Ben: Perley Poore observed, "where the eminently respectable *National Intelligencer* and the ponderous *Globe* failed to satisfy the reading community."[1]

The editor's familiar "H. G." often appeared under a Washington dateline, but management of the *Tribune* forced him to spend the greater share of his time at its New York offices. To cover the news in the capital, he hired a string of aggressive and talented Washington correspondents. Like the rest of the *Tribune's* staff they were, said one, "resolute, brilliant, capable, irresponsible, intolerant— [and] not above setting things on fire for the fun of seeing them burn."[2]

Greeley and his Washington correspondents reflected the political ferment of their era, which saw the rise and fall of the Whigs, the vigorous but short-lived campaigns of the Liberty, Free Soil, and American (Know-Nothing) parties, and the emergence of the Republicans as a permanent opposition party to the Democrats. The earlier party system had made the journalism of Gales and

Seaton, but Greeley's *Tribune* helped to make the party system of his day. The editor threw open its pages to the spirit of reform, gave voice to popular sentiments and dissatisfactions, and helped to whip up party spirit to win elections. Much of his paper's attention focused on Congress, an institution which Greeley never held in particularly high esteem. Yet Congress drew him back repeatedly. Addicted to politics, the editor went to Washington as much to lecture the legislators as to report on them.[3]

The *New York Tribune* stood financially independent of any political party, although not entirely by choice. Greeley had earned his spurs editing Whig campaign papers under the tutelage of Thurlow Weed, the Albany editor and kingpin of New York Whig politics. Eventually he bristled at being treated "like a school boy" and rebelled against Weed's efforts to mold his thinking. The last straw came in 1840, when Greeley received no political reward for his efforts in electing the Whig ticket. Too proud to ask, and insulted over being neglected, Greeley vowed to "burn incense at the feet of no man." In April 1841, he established the *Tribune* as an independent newspaper. Although prominent Whigs had encouraged him to launch a penny paper aimed at working-class

Horace Greeley as he appeared in the 1840s.

readers, Greeley collected only thirty dollars in Whig advertisements during the paper's first month. "The *Tribune* never cost the Whig party anything," he asserted; "and we never asked for favor of it but pay for its Advertisements in our columns—and even that we have failed in part to obtain." Salvation came not from a political party but from a financially astute New York lawyer who took over as the *Tribune's* publisher and freed its editor from worrying about how to pay his bills.[4]

Financial independence saved the *Tribune* from "sterile partisanship" and made it an unpredictable newspaper, one that could hire Margaret Fuller as literary editor and Karl Marx to cover British politics. Editorially, the *Tribune* promoted the Whig party, Henry Clay's American System, the antislavery cause, prohibition, pacifism, vegetarianism, and any number of other social issues that intrigued its editor and dismayed conservative Whigs like Thurlow Weed.[5]

When Lord Acton visited New York he puzzled over the *Tribune*, "ultra-democratic in every question, without being Democratic." Touring its headquarters with Greeley, Acton described his host as a "half-cracked" editor who pushed his causes to extravagance, and yet who defended them no matter how unpopular. By contrast, Greeley's chief rival, James Gordon Bennett, charted his editorial course whichever way public opinion inclined. Still, Bennett was an innovative editor and tough competitor. His *New York Herald* devoted much news space to sex, scandal, and sensationalism and could afford to hire a squadron of aggressive reporters and correspondents. In the 1840s, the *Herald's* circulation in the penny paper market far surpassed the *Tribune*.[6]

Having himself reported on the New York State legislature for Weed's *Albany Evening Journal*, Greeley intended to compete with the *Herald* in covering the national legislature. In June 1841, he sent his first correspondent to Washington for the special session of Congress. Greeley soon joined him to file his own reports from the galleries. In an era of personal journalism, readers attributed anything that appeared in the *Tribune* to Greeley or assumed any story represented his own views. The editor tried to remind readers that many hands wrote for his paper. He made a point of initialing his own reports and recommended that reporters do the same, so that everyone connected with the *Tribune* would become known to the public. But, mindful of libel suits and politicians armed with pistols and walking sticks, his correspondents relied on fanciful aliases for their letters. Greeley's first Washington correspondent signed himself "Argus," after the mythical giant with a hundred eyes.[7]

"Argus" wrote in a dry, straightforward manner, suggesting that behind the pseudonym stood a stenographic reporter who wrote political commentary on the side. It fell to the editor to provide the paper's more pungent Washington correspondence. This pattern continued until 1844, when Greeley's beloved Henry Clay lost the presidency to James K. Polk, and the Democrats recaptured majorities in both the House and Senate. Wanting to seize the offense, Greeley replaced "Argus" with William E. Robinson, who quickly won fame as "the naughty, malicious, fun-loving correspondent 'Richelieu.'" No reader ever had to guess where "Richelieu" stood on the issues. "Dear Greeley," began his first letter to the *Tribune* on 12 December 1844: "We shall soon have hot work on the Texas question. The Abolitionists labored so faithfully against Mr. Clay, and for Texas and Slavery, during the recent Presidential contest, that the Loco-Focos [Democrats] feel themselves in duty bound to extend the limits and perpetuate the region of human slavery."[8]

An Irish-born, Yale-educated poet trained in the law, William Ergina Robinson became a superb correspondent once he overcame tendencies to lapse into Latin and to sprinkle his reporting with classical allusions. Although the alias "Richelieu" suggested a haughty demeanor, Robinson mingled easily with Whig party leaders. He wrote in an aggressively partisan style but also distanced himself from the politicians. After his first session of reporting on Congress, "Richelieu" notified his readers that he left the capital "with a lower estimate of human nature and its tendency to improvement, than I entertained when I went there"—a sentiment in sharp variance from the respectful reporting of his fellow Whig journalists, Gales and Seaton.[9]

When Robinson returned to Washington with the next Congress, the *Tribune* inaugurated a new column called "Rumors and Humors in Washington," signed "Persimmon." Since the *Tribune* could afford only one Washington correspondent at that time, Robinson wrote both as "Richelieu" and "Persimmon." The second identity added another layer of protection while he poked fun at congressmen. "Persimmon's" identity became a matter of public debate after his second letter appeared in February 1846 with a burlesque of the dining habits of Ohio Democrat William E. Sawyer:

> Every day at 2 o'clock he feeds. About that hour he is seen leaving his seat, and taking a position in a window back of the Speaker's Chair, to the left. He unfolds a greasy paper in which is contained a chunk of bread and a sausage or some other unctuous substance. These he disposes of quite rapidly, wipes his hands with the greasy paper for a napkin, and then throws it out of the window. —What little grease is left on his hands he wipes on his almost bald head which saves any outlay for Pomatum. His mouth sometimes seems as a finger glass, his coat sleeves and pantaloons being called into requisition as a napkin. He uses a jackknife for a toothpick, and then he goes on the floor again to abuse the Whigs as the British Party, and claims the whole of Oregon as necessary for the spread of Civilization.[10]

Representative Sawyer foolishly responded to his tormentor. Sawyer's denunciation of "Persimmon" persuaded fellow House members to expel the *Tribune*'s correspondent from the reporters' desk, by a vote of 119 to 46, an overreaction that drew national and international attention and made "Sausage Sawyer" infamous. Washington hotels featured *Sausages a la Sawyer* on their menus, and Whig congressmen littered their speeches with sausage references, until the beleaguered Sawyer retreated from national politics.[11]

Horace Greeley stormed against the gag rule on his correspondent, charging that it was rare for the House to do "as good a day's work for the Country as the least efficient of the Reporters." Meanwhile, William Robinson tried to dissociate himself from "Persimmon's" humor. The remarks were "such as I would not use in my letters," "Richelieu" wrote ambiguously. Since Robinson was the only visible *Tribune* correspondent, he was banished from the House floor. However, Representative John Quincy Adams escorted Robinson to a gallery reserved for the guests of House members. In that perch, he remained until the next session when the House lifted its ban on the *Tribune*.[12]

During the months that Robinson was denied the "worthless privileges of the House," he made himself obnoxious to the Senate by publishing a still-secret treaty on the Oregon boundary. For expansionists who supported Polk on the belief that he would settle for nothing less than all of Oregon to the 54'40° boundary, the administration's compromise with Britain came as a shock. Robinson gave them no relief from their misery. On the day that Polk first received word that the British would settle on the forty-ninth parallel, Robinson sent an "important rumor" to the *Tribune* announcing the deal. "The 54'40° men feel that they have made themselves bigger fools than nature intended them for—and she was pretty bountiful to them at that," Robinson mocked. Before the Senate lifted its injunction of secrecy from the ratified treaty, Robinson published a synopsis of it in the *Tribune*. In his haste to transcribe the treaty, he accidentally omitted three words. The *Tribune* later used this error to embarrass other newspapers that published the synopsis, omissions and all, without attribution. Among those caught stealing was "D. A. G.," the Washington correspondent for the *New York Express*, who soon found a way to get even.[13]

Three weeks later, the *Philadelphia North American* published the complete text of the treaty along with the president's confidential message to the Senate. "Richelieu" cited the full text with satisfaction, since it verified his synopsis. By contrast, Polk's official paper, the *Washington Union*, refused to reprint the documents until the Senate released them. "We are utterly at a loss to know from whom the Washington correspondent of the *North American* obtained them," declared the *Union;* "or if they be obtained from (what we cannot believe) a senator of the United States, we cannot see on what principle this publication of a confidential document can be reconciled to his service of a public duty."[14]

It was no secret that the *New York Tribune* and the *Philadelphia North American* frequently cooperated on stories, so Senate investigators pursued both papers' Washington correspondents, "Richelieu" and "Independent," the pen name for James E. Harvey. When the editor of the *North American* was called to testify, he claimed merely to have received a package of documents in the mail signed "A Friend." He failed to mention that this was the familiar salutation of James Harvey.[15]

William Robinson swore that he pieced together his synopsis from more than one source. James Harvey also insisted that his information came from "various sources in the political circles in which I mingle." Then the investigating committee heard from George A. Dwight, who wrote for the *New York Express* as "D. A. G." Still smarting over the mocking he had gotten from the

Tribune for reprinting its synopsis, Dwight ridiculed the notion that such a long document could have been accurately reproduced from assorted conversations and insisted that it must have come from an actual copy. Dwight recalled how Robinson had given him the synopsis and boasted that he could get the president's confidential message as well. Called back to testify, Robinson admitted promising the confidential message in a "jocular spirit" but steadfastly refused to reveal his sources. With the Senate about to adjourn, the investigating committee concluded its work without making any formal accusations. "They have discovered nothing," "Richelieu" reported to the *Tribune*.[16]

Victorious but bruised, William Robinson had his fill of Washington correspondence. The new Whig majority in the House offered the hope of a federal appointment, but Robinson discovered that he had made himself too controversial. "You don't have to tell me what luck you have had about that Deputy Clerkship," Horace Greeley consoled his "unappointed friend," while at the same time counseling against patronage. "Next to marrying a very cross old maid for a fortune, getting an office to live by is the poorest business I can think of," the editor advised. Because he did not want it to appear that "Richelieu" had fallen out of favor with the *Tribune*, Greeley urged him to remain in Washington until the end of the congressional session. "Richelieu's" letters continued but lacked their old fire. The increasing use of the telegraph also eroded some of their purpose. It took Robinson's letters two days to reach New York, while his telegraphic dispatches could be published the next morning. Once, while reporting a senator's impending speech, Robinson noted that "the Telegraph will overtake this letter and tell you what he *did* say." Disappointments dogged him. He lost the Whig nomination for Congress from his New York district by a single vote. A newspaper he founded folded after six months, and he abandoned journalism to practice law. Success eluded William Robinson for another twenty years, until he won election to the U.S. House of Representatives and took a seat in the body that had once banished "Richelieu" and "Persimmon."[17]

As Robinson disengaged from the *Tribune*, Greeley hired a Washington correspondent who signed himself "M." Behind the initial stood Charles W. March, thirty-three, a Harvard graduate and politically ambitious lawyer. March had corresponded for the *New York Evening Post* and *Boston Courier*, before purchasing an

William E. Robinson, "Richelieu" and "Persimmon."

interest in the *Tribune* and writing its Washington correspondence. His chief objective was to promote an old family friend, Daniel Webster, to the presidency.[18]

Joining "M" in Washington was Greeley himself, who in 1848 won a short term in the House of Representatives as a New York Whig. Since his successor had been chosen in the same election, the editor spent his entire three-month term in Congress as a lame duck. Harboring few expectations, Representative Greeley still felt keenly disappointed with his inert and cynical colleagues. They in turn ridiculed him as a comic amateur. Greeley accomplished nothing legislatively in his short term, but he labored daily on his letters to the *Tribune* and used his congressional privileges to uncover news for his paper. In particular, he obtained access to other

House members' travel vouchers and then compared the routes for which they claimed reimbursement to the most direct mail routes and calculated the differences. Published in the *Tribune*, the results embarrassed members of both parties, including Illinois Representative Abraham Lincoln, whom Greeley accused of over-billing the government by $676.80. The exposé raised cries of protest and brought "a whole swarm of hornets" about Greeley's ears. His short term, in his own words, made him "the most thoroughly detested man who ever sat in Congress." Still, he counted the experience worth his while. "I thought it would be a nuisance and a sacrifice for me to go to Congress," he later advised a country editor named Schuyler Colfax, who contemplated running for the House; "but I was mistaken; it did me lasting good. I never was brought so palpably and tryingly into collision with the embodied scoundrelism of the nation as while in Congress."[19]

Retirement from Congress meant the loss of the *Tribune's* best Washington correspondent, editor Greeley himself. After Charles March also left, the paper had little luck with their new correspondent, "D. H." The New York editors once appended a note to the bottom of "D. H.'s" letter: "Our correspondent will oblige us by writing on one side only of the paper and by confining himself to facts, leaving comments to the Editors." This was not necessarily a call for that later journalistic goal of "objectivity." The *Tribune's* editors had less interest in limiting news to facts than in making their correspondent toe the editorial line. As long as Greeley's correspondents agreed with him on political issues they were free to make whatever commentary they wanted. His next Washington correspondent, who signed himself "Roger Sherman" after an anti-slavery signer of the Constitution, kept up a running assault on the South. "Roger Sherman" warned that Texas would be carved into several states to give the South a voting majority in the Senate. "Some will say it is impossible," he wrote; "but if they saw this Congress as I see them . . . they would try to stop the evil before it becomes incurable."[20]

In April 1850, Greeley celebrated the *Tribune's* ninth anniversary by expanding the paper from four to eight pages, and from twenty-eight to fifty-eight columns. Among the first beneficiaries of this expansion was Jane Grey Swisshelm, editor of an abolitionist weekly in Pittsburgh, who dreamed of reporting from Washington. News that Senator Daniel Webster had defected to the "Slave

Power" by endorsing the Compromise of 1850, roused Swisshelm to action. "The danger was imminent, the crisis alarming, and the excitement very great," she wrote. "I longed to be in Washington." Boldly, she contacted Horace Greeley, offering herself as a Washington correspondent. Greeley, whose many interests included women's rights, liked the novelty of a woman political reporter and hired her at five dollars a letter. Her first Washington letter appeared on an inside page in the *Tribune* on 12 April 1850. Within three days, "Mrs. Swisshelm's Letters" had made it to the front page.[21]

"There is a great deal of profound logic and quite a number of handsome crepe shawls in Washington," she wrote. "As I have an ear for one and an eye for the other, I get sadly confused between hearing and seeing. It is rather difficult to keep the run of all that is said on the floor in Congress and all that is displayed in the galleries." Jane Swisshelm campaigned to gain a seat in the press gallery, the front row of seats reserved for reporters and correspondents directly above the presiding officer's chair. Vice President Millard Fillmore, who controlled access to the press gallery, did what he could to dissuade her. No woman had ever sat in that male bastion, he cautioned; she would find it unpleasant; she would attract undue attention. When Swisshelm held her ground, Fillmore at last relented.

Jane Swisshelm's appearance in the Senate press gallery on 17 April caused only a minor stir, for it was overshadowed by more dramatic actions down on the floor. That same day an enraged Senator Thomas Hart Benton stalked the diminutive senator from Mississippi, Henry S. Foote. Foote drew his pistol for protection. "Stand out of the way and let the assassin fire!" Benton bellowed as other senators intervened. "I sat in the reporters' gallery, directly opposite the gentlemen," Swisshelm told her readers, "and saw it all."[22]

Despite an auspicious beginning, Swisshelm's first letter from the press gallery was also her last. She sacrificed her career as a correspondent to achieve her goal of destroying Daniel Webster. In the gallery she collected gossip that portrayed the "God-like Daniel" as a drunkard and the father of illegitimate mulatto children. Other correspondents disdained to reveal the private lives of public men and would have nothing to do with these stories, but Swisshelm confessed she was "a little thick in the skull and never

Jane Grey Swisshelm, the first woman admitted to the Senate press gallery.

could understand nice distinctions in etiquette or ethics." The abolitionist congressman George W. Julian counseled her against publishing the story. "It would ruin you, ruin your influence, ruin your work. You would lose your *Tribune* engagement," Julian warned. Unmoved, she decided to publish it "and let God take care of the consequences."

The blunt little article was "copied and copied" by the nation's press, but although Swisshelm had published it in her Pittsburgh weekly, she was identified as Washington correspondent for the *New York Tribune*. When public condemnation fell upon Greeley, the editor swiftly fired his correspondent. Ejected from the press gallery, Jane Swisshelm migrated westward as a frontier editor. In later years, she was pleased that Greeley bore her no grudge, "after I had wronged you."[23]

With American politics in crisis, Greeley lacked the right person in Washington. None since "Richelieu" had filled the job adequately. Then Greeley learned of a dispute between the Washington correspondent for the *Boston Courier* and its editors. James Shepherd Pike, a successful businessman and failed politician, was a forceful writer who assailed all compromise with slavery. Pike damned Daniel Webster's defense of the Compromise of 1850, with its fugitive slave provisions, which brought an editorial reprimand. "You know the *Courier* has taken the side of Webster in the California and [Wilmot] Proviso question," his editors reminded him. "People are quoting your letters against us." The rebuke made Pike receptive to an invitation from the *Tribune*. "What I want is a daily letter (when there is anything to say) on the doings of Congress, commenting on anything spicy or interesting, and letting the readers make the right comments, rather than see that you are making them," Greeley explained. "What I am after is news."[24]

Days later, the first "J. S. P." lettered appeared in the *Tribune*, denouncing Henry Clay's omnibus compromise proposal. "The truth is, the whole scheme of the Omnibus bill is a broad trap to catch the Whig Party," wrote Pike. "I protest earnestly that no Whig should so stultify himself as to lend a hand to this scheme." This was strong stuff even for editor Greeley. A *Tribune* editorial welcomed its new Washington correspondent, but added: "J.S.P. seems mainly intent on proving that Northern Whigs ought not to sustain the proposed compromise. As barely one of them (Mr.

Webster) has indicated a purpose of so doing . . . our correspondent seems to be calling rather the righteous than sinners to repentance." Greeley sent Pike a private note, advising him not to mind the editorial objections to his letters, "but let us know sometimes what Congress, the Cabinet, etc. are about to do, as well as what they ought to do."[25]

In spite of their disagreements, Greeley felt satisfied with Pike's performance and promoted him to associate editor. "We want an editor permanently at Washington who will do the chores there," explained Charles A. Dana, Greeley's managing editor, "as we can't get them done by a hired correspondent." In addition to his "J. S. P." letters, Pike would supervise a growing mix of lesser Washington correspondents for the *Tribune:* "Tim O'Brien," "Alpha," "Typo," "B," "K," and "W." Most of all, Pike was expected to remain controversial and colorful. "I hope you will send us a rocket to flash up our sky," Dana encouraged him. "You will thus save the country, not to speak of saving me from making a stupid paper."[26]

As chief representative at the Capitol of the nation's leading antislavery paper, James Pike could tap cooperative congressmen for news, among them Elihu Washburne, Israel Washburn, Schuyler Colfax, and Ben Wade, whom he gave good press in return. The *Tribune* also celebrated New York Senator William Seward, but that relationship soon became entangled in its rivalry with a new paper, the *New York Times*. Henry J. Raymond, Greeley's former associate editor, founded the *Times* in 1851 and began competing with the *Tribune* for Whig advertising and readers. Raymond hired an experienced and aggressive Washington correspondent, James W. Simonton, who often beat Pike in getting the news. Greeley was especially outraged when Simonton obtained advance copies of Senator Seward's speeches. It was beginning to appear as if the *Times* had become "your special organ," Greeley chided Seward. "I do not dispute your right to *make* it your organ . . . but unless you intend that, I object to whatever gives a false appearance of it."[27]

The Whig defeat in the elections of 1852 convinced Greeley that the party was doomed. More cautious New York Whigs, under Seward and Weed, clung to the wreckage of the old party, but Greeley sought a new political coalition united through its opposition to slavery. In 1854, Democratic Senator Stephen Douglas handed him a rallying cry by sponsoring legislation to organize the

Kansas and Nebraska territories and to void the Missouri Compromise, allowing settlers to decide whether to admit slavery. The maelstrom of northern opposition to the Kansas-Nebraska Act created the Republican party. At the same time, and for the same reasons, circulation of the *Weekly Tribune*, Greeley's national edition, shot up from 75,000 to 112,000 during the first six months of 1854. "Congress was never more sensitive to the public voice than it is to-day upon this measure," wrote "J. S. P." in the *Tribune*, who used his letters to stir public passions and "shake the pillars of the Capitol."[28]

Unable to remain just a journalist, Pike intervened in the congressional fight against the Kansas-Nebraska bill. When Maine elected William Pitt Fessenden to the Senate, Pike notified him: "Every possible speech is wanted and you are set down for one already." Fessenden should hurry to Washington to "give the boys aid and comfort," Pike advised. "We'll give the rascals hell in the *Tribune*." Not surprisingly, "J. S. P." praised Fessenden's maiden speech lavishly: "He commanded strict attention from all sides, and enforced the conviction on all senators present that not only had a new member come among them, but that a champion had made his appearance in the body."[29]

As the *Tribune* acclaimed Senator Fessenden, it took more hostile aim at Senator Edward Everett. A former president of Harvard, Everett had assumed Daniel Webster's mantle in the Senate and was frequently mentioned as a Whig presidential candidate, but he made the mistake of retiring to bed too early and missing the vote against the Kansas-Nebraska bill. When the *Tribune* published its dishonor roll of those absent, Everett headed the list. "If his devotion to slumber is the main reason," the *Tribune* thundered, "he ought to have remained President of Harvard." Everett sought out Senator Seward to ask "why he allowed his organ to abuse me at that rate?" But even a letter from Seward, testifying to Everett's ill health on the night of the vote, failed to mollify Greeley. The damage done and the stigma attached, Everett resigned from the Senate.[30]

James Pike's blistering letters on the Kansas-Nebraska Act showed him a better commentator than reporter, and the *Tribune* still lacked someone with the primary objective of collecting the news. "Not to write prosy vacuities, like some, or to make himself notorious and absurd like others. But a shrewd, inventive, omnipresent fellow," Charles Dana explained to Pike. "You know just what we need. Can you hunt him up for us?" Greeley wanted someone who could fish secrets out of the Senate's many closed sessions. "Everybody, from Mother Eve's time down, has been especially anxious to know what ought not to be known, and we must get some of it into the *Tribune* or be voted dull, indolent, and behind the times." Pike compounded the problem by his relentless attacks upon the Democrats, who shut doors all over Washington to him during the Democratic administration of Franklin Pierce. Greeley suggested that they look for someone like the Washington correspondent for the *Philadelphia North American*, James Harvey, who maintained ties with both parties. Unable to find anyone like Harvey, they hired Harvey. He would continue to write as "Independent" for the *North American* and become "Index" for the *Tribune*.[31]

Pike and Harvey made an effective team, for all their differences. Pike courted notoriety; Harvey remained obscure to all but Washington insiders. Pike was a northerner, so hostile to slavery that he advocated disunion rather than compromise; Harvey had been born and raised in South Carolina, and throughout a career in Philadelphia and Washington considered himself southern. Pike disdained the Irish Catholics, who voted against his Whig candidacies in Maine; Harvey was the son of Irish immigrants and had been educated in Catholic schools. Pike maintained close ties with the radical wings of the Whig and Republican parties; Harvey gravitated toward more conservative politicians and won entry into the back rooms of both Whig and Democratic administrations. Pike was a passionate man; Harvey a "calm but not a disinterested spectator." Between them, they worked out an arrangement by which Pike wrote commentary and Harvey acted more as a reporter, ferreting out facts, developing leads, and building sources. "Harvey is our regular correspondent," Pike explained; "I am rather an amateur—I come and go when I please."[32]

Editor Greeley similarly came and went as he pleased. Generally, he visited the capital for only a few days at a time, but during the winter of 1855–56, he resolved to remain there as long as necessary to elect an antislavery man Speaker of the House of Representatives. Republican strategists saw the Speaker's ability to appoint members of House committees, and to keep the legislative agenda and national attention focused on antislavery issues, as vital ingredients for the formation of a national party organization. At noon on the first Monday in December, when the roll of the Thirty-Fourth Congress was called, Greeley sat at a reporter's desk in the chamber. Each day thereafter he filed telegraphic dispatches and letters, recording vote after vote, as none of the parties could muster a majority behind any candidate. He made it clear that he favored Representative Nathaniel Banks of Massachusetts and worked in Banks's behalf in the cloakrooms as well as in the columns of his newspaper.[33]

At times, Greeley fretted that his own paper was working against him. Being on the scene in Washington made him more pragmatic than his editors in New York. He complained that their partisan blasts were interfering with getting the news. "We must have friends, not only in one party but in all parties," Greeley cautioned Dana, who was in charge during his absence. One night Greeley had sent the *Tribune* an erroneous report on a Democratic caucus, based on the overheard conversation of a Democratic congressman. "Now, don't you see," Greeley wrote Dana, "that I can't get into Democratic caucuses; I must learn what they do from somebody; and if we pick a quarrel with all opponents personally, what chance do we have for news?" Greeley warned his New York editors to stop abusing Senator John M. Clayton. "I don't particularly want to use Clayton," he said, "but Harvey does, and he is about the best man to pump in the Senate."[34]

Greeley suffered physical and emotional pain for his intervention in the race for Speaker. After the House cast its 118th unsuccessful ballot, Arkansas Democrat Albert Rust proposed that all leading contenders withdraw in favor of a compromise candidate. Greeley reacted indignantly to Rust's effort to block Banks's election. "I have had some acquaintance with human degradation," he wrote to the *Tribune;* "yet it did seem to me to-day that Rust's resolution in the House was a more discreditable proposition than I had ever known gravely submitted to a legislative body." The day after the letter appeared, Greeley unfortunately encountered Rust on a snowy path across the Capitol grounds. The powerfully built congressman made his editorial reply with his fists on Greeley's head.[35]

"I must give it up and go home," a dispirited Greeley wrote from his hotel room, his sore head swathed in wet cloths. "You are getting everybody to curse me," he blamed Dana. "I am too sick to be out of bed, too crazy to sleep, and am surrounded by horrors." But after a little rest Greeley was back in the House in time to cover Banks's election on the 133rd ballot. He decided to remain in Washington for a few more weeks. "Of course I shall stay in this infernal hole," Greeley told Pike. "Did you ever stay in a place where you didn't dare look in the glass when you got up in the morning for fear of seeing a scoundrel?"[36]

The southern congressman's assault on a northern editor was soon followed by another southern congressman's caning of Massachusetts Senator Charles Sumner at his desk in the Senate Chamber. "Probably a majority of the members of Congress went to their seats armed to-day," reported "J. S. P." "The South is at war against the North for trying to prevent the spread of slavery, and the habits of many of her children are the habits of barbarians."[37]

In the 1850s, every national issue, including the debate over the route of the first transcontinental railroad, became a regional dispute. The *Tribune* favored a northern route for the railroad as a stimulus for the westward movement, but the paper's Washington correspondents sensed trouble. "Index" warned of suspicious lobbying efforts in favor of the Pacific Railroad bill. "J. S. P." saw the bill as just a trap to "catch Uncle Sam" for his land and money. Pike had picked up signals that the bill's supporters would pay for his support. "You and Harvey . . . must have a section of land," New York Republican Representative O. B. Matteson suggested to Pike one day in the House chamber. When Pike made no reply, the congressman added: "Well, some of these sections are pretty valuable—worth as much as ten dollars an acre." An offended "J. S. P." began to contradict Greeley's editorials by warning of corruption in the railroad bill. If the new Republican party did not stand above suspicion, Pike argued, the moral force of its principles would be lost, and it would sink into contempt.[38]

The scandal broke not in the pages of the *Tribune* but in the rival *New York Times*, whose correspondent "S" (James Simonton) denounced the Pacific Railroad bill as a "football of cliques who would use it for their own purposes." Lobbyists, "whose hands reek with the slime of congressional corruption," had shaped the bill to pillage federal lands. An accompanying editorial in the *Times* charged that some thirty to forty members of the House stood to profit by their votes on the bill. Angry House members directed their fire against Simonton until a freshman representative revealed that another member had offered him $1,500 to vote for the railroad land grant. Chagrined, the House appointed a select committee to investigate the charges.[39]

James Pike cooperated as a witness at the hearings, naming Representative Matteson as his tempter. Simonton, however, proved more coy on the stand than in his dispatches. He had no "legal evidence" of corruption in the House and had gathered his story from rumors and inferences. A former congressman, George W. Chase, had offered him a stake in the land bill, and Simonton had later seen Chase whispering in the ears of various House members before the vote. Simonton also testified that two representatives had approached him to act as an intermediary to sell their votes, but they made him promise not to reveal their names. "In my profession," he explained, "such questions are put to me every day." Only after he was arrested by the House Sergeant at Arms and brought to the House chamber did Simonton agree to name names privately, stipulating that his information not be used as evidence against them. The investigating committee recommended that Matteson and three other House members be expelled, but they resigned before the House took action. Instead, the House expelled James Simonton.[40]

The *Tribune* saw nothing noble in Simonton's defense of his confidential sources. "If the press exercises a gigantic influence, it has commensurate responsibilities," the *Tribune* loftily proclaimed. "Members of Congress are still human beings, and ought not to be libeled, ought not to be attacked for the fun of the thing, ought not to be used simply to create a sensation and sell newspapers." Greeley's paper had other reasons to doubt James Simonton's civic virtue. A decade earlier, "Richelieu" had exposed Simonton—then a reporter for the *Washington Union*—for offering to sell secret Senate documents to whichever newspaper met his price. Under examination by a Senate committee, Simonton had confessed to helping a friend get a claim through Congress, for a "small" compensation. He also admitted to lobbying for a Wisconsin land bill. Under this cloud, Simonton left Washington and went west to cover military campaigns. (In later years, a reformed James Simonton returned to prominence as director of the New York Associated Press, where he helped expose scandals in the Grant administration.)[41]

The *New York Times,* sore from its bruising during the Simonton affair, struck back by accusing the *Tribune's* "principal Washington correspondent" of peddling disunion. James Pike had indeed written that the North should withdraw if the South refused to abolish slavery. Editor Greeley suppressed "J. S. P.'s" disunionist letters during the presidential election of 1856 but allowed them to be printed after the Democratic victory. Responding to the *Times,* Greeley pointed out that his paper regularly carried opinions with which he did not agree and that Pike was just an occasional writer rather than his principal Washington correspondent. Feeling cut adrift by his editor, Pike wrote that he did not desire disunion, but that if the "Slave Power" continued to dominate the federal government, antislavery forces would be left with a choice of submission or separation. Greeley published the letter but tagged it "a very circular piece of logic."[42]

Despite the strains between them, Pike continued to write as Greeley's "Special Correspondent" for another four years. Instead it was "Our Own Correspondent," James Harvey, whom the *Tribune* lost. In 1856, Harvey scored his greatest journalistic coup by penetrating the secrecy of the Supreme Court. Harvey had long promoted the presidential candidacy of Supreme Court Justice John McLean, and saw the court's handling of the Dred Scott case as the vehicle for winning him the Republican nomination. Justice McLean cooperated by providing the reporter with unprecedented access to the court's deliberations. "All our opinions were published in the New York *Tribune* the next day after the opinions were expressed," complained Justice John Catron. "This was of course a gross breach of confidence, as the information could only have come from a judge who was present." Perhaps because of his triumph, Harvey's relations with the *Tribune* soured. The tight-fisted Greeley would not raise his salary, and Harvey returned to the *North American.*[43]

With Harvey's departure the quality of the *Tribune's* reporting from Washington noticeably declined. Pike continued his commentaries, but none of the paper's day-to-day reporters met the editors' standards. When important news broke during the struggle between President James Buchanan and Congress over the Kansas constitution, the *Tribune* often had to run Associated Press stories because its own correspondent was absent. The *Tribune* then hired a Massachusetts abolitionist and temperance lecturer, Simon P. Hanscom, who came strongly recommended by Indiana Representative Schuyler Colfax. Pike considered Hanscom a fool, and Harvey thought him a crook, but according to managing editor Dana, "Colfax, who is a special friend of Greeley's, never ceases urging Horace to give him a chance. That's the secret of his engagement, which, I am happy to say, is only to the end of the session." When Hanscom's contract was not renewed, he justified all suspicions by switching allegiances and becoming Washington correspondent for the arch rival *New York Herald*. In his wake, the *Tribune's* correspondence appeared without even the customary pseudonyms, indicating the interchangeability of its authors.[44]

The politics of 1860 achieved everything for which Greeley and the *Tribune* had labored. At the Republican convention, the editor led an "anyone but Seward" movement to deny William Seward the presidency. Greeley grinned broadly and Thurlow Weed was reduced to tears as the convention nominated Abraham Lincoln. (Later, when Lincoln appointed Seward secretary of state, Weed exacted his revenge by blocking Greeley's bid to fill the vacant seat in the Senate.) The Republicans won on a platform that embraced the *Tribune's* favorite issues: free labor, a homestead act, a protective tariff, and a transcontinental railroad. But the election also triggered secession and the threat of war. In its twentieth anniversary issue, on 10 April 1861, the *Tribune* carried reports of the naval fleet on its way to reinforce Fort Sumter.[45]

The wages of political journalism were patronage. Editor Greeley lost his chance for a Senate seat, but his former Washington correspondents won a generous share of political plums from the new Republican administration. "Richelieu" became assessor of internal revenue in the third district of New York. Mrs. Swisshelm took a clerkship in the Treasury Department. "J. S. P." received a long-desired diplomatic appointment as minister to The Hague. "Index" also went overseas. James Harvey believed himself due an appointment in recognition of his "twenty years of hard political labor," but turned down The Hague, "plainly because I am poor," to become minister to Portugal.[46]

Their departures cleared the way for Greeley's most disastrous choice of a Washington correspondent. At the height of the secession crisis, in early 1861, the *Tribune* sent to Washington a hotheaded Iowa abolitionist, Fitz Henry Warren. Soon Warren's rooms near the Willard Hotel became the gathering place of the most radical congressional Republicans, who traded rumors and cursed the inactivity of the Union army. Warren's circle suspected Abraham Lincoln of having no intention of suppressing the rebellion and of simply delaying in order to achieve a compromise with the South. The radicals demanded a short, sharp campaign aimed at the rebel capital of Richmond. [47]

"On to Richmond!" cried Warren's letters to the *Tribune* throughout May and June. Daily, the paper ran the banner: "Forward to Richmond! The Rebel Congress must not be allowed to meet there by the 20th of July!" As the chant spread through the North, it pressed the Lincoln administration to launch an offensive. So at dawn on 20 July 1861, congressmen and correspondents stood together on the streets of Centreville, Virginia, to watch the Union army march confidently toward Bull Run. Throughout the day, reporters dashed from the front lines to the telegraph offices with news of the latest Union advances. *New York Times* editor Henry Raymond had just sent off another optimistic report when he confronted Union troops fleeing from battle. Unexpected Confederate reinforcements had turned the tide, sweeping correspondents and congressmen into the pell-mell of retreat back toward Washington. [48]

Much blame for the Union army's defeat fell upon the *Tribune's* "On to Richmond!" agitation. A stunned Horace Greeley disavowed any connection with the campaign and, in a signed letter, promised to bar any criticism of army tactics in his paper. "Correspondents and reporters may state facts, but must forebear comment," he instructed. Fitz Henry Warren submitted his resignation as Washington correspondent and returned to Iowa, where he raised a cavalry unit. Charles Dana resigned as managing editor, having lost Greeley's favor for his share in the blunder. Dana always insisted that the "On to Richmond!" cry had simply repeated Greeley's own exhortations to his Washington correspondent, which the editor had allowed to be repeated daily through his columns. [49]

From 1841 to 1861, Greeley's *New York Tribune* had fielded an impressive roster of Washington correspondents, who had variously demonstrated the complex relationships involved in Washington reporting. On the level of relations between editors and correspondents, Greeley and Dana set the tone for their paper, dispatching writers who reflected their views, upbraiding them when they deviated from the editorial line, and exhorting them to set off enough journalistic fireworks to sell papers. Another level of relations existed between the *Tribune*'s Washington correspondents and those representing other papers. As in the case of William Robinson and George Dwight, they sought to beat each other for news but also traded information between themselves. Correspondents banded together to sort out truth from rumor, read and evaluated each other's stories, and covered for each other during absence, illnesses, and hangovers. They developed the practice of "blacksheeting," by which a reporter lent carbon copies of his stories to fellow journalists—so long as they corresponded for papers from other cities—and could count on reciprocal favors when needed.

A third level of relations existed between Washington correspondents and the politicians they covered. Like the reporters of debate, the letter writers devised their own set of unwritten rules. Jane Swisshelm had violated these rules when she exposed Daniel Webster's private indiscretions. William Robinson had upheld them when he refused to divulge his sources to a Senate investigating committee. Being dependent on a small body of political leaders for news, Washington journalists played by the rules or got little inside information. Horace Greeley learned this lesson during the Speakership fight. When his paper attacked on a strictly partisan basis, it lost important sources inside the other party.

The pulls and pushes of these various relationships helped move news reporting toward greater balance, in spite of editors' partisan leanings. Greeley's managing editors at the *Tribune* promoted "objectivity" by showing displeasure over their Washington correspondents' editorializing and by hiring James Harvey to obtain straight reporting to accompany James Pike's commentary. Nevertheless, Greeley undermined these efforts through his compulsion to intervene in the political process, to shape political events, to build political parties, and to lead political movements. If Horace Greeley never achieved the type of reporting he desired from the capital, it was largely because of the mixed signals he sent his Washington correspondents.

3

Horace White Speculates on the War

THE PRESS and public men achieved nearly "universal accord," in the words of one Civil War correspondent, "so long as active war was waged along the Union front." Congress and its correspondents were observers of a war fought at times within earshot of the city and conducted under a commander in chief unafraid to use unprecedented executive authority. The conflict introduced a generation of talented journalists to political reporting and to the leadership of the Republican party, just coming into control of the federal government. Washington's press corps swelled with newcomers, among them the *Chicago Tribune*'s Horace White, who shared cramped boardinghouses with the congressmen he covered, and built friendships that led to valuable sources of information and patronage. Mutually dedicated to a Union victory, both politicians and reporters also recognized that fortunes could be won in the speculative wartime capital.[1]

After a decade of political turmoil, the Civil War ushered in an era of Republican ascendancy. Southern Democrats seceded, while northern Democrats were stigmatized for their antiwar sentiments. The federal government grew to meet the emergency, and the new Republicans enacted a program of land distribution, protective tariffs, and currency and banking reforms that ran contrary to the old Jeffersonian Republican creed of limited government. While the northern press largely embraced these changes, Washington reporters found evidence that an expansive government fostered corruption. Still partisan by nature, correspondents were torn between telling what they saw and telling what they believed would advance their party.[2]

Secession forged unity between the press and politicians. Southern Democratic senators and representatives withdrew from Con-

gress with their states, leaving Republican members virtually un-
opposed. Similarly, in the absence of reporters to Democratic
papers, the press galleries largely reported for the northern Republican press. In 1860, ten correspondents worked exclusively for
southern papers. By 1861, all were gone, including Eliab Kingman, the dean of the Washington press corps whose loss of southern clients forced his retirement. By contrast, the number of
northern and western papers represented in Washington multiplied to meet the public appetite for war news. Only a handful
of Democratic correspondents remained to struggle against the
odds.[3]

The war brought "a new class of news-gatherers into service," as
Ben: Perley Poore discovered. The veteran Washington correspondent had spent the early days of the war drilling Massachusetts
troops on a field near Annapolis. Mustered out after his three
months' service in August 1861, Major Poore returned to the capital to find that "a corps of quick-witted, plucky young fellows" had
entered his business. Established correspondents such as James
Harvey resented the new type of reporters pouring into Washington. Harvey complained of those "cheap chaps" competing against
him: "No man who does his whole duty properly, and has the necessary faculties, can afford to give his time and labor at the price
these Bohemians do, who have degraded journalism and damaged
the papers with which they have been connected."[4]

To James Harvey, the "Bohemian" reporters lacked principles.
His was a generational complaint against younger men less set in
their ways and willing to work for less pay. The newcomers were
better journalists than Harvey could admit. They had left jobs as
schoolteachers, lawyers, and small town editors to witness a monumental war firsthand. Young, free-spirited, and literary-minded,
they adopted the label "Bohemian," which had gained popularity
among New York journalists before the Civil War. The Bohemians
contained their share of adventurers, entrepreneurs, and spoils-
men. Unlike the *New York Tribune* and a few other metropolitan
dailies, most newspapers could not afford the exclusive services of
a Washington correspondent, and none considered it worthwhile
to pay a reporter to remain in Washington during the long months
that Congress was out of session. By necessity, correspondents became independent operatives, selling their stories to whatever
papers would buy them, regardless of their editorial policy, and

seeking outside sources of income from patronage, lobbying, and speculation.

Few journalists embodied these contradictions more thoroughly than did Horace White, ardent abolitionist and financial speculator, who came to Washington in 1861 for the *Chicago Tribune*. Born in New Hampshire in 1834, White moved as a child to the frontier town of Beloit, Wisconsin, founded as a colony of the New England Emigrating Society by his enterprising father. After his father's death, young Horace was raised by a pious, Calvinist stepfather, who scorned dancing, theater going, card playing, and fiction reading. By the time Horace White entered Beloit College, he was ripe for rebellion, and there he earned a suspension for "intemperance, gaming, falsehood and being under the imputation of theft." Following some reflection and repentance, he returned to the school and graduated in 1853, without completely losing his gaming spirit.

Once a paperboy for the *Beloit News*, Horace White looked to a career in journalism, in a bigger city that offered better chances for advancement. He applied for a job on the *Chicago Journal* and was appointed city editor. The paper had a staff of three and, whenever it could afford to, paid him a weekly salary of five dollars. Outside financial deals kept him better funded. Convinced that great fortunes waited "for those who know how to get at them," White devised elaborate schemes to get rich by investing in Illinois coal lands. He planted stories in the *Journal* to stimulate public investment in his property and then sold out before the mines became operational. If other investors could not "go on and manage the thing as judiciously as we did, they will suffer the consequences of their own stupidity or perverseness," he reassured uneasy partners.

Horace White abandoned reporting in 1856 to join the Chicago-based National Kansas Committee, an organization that purchased arms, ammunition, and supplies for antislavery settlers, outfitting John Brown among others. White's passionate commitment to the Free Soil cause did not prevent his speculation in Kansas land. The Panic of 1857, however, dashed his financial plans and sent him back into journalism.[5]

Joining the staff of the Republican *Chicago Tribune*, White was assigned to cover the Illinois senatorial campaign between incumbent Stephen Douglas and challenger Abraham Lincoln. For all his materialistic ambitions, White took his politics seriously, convinced that "all the work of saving the country had to be done then and there." His reporting of the Lincoln-Douglas debates promoted Abraham Lincoln's national reputation far beyond a losing Senate race. In February 1860, White advised Lincoln to get into "training for the Presidency," and the next year he followed the new president to Washington.[6]

As the *Chicago Tribune's* new Washington correspondent, Horace White took residence in Mrs. Chipman's Republican-leaning boardinghouse, whose messmates included Representative Elihu Washburne of Illinois, Senator William Fessenden of Maine, and Senator James Grimes of Iowa. Nearby was the private home of Illinois Senator Lyman Trumbull and his family, with whom White soon developed "terms of intimacy." In making congressional friendships, White had a distinct advantage over his bachelor rivals in the press corps. His attractive young wife, Martha, had accompanied him and became a favorite of the congressmen and their wives.[7]

Horace White's impressions of Washington differed sharply from those of his predecessor, Joseph Medill, who had thought the capital a dull town populated with idle folk. After Lincoln's inauguration, the city transformed itself into a teeming wartime center. Even the shape of the Capitol Building was changing, to the correspondents' advantage. Prewar western expansionism had added so many states, and so many congressmen, that the Senate and House outgrew their quarters. In the 1850s, massive new wings were constructed on the north and south ends of the Capitol to provide larger chambers. But the new chambers were acoustical disasters. Sound bounced off recessed walls and was absorbed through glass ceilings. One representative described the House chamber as "the worst place in America for a man to speak," into which many fine orators entered, never to be heard from again.[8]

Reporters and correspondents had a harder time hearing the debates, but in other respects the new chambers suited them comfortably. Both the House and Senate reserved prominent sections of their galleries exclusively for journalists. Located immediately above the presiding officers' rostrums in both chambers, these press galleries afforded correspondents a panoramic view of the members at their desks. Behind the galleries, through etched glass doors, were spacious lobbies fitted with tables and chairs, pens and

Horace White, the *Chicago Tribune*'s correspondent and editor.

ink, and stationery and other amenities, furnished at public expense. The new press galleries also housed telegraph offices, to save the correspondents a trip downtown. "By this means," a House planning committee predicted, "the report of an hour's speech might be completely set up in New York within fifteen minutes of its delivery." Accredited journalists drew desks according to old traditions. The *Congressional Globe's* reporters of debate occupied a table on the floor and the front row of desks in the press gallery. Beside them sat the reporters of the *National Intelligencer* and other Washington papers. In rows behind them were desks reserved for the reporters for the Associated Press, and further back sat Horace White of the *Chicago Tribune*, together with correspondents for other out-of-town papers.[9]

Expansion of the Capitol Building created space for committee rooms and permitted the hiring of staff. By 1860, every congressional committee with substantive business could hire a clerk for the duration of the session. The few committees—Finance, Ways and Means, Printing, and Claims—that received material after Congress had adjourned, employed year-round staff. Who better to hire as clerks than newspaper correspondents? They were literate, hungry for additional salary, and in town exactly the same months as the Congress. The first committee clerks did little more than handle mail and official documents, leaving ample time for correspondents to write their dispatches.[10]

Horace White secured his clerkships from his messmates. Representative Elihu Washburne first found him a post at the Treasury Department, until the *Chicago Tribune's* editor, Joseph Medill, objected that a year-round position would prevent White from returning to Chicago during congressional recesses. Senator Grimes then appointed White clerk of the Senate Committee on the District of Columbia, for an extra six dollars a day. Naturally, White treated his sponsors favorably in his dispatches to the *Tribune*, but the patronage left him open to attack from senators he treated less favorably. Wisconsin's James R. Doolittle took the Senate floor to complain that he could not "pension" correspondents like White and purchase the praise "by which great men and heroes are manufactured here."[11]

Along with Horace White, a small army of practicing journalists drew second salaries as committee clerks. Whitelaw Reid, who reported as "Agate" for the *Cincinnati Gazette*, was clerk of the

House Military Affairs Committee and House librarian. David Bartlett, of the *New York Evening Post*, served as clerk of the House Committee on Elections. The *New York Times*'s Lorenzo Crounse clerked for the House Committee on Banking and Currency, and Uriah Painter of the *Philadelphia Inquirer*, for the House Committee on Post Offices and Post Roads. J. A. McKean of the *Chicago Post* served as clerk of two House committees, while Richard Hinton, correspondent for the *Worcester Spy*, indexed private claims for Congress.[12]

The *Boston Journal*'s Ben: Perley Poore took his first clerkship in 1859 with the House Foreign Affairs Committee and remained on the congressional payroll almost perpetually for the next quarter century. In 1862 he gave up clerking for the Senate Foreign Relations Committee to become clerk of the Committee on Printing and Records. Inside information on foreign policy might have provided more news for a correspondent, but the Printing Committee offered something even more valuable: regular government printing contracts. In truth, secrets learned as a committee clerk often inhibited a correspondent. Poore could not overtly leak information that came across his desk if he hoped to retain his position. As one of Poore's officemates once commented, he felt "rather sensitive about speculating as to what the opinion of the Senate may be, as he himself is an officer of the Senate, and it might embarrass him."[13]

For such favored correspondents, committee clerkships provided salaries, access to the House and Senate floor and members, and advance notice of committee business. Some committee clerks also made a profitable business out of selling committee secrets. For instance, the correspondents knew the clerk of the House Ways and Means Committee, George Bassett, to be corrupt. "He did sell confidential news contrary to his oath, and he plays broker," correspondent E. B. Wight informed his editor. Simon Hanscom once notified the *New York Herald* that he had been unable to send full details of a tax bill in the Ways and Means Committee because its clerk had been absent from the closed session.[14]

Patronage for some stirred resentment among the rest of the press gallery. Noah Brooks objected to his confinement in the gallery while other correspondents circulated below on the floor, "where they have managed to be smuggled in as Committee Clerks to the disgust and envy of their less fortunate or less pushy brethren." Brooks earned $2,000 a year from the *Sacramento Union,* an amount he sought to double by running for election as House postmaster, at $2,500 annually. Heading his ticket were two other journalists, Indiana editor Schuyler Colfax for Republican Speaker of the House, and Pennsylvania editor Edward McPherson for Clerk of the House. Colfax and McPherson won, but Brooks had to settle for the clerkship of a minor committee. The consolation job paid "quite as well," he conceded, "and has neither work or responsibility in it, so I have no reason to complain." As a committee clerk, Brooks had an office located conveniently near the House chamber, easy access to the House floor, and funds to live in high style.[15]

Besides patronage, correspondents' friendships with politicians aided them in dealing with telegraph censorship. By the 1860s, the telegraph dictated a Washington reporter's work patterns. Wartime public demand for news put the slightest information at a premium that justified paying telegraph tolls. Editors forgot earlier objections to telegraph bills and demanded instant reporting. For a West Coast correspondent like Brooks, telegraph expenses still kept his dispatches down to brief notices of the most important events. Brooks's fuller accounts went out by letters, carried by stagecoach or steamboat via Panama—either way taking a month to reach his paper. For eastern and midwestern reporters, the charges were less onerous, and publishers paid for whatever they could get. But their increased use of the telegraph put the correspondents at the mercy of arbitrary government censors.[16]

Newspaper correspondents accepted military censorship as a necessity of the war and pledged to suppress information that might aid and comfort the enemy. But they chafed at political censorship. The Department of State, which at the beginning of the war supervised telegraph censorship from the capital, steadily widened its nets to prohibit unfair criticism of the civil government. What constituted legitimate and illegitimate criticism remained ambiguous. Censors scrutinized dispatches to eliminate anything remotely critical of the Lincoln administration and took the privilege of adding or subtracting material from stories, which were then published "in the most absurd style." As stories ended in government wastebaskets, editors complained of hearing nothing from their correspondents. Republican correspondents sympathetic to the administration had less trouble getting their stories accepted, but George W. Adams, who wrote for a Democratic paper, complained of it being "impossible to send a word against anyone connected with the Government, however merited and just, and however slight it may be—by telegraph." Even Sam Wilkeson, correspondent for the Republican *New York Tribune,* found deletions in his dispatches. Once he telegraphed an account of congressional uproar over the cost of printing treasury notes. When the story appeared, Wilkeson noticed that the censors had eliminated one line: "Wait till the bills come in for engraving and printing a useless diploma of honor for all the soldiers enlisted during the war—a job authorized by a department which has nothing to do with soldiers or sailors." The unnamed department had been the State Department, whose censors killed the reference.[17]

Stories that a reporter could hear in any Washington hotel would not pass the telegraph censors. Censors once deleted an item that George Adams had simply copied from a Washington newspaper. More disturbing to Adams was the revelation that the censors were approving stories for Republican papers while killing the same items when he tried to send them to the Democratic *New York World.* In December 1861, members of the press gallery appealed to friends on Capitol Hill. The House Judiciary Committee obligingly held hearings and called such disgruntled correspondents as Ben: Perley Poore, Sam Wilkeson, and George Adams. But committee members were particularly interested in hearing from the one correspondent to whom the censors gave no trouble. Why had the Department of State specifically exempted Associated Press reporter Lawrence Gobright from censorship? "I have no complaint to make of the censor," the veteran correspondent replied, offering this explanation: "My business is merely to communicate facts. My instructions do not allow me to make any comment upon the facts which I communicate. My despatches are sent to papers of all manner of politics, and the editors say they are able to make their own comments upon the facts which are sent to them. I therefore confine myself to what I consider legitimate news." In a sense, Gobright defined himself as an "objective" reporter, in that he did not "act as a politician belonging to any school, but [tried] to be truthful and impartial. My despatches are merely dry matters of fact and detail."[18]

Secretary Seward's growing unpopularity among the more radical Republicans in Congress helped the reporters' cause. Declaring the telegraph "a most important auxiliary to the press of the country," the House Judiciary Committee demanded that the wires be uncensored for all but military matters. No one mentioned that many members of Congress were making the same types of criticisms of the administration that the censors were excising from newspaper dispatches. Before Congress could act further, however, Lincoln muted the issue by transferring telegraphic censorship from the State to the War Department.[19]

Military censorship carried its own burdens, since military and political news were inextricably mixed. Military censors considered the *New York World* a traitorous "Copperhead" paper, and viewed George Adams's dispatches as suspiciously as had the State Department. Shrewdly, Adams cultivated the friendship of a young military censor, Benjamin Snyder. "When I tell you that I once narrowly escaped being sent to jail by Secretary [of War Edwin] Stanton, by allowing a dispatch to be sent, you can realize the extent of the confidence which I reposed in Mr. Adams' judgment and word," Snyder later confessed. Adams's impersonal style of reporting warranted the censor's trust. The unassuming and taciturn George Adams refrained from florid adjectives or violent criticism. His stories rarely were published with his name or initials. Republicans as well as Democrats regarded Adams as fair and judicious, and as a man who could hold confidences. A permanent resident of the District of Columbia, Adams endeared himself to Republican correspondents by covering news for them during their absences from the city. With this combination of reputation and well-placed friendships, he was able to congratulate himself on how much he got past the censors.[20]

Neither did the mails escape the censors. In March 1862, Horace White learned that the Post Office Department had adopted rules against mailing news of military movements. White complained to the first assistant postmaster general, John A. Kasson, that the new order was so vague that "no two postmasters or publishers could ever construe it alike." Writing to the *Chicago Tribune* editors, White reported that "Kasson don't know what the order means—that is he *presumes* it means so & so, but he admits that the language is vague & mischievous, & moreover that the whole thing is illegal." Nevertheless, mail censorship became a reality under which the correspondents had to live. When editors of the *New York Herald* complained that they had heard nothing from

Henry M. Flint, the correspondent replied: "I have written daily, ever since last Saturday, and almost every day, twice a day; namely by the 8:30 mail in the morning and the 5 o'clock mail in the afternoon." He could only conclude that the Washington post office had detained his letters.[21]

In battles with the censors, the press found champions among journalists who served in Congress. Schuyler Colfax's election as Speaker had brought special pleasure to the press gallery. Now one of their own—the proprietor and occasional letter writer to the *South Bend Register*—presided over the House of Representatives. Other House members included the Democratic leader, James Brooks, once a Washington correspondent and editor of the *New York Daily Express*, and a promising freshman from Maine, James G. Blaine, former editor of the *Portland Advertiser*. In the Senate sat Republican Henry Anthony, owner of the *Providence Journal*, and Democrat B. Gratz Brown, editor of the *Missouri Democrat*. The election of 1864 brought ten more journalists into the House, including Henry J. Raymond, editor of the *New York Times*. Although vastly outnumbered by lawyers, merchants, and farmers, the journalist-congressmen became less of an oddity during the war.[22]

To celebrate Colfax's election as Speaker, the Washington press corps hosted a dinner in his honor, one of the first of what became a favored device for bringing together reporters and politicians in a social setting. "We journalists and men of the newspaper press do love you, and claim you as bone of our bone and flesh of our flesh," said toastmaster Sam Wilkeson. "Fill your glasses, all, in an invocation to the gods for long life, greater success, and ever-increasing happiness to our editorial brother in the Speaker's Chair." Responding, Colfax thanked his press hosts for their "generous forbearance to all my shortcomings," and their sustaining of him through all of his elections. Having sprung from the press, Speaker Colfax applied the lessons of his profession skillfully, making himself always available for interviews, planting stories, sending flattering notes to editors, suggesting editorials, and spreading patronage. He intended to parlay his popularity with the press into a national following that would make him the first journalist in the White House.[23]

While Colfax presided over the House, another journalist held the chief staff office on the Senate side. John W. Forney, publisher of the *Philadelphia Press* and *Washington Sunday Chronicle*, failed to win a Senate seat from Pennsylvania but was elected Secretary of the Senate in 1861 (he previously served as Clerk of the House). A political freebooter of the first rank, Forney had bounced from faction to faction within the Democratic party before leaping with his newspapers into the Republican camp. Whatever his party, Forney was the perennial insider, fixer, and arranger. His spacious chambers in a Capitol Hill boardinghouse drew congressmen, cabinet secretaries, clerks, lawyers, and clergymen for evenings of political gossip and cards. As Secretary of the Senate, his control of patronage made him a consequential contact for the Washington press corps. Forney's Washington correspondent, John Russell Young, compared him to "a general in command at the Front." Despite his Senate post, he continued to send "daily and hourly messages" to his Philadelphia and Washington editors.[24]

President Lincoln intervened personally to assure Forney's election as Secretary of the Senate, and Forney's *Washington Chronicle* became as close to an official organ as the Lincoln administration would have. The *Chronicle*, which became a daily paper in 1862, lived off of government printing contracts and government purchases of ten thousand copies a day for distribution among the Army of the Potomac. To build public support for his administration, Lincoln spread government printing and advertising among a host of papers throughout the Union and appointed more editors, publishers, and Washington correspondents as diplomats, customs collectors, postmasters, and provost marshals than had any of his predecessors. While rewarding friends, the administration denied postal service to antiwar "Copperhead" papers, seized issues, and arrested editors.[25]

At the White House, Lincoln astutely left his door open to correspondents. He would talk to them at all hours of the day or night, although according to custom they could attribute nothing to him directly. One Canadian reporter expressed surprise over his easy entry into the president's office. "Yes," Lincoln replied, "this ready means of access is, I may say, under our form of government, the only link or cord which connects the people with the governing power; and, however unprofitable much of it is, it must be kept up."[26]

The channels of communication between the press and public men transmitted both ways. Reporters regul ahead of politicians. Congressmen tapped friendly journalists for the latest intelligence, and committees called them in to testify. In 1862 the Joint Committee on the Conduct of the War heard Uriah Painter, correspondent for the *Philadelphia Inquirer*, denounce the tactics General George McClellan had employed during the Peninsular campaign. As the committee pressed its investigation of McClellan, the *Inquirer* published regular reports that electrifying news would soon be released. Democratic papers accused Chairman Ben Wade of deliberately and systematically spreading such stories to poison public opinion against the general even before the committee released its report. Painter, who remained a close adviser to Senator Wade for years after, most likely coached the chairman on how to deal with the press. Wade at last released the report to the Associated Press and major metropolitan dailies on a Saturday, with an embargo against its publication until Monday. This gave sympathetic publishers time to set the entire report in print and prepare their editorials. The Joint Committee's report boosted Union army morale while undermining the political standing of the Democratic General McClellan, becoming a useful Republican campaign tool.[27]

Those possessing and seeking information gathered frequently at the Washington home of Henry D. Cooke. The Ohio editor had come to Washington in 1860 ostensibly as the correspondent for the *Ohio State Journal* but more as Washington agent for his brother, financier Jay Cooke. Even after he gave up reporting, Cooke entertained his "editorial friends" and traded news and stock tips with them. Cooke took under his wing the young correspondent of the *Philadelphia Inquirer*, Uriah Painter, and helped him recognize the monetary value of the news he collected. Using his knowledge of troop movements, Painter speculated in the gold markets, which rose and fell in reaction to battlefield events. Painter scored highly as a speculator, until he was caught short in the gold market's reaction to the unexpected news of Lincoln's assassination.[28]

As avid a speculator as Horace White was stunned to see the pervasive corruption in Washington. Having condemned the ethical laxity of the Buchanan administration, the *Chicago Tribune* had predicted that Lincoln's election would usher in an "age of purity." But in 1862 its Washington correspondent reported that "the tone of morality here is considered lower than it ever has been before."

Wartime federal spending magnified the plundering of the public treasury during the previous decade. White charged that "for every dollar wrongfully taken by a contractor, five have been taken by public servants," and accused Republicans and Democrats alike in raiding the treasury. "Congress has its due proportion of vagabond politicians, who think they will never have another chance, and who are bound to have 'their share.'"[29]

Accurate information in wartime Washington was a precious commodity, not only to Congress and the press but to the lobbyists, contractors, and speculators who crowded the Capitol corridors. A French officer serving with the Union army recalled how lobbyists, like a cloud of locusts, "continually besieged the bureaus of [the] administration, the doors of the Senate and House of Representatives, wherever there was a chance to gain something." Temptations abounded, which many journalists found hard to resist. Francis Richardson, who came to Washington as a journalist in 1865, learned that the correspondents had "constituted a kind of close corporation, and in association with various members of Congress profited by their early knowledge of legislation affecting the taxes, to make speculative ventures which brought them large gains."[30]

Although his Washington letters adopted a tone of moral disapproval, Horace White could not resist dabbling in wartime speculation. Acting on a tip that Congress would raise whiskey taxes in 1863, he invested in liquor stocks. When the tax was imposed, liquor prices rose sharply, and White reaped handsome profits. It was the beginnings of the fortune he had long sought. In later years, White strenuously denied having misused his official positions for profit, by which he meant that he acquired his inside information not as a committee clerk, but as a journalist. By the ethics of the day, the latter was entirely legitimate.[31]

Washington correspondents like White could rationalize their outside business dealings as long as it did not interfere with their newspaper responsibilities. Despite the war, the slow pace of the federal government left correspondents time for both reporting and financial speculation. Military news predominated over political reporting. "There is very little disposition now to print or reprint anything that does not describe a battle," Senator Charles Sumner complained in 1864. Noah Brooks described the congressional correspondents lounging in the press galleries, while "the progress of legislation would go droning on with a dreary monotony that lulled the few drowsy spectators, and gave the newspaper men an opportunity to bring up their arrears of work."[32]

By 1864, Horace White's differences of policy and personality with editor Joseph Medill had caused him to resign as the *Chicago Tribune*'s Washington correspondent. He organized the Independent News Room, with Henry Villard and Adams Hill, who had quit jobs as correspondents for the *New York Tribune* after quarreling with Horace Greeley. Their small wire service was among the first to challenge the powerful New York Associated Press. In fact, they primarily sought western papers unhappy with limited access to the Associated Press and with the high prices it charged. Gathering these subscribers, the three young reporters earned a "pleasant, lucrative and independent" living. But the powerful Associated Press went to great lengths to put its new competitor out of business, including accusing the Independent News Room of having distributed false and incendiary reports about the draft. The War Department arrested Villard, put Hill under surveillance, and called White in for questioning, but after Secretary of War Stanton became convinced of their innocence, he leaked information to the small news bureau as his means of apology.[33]

By war's end, the swelled ranks of newspaper correspondents settled permanently into Washington, considerably expanding the little band of prewar letter writers. Every editor of a major daily, and many minor ones as well, wanted his own "special correspondent" at the capital. Those who covered the war lingered to cover the political battles and watched the generals they had followed in the fields take seats in the chambers below them. New rules and traditions had also developed to govern the relations between the politicians and the press, particularly to accommodate press patronage. The House and Senate regularly voted for a bonus for congressional staff at the end of each Congress, and members found it unwise to challenge its propriety. When the fiscally conservative John Sherman led a movement against such "wild recklessness" with the public's money, he paid for his labors with bad press. "The truth is," Sherman griped to Horace Greeley, "that many of the most influential writers are connected with Congress either as Clerks to Committees or in the several offices. Many of these feel that their compensation is inadequate and as I felt it my plain duty to prevent their getting extra compensation in violation of laws they are determined to punish me."[34]

At war's end, some correspondents abandoned Washington for more prestigious editorial posts. John Russell Young, still in his twenties, became managing editor of Greeley's *New York Tribune*, until he was succeeded by another wartime correspondent, Whitelaw Reid. George Adams entered the management of the *Washington Evening Star*. Horace White took his accumulated business and speculative earnings back to Chicago where he purchased a twenty-percent share of the stock in the *Chicago Tribune*, an amount sufficient for him to displace Joseph Medill as editor-in-chief. As editor of the midwest's most influential Republican paper, White at last achieved the influence, fame, and fortune he sought. He built an impressive mansion for his family and oversaw construction of a new headquarters for the *Tribune*. On 9 October 1871, at the pinnacle of White's success, fire devastated the city of Chicago, burning White's mansion to the ground and gutting the uninsured and supposedly fireproof *Tribune* building. As he surveyed the carnage, White's thoughts inevitably returned to the Civil War. A single night of fire had "reduced the rich to poverty," he wrote in a *Tribune* editorial. The conflagration made painfully clear to him that "the War, with its sudden fortunes, its speculations, and the hot-house growth given to certain pursuits, gradually led us into habits of extravagance."[35]

White turned the editorial reigns of the *Chicago Tribune* back to Joseph Medill in 1874. In later years he engaged in railroad building with Henry Villard and regained his editorial voice through Villard's newspaper, the *New York Evening Post*, and magazine, the *Nation*. During the closing decades of the nineteenth century, the Civil War speculator and partisan journalist became a leading national spokesman for independent journalism, anti-imperialism, anti-inflationism and other liberal causes. When Horace White died in 1916, President Woodrow Wilson mourned his passing as "a loss which the whole country must feel" and credited his career as "one of moral as well as intellectual distinction."[36]

4

Ben: Perley Poore and the Bohemian Brigade

AFTER THE CIVIL WAR the "Bohemian Brigade" of hard-drinking, battle-scarred, nose-for-news war correspondents stayed in the capital as political reporters. The *Boston Journal's* Ben: Perley Poore identified true Bohemians as "willing to work hard that they may have money to spend; not caring a pin for what Mrs. Grundy may think, yet jealously sensitive about the paper they are 'on,' philosophically jolly when possible, and bestowing no thought on the future, provided they are not behind on the news of the day." For all their Bohemian self-imagery, the "special correspondents in Washington" were well-educated, middle-class professionals. If they ranked lower in social status than their attainments warranted, the fault was less the individuals' than their profession's. The nature of the Washington correspondent's labor, wrote *Harper's Weekly,* made him "unobtrusive, though prying; quiet, though busy, a listener rather than a talker; the observer rather than the observed; his identity is swallowed up in that of his journal; he is known less by his name than his title."[1]

At war's end, only six of the fifty-three correspondents who sat in the Senate and House press galleries could date their Washington service back to the antebellum era. Lawrence "Pops" Gobright claimed the longest tenure, having arrived as a correspondent during Andrew Jackson's presidency, in advance of either the railroad or telegraph. Second in seniority stood the *Boston Journal's* Benjamin Perley Poore, who had corresponded from Washington since 1847. William B. Shaw started as a government printer in 1851, before becoming the *New York Herald's* Washington correspondent. Still in his thirties during the 1860s, Shaw counted himself among the old-timers, as his pen name "Nestor" suggested. David

73

Bartlett came to Washington as editor of the *Washington New Era*, an antislavery daily paper, before taking a seat in the press gallery in 1857 as correspondent for the *Springfield Republican* (of Massachusetts).[2]

Youth was the most common attribute among the new additions to the press corps during the Civil War. Uriah Painter was twenty-two when he boarded Lincoln's inaugural train to cover Washington and the war for the *Philadelphia Inquirer.* Whitelaw Reid was twenty-four when the *Cincinnati Gazette* sent him to report on Washington and the Army of the Potomac in 1862, the same year that the *Chicago Tribune* sent twenty-eight-year-old Horace White. William Wallace Warden was a mature thirty-six and a former editor of *Pen and Pencil* when the *Cincinnati Enquirer* hired him to report from Washington in 1863. Also joining the Washington press corps that year was Joseph McCullagh, twenty-one, who had previously covered the western military campaigns. Twenty-nine-year-old Henry Van Ness Boynton, brevetted a brigadier general after being severely wounded at Missionary Ridge, replaced Whitelaw Reid as correspondent for the *Cincinnati Gazette* in 1865. At the beginning of the Thirty-Ninth Congress, which met in December 1865, the average age of the correspondents in the Senate press gallery was thirty-four, ranging from Thomas Flowers at fifty-four to James Rankin Young at nineteen.[3]

"Thoroughly popular with both old and young men," Ben: Perley Poore bridged the generations. His gregarious manner captured the Bohemian spirit of the press, but his origins were far more genteel. Poore was born on 2 November 1820, at his family's four-hundred-acre farm, Indian Hill, outside Newburyport, Massachusetts. His father, a dry-goods merchant, had married a young woman from Georgetown, so Poore could date his Washington experiences back to childhood visits to his grandparents, during the administration of John Quincy Adams.[4]

A military school student, the boy rebelled against his father's plans to send him to West Point and ran off to apprentice himself as a printer. Two years later, the elder Poore became resigned to his son's civilian inclinations and bought him ownership of a weekly newspaper, the Athens, Georgia, *Southern Whig*. At eighteen, Perley Poore set out to make his paper the Whig voice in the South. In Athens he also studied law, campaigned unsuccessfully for office, and was prosecuted for "dancing, carousing, hugging and embracing slave women" during a party at his home. Although acquitted, Poore sold the *Whig* and abandoned the South. He went abroad as diplomatic attaché in Brussels and toured Europe and North Africa, sending occasional travel letters back to New England newspapers. Returning to the United States in 1847, he was hired as Washington correspondent for the *Boston Atlas*. Next followed ventures as editor of the *Daily Bee* and *Perley's Sunday Picnic*, as biographer of Napoleon and Louis Philippe, and as author of a string of unmemorable novels, until Poore resumed his Washington correspondence for the *Boston Journal* and any other papers that would pay for his letters. Mixing political news, gossip, social commentary, and personality profiles, he called his weekly columns "waifs," for "things found and not claimed."[5]

By the late 1850s, Poore's wit and drawing room charm had gained him access to Washington's most influential men, whom he tapped as sources of news and financial support. Poore had inherited Indian Hill, the family homestead that he then expanded steadily over the years into a sixty-four room mansion with gables, turreted towers, vine-covered stone walls, and a red-shingled roof. Into its myriad rooms, corridors, and stairwells he crammed the antique furniture, china, paintings, firearms, tools, books, and autographs that he collected indiscriminately on his travels. One of America's first antiquarians, Perley Poore built an impressive and expensive collection that reflected romantic notions of the past. Meanwhile in Washington he maintained rooms at fashionable hotels, and his full figure displayed a taste for fine food and drink.[6]

Poore's appetites were hard to satisfy on a reporter's salary, given that the *Boston Journal* paid its Washington correspondent only for the months when Congress was in session. (When Congress adjourned, Poore told his readers, Washington became as "silent as a theatre when the performances are concluded, and the spectators have gone home.") To make ends meet, he wrote speeches for congressmen, clerked for three committees, and collected more than his share of federal patronage and subsidy. Poore spent the money as fast as it came in. His debts, and his compulsions to collect, led him into temptation. Southerners pictured Poore as a scavenging magpie who had helped himself to captured Confederate documents, in the custody of the Senate Committee on Printing and Records, to augment his celebrated autograph collection. The catalog of Poore's holdings at the time of his death amply verified

Ben: Perley Poore of the *Boston Journal*.

these accusations. His "relics" contained manuscript copies of congressional messages from every president during his clerkship, Buchanan's manuscript inaugural address, and other purloined government documents.[7]

The Printing Committee, chaired by Rhode Island's Senator Henry Anthony (the publisher of the *Providence Journal*), hired Poore as its clerk and issued regular contracts for him to edit government publications. He expanded and redesigned the annual *Congressional Directory*, produced a handy guide to government documents, and created the *Biographical Directory of the American Congress*. The latter directory, with its short biographies of every person who had served in the Senate, House, and Continental Congress, involved a substantial degree of plagiarism. Charles Lanman, who supported himself by compiling privately published biographical dictionaries of Congress, was astonished to discover that Congress had published its own volume in direct competition with his. Lanman found that the government volume had lifted biographical entries wholesale from his own book and "was *copyrighted* and dedicated to Senator H.B. Anthony" by the clerk of Anthony's committee, Ben: Perley Poore.[8]

During the Civil War, the demand for Poore's writings spiraled, and he added more newspapers to the list receiving his dispatches, under assorted pseudonyms. By the 1860s it was not unusual for a metropolitan daily to run two pages of Washington reports. The *New York Herald,* for example, seldom published less than a column of Washington "specials," telegraph dispatches of its own correspondents, and several columns of congressional floor proceedings from the Associated Press. The *Herald* paid five cents a word for telegrams from its correspondents, but only a fraction of a cent per word for its share of Associated Press reports. Still, the "specials" gave each paper its unique personality and its competitive edge. This accounted for the higher salaries that Washington correspondents received—an average of twenty-five to fifty dollars a week during the congressional sessions. Several correspondents boasted salaries exceeding the ninety-six dollars a week paid to members of Congress.[9]

Poore's daily routine as a Washington correspondent during the 1860s saw his mornings spent in committee rooms and afternoons in the press galleries. In their lobby behind the press gallery, he and other reporters held their own informal sessions, commenting in a "not overcomplimentary" manner on the chamber proceedings. Whenever the floor debate percolated, or a vote was called, the reporters took their seats in the gallery, scribbled notes, .and then raced to the telegraph operators.[10]

Leaving the Capitol late in the afternoons, Poore would tour the city's major hotels where politicians, military officers, and journalists met at the bar, and no one thought or talked "of anything else but politics." The Willard and Ebbitt hotels anchored opposite ends of Fourteenth Street, off Pennsylvania Avenue. During the war this stretch took the name Newspaper Row for its many ramshackle newspaper offices. Correspondents gravitated to "the Row" because the telegraph office stood at its corner, it lay within walking distance of the executive departments, and the horse-drawn F Street trolley connected it to Capitol Hill.[11]

When correspondent Henry Villard sought out the *New York Tribune*'s office on Newspaper Row in 1862, he found it in a small, one-story brick building opposite the Willard. Its entire staff consisted of Sam Wilkeson and his young, Harvard-trained assistant, Adams S. Hill. As the *Tribune*'s war correspondent, Villard operated entirely independent of the paper's Washington bureau, stopping at the office only to file his telegraphic dispatches over their wires. The muddy, overcrowded, inelegant city left Villard unimpressed. Similarly, Franc Wilkie, who wrote as "Galeway" for the *New York Times*, dismissed the wartime capital as a cesspool of contractors, office seekers, confidence men, and courtesans. Military censorship of the telegraph made Washington "a dull point for news" for Wilkie, who departed for the front lines. He held the reporters he left behind in low regard. "Excepting Whitelaw Reid and Ben: Perley Poore," Wilkie scoffed, "the correspondents there were nobodies."[12]

Unless Congress held a night session, Poore spent his evenings on Newspaper Row, writing dispatches from nine to midnight. During these evenings, members of Congress would drop by to read early news reports or to pass along the latest tip. Such personal contacts had grown increasingly essential for a correspondent's success. Associated Press reports supplied their newspapers with the straight facts of any day's session in Congress, leaving it for the correspondent to provide a meaningful interpretation, slanted to the local interests of his readers. A correspondent's inside knowledge therefore justified his professional existence and higher-than-average salary.[13]

The typical Newspaper Row bureau consisted of an anteroom, reading room, reporters' room, and chief correspondent's room, the "sanctum sanctorum" guarded by a trusty janitor. Late night visitors could divulge confidential information in these back rooms without interlopers interrupting or recognizing them. Correspondents maintained high security to protect their sources from other journalists. "Each correspondent is on the alert, anxious not to be 'beaten' by some rival," Ben: Perley Poore explained. Despite their rivalry, a camaraderie existed among the competitors. They referred to themselves as a fraternity and "reportorial brotherhood." They were neighbors in the fullest sense of the word, occupying desks beside each other in the press galleries and offices next to each other on the Row, and standing shoulder to shoulder at the hotel bars. Their impulse to crowd together put space on Newspaper Row at a premium, both inside and outside their modest buildings. Perley Poore noted that some correspondents represented so many newspapers simultaneously that they had difficulty finding room to hang all the identifying signs that publishers sent to their "own correspondent."[14]

As a Washington old-timer, Poore had at first scoffed at the offices springing up along the Row, but eventually he felt compelled to keep up with the competition. When other Boston papers opened offices, Poore set out to convince his tight-fisted publishers that the *Boston Journal* needed a Washington bureau outside his hotel room. "I can get a decent office on 14th Street, in 'the row,' exclusive for $30 pr month," he wrote, "and it will cost about $200 for signs, furniture, &c in good shape." He estimated that the rent cost only one quarter of what the larger New York papers were paying for Washington offices. "There will be no extravagance, but the place will be worthy of the paper," Poore promised.[15]

As congressional visitors flowed nightly into the offices along the Row, they could talk of little beside their rift with President Andrew Johnson. Everything had changed since Johnson inherited the presidency from the assassinated Abraham Lincoln. Initially, Johnson counted on strong support from Republicans in Congress and from their allies in the press galleries. Correspondent David Bartlett, an abolitionist before the war and radical reconstructionist after, cautioned readers of the *New York Independent* not to make hasty judgments of the new president. "Personally, he favors negro suffrage," Bartlett wrote with assurance. "He has said so repeatedly of late." Colonel John W. Forney, seeking to keep his patronage lines open to the new administration, appraised Johnson as a "practical statesman" whose policies offered "a common ground upon which all earnest loyalists can meet." Forney judged that "the overwhelming majority of the Union masses are with President Johnson."[16]

The president's honeymoon with Republican congressmen and journalists ended when he vetoed the Freedman's Bureau bill in February 1866. In Congress, Republican moderates constructed the bill to unite their party and passed it by overwhelming majorities in both houses. Forney, still serving as Secretary of the Senate, had expected the president to sign the bill to protect the freedmen against "the intrigues and cruelties of their late masters." But when Johnson vetoed the bill on grounds that the states it most affected remained excluded from Congress, a stunned Forney damned the president as a Copperhead. Forney's defection did not escape Johnson's notice. When a cheering crowd of his supporters outside the White House shouted "Give it to Forney!" Johnson responded: "I do not waste my ammunition upon dead ducks."[17]

Johnson's belligerence toward congressional reconstruction united moderate and radical forces against him. "He has broke the faith, betrayed the trust, and must sink from detestation to contempt," cried Senator Fessenden, author of the Freedmen's Bureau bill, a sentiment echoed by the Washington correspondents. D. F. Drinkwater, House correspondent for the United Press Association, decried Johnson's "sympathy with treason and traitors and his persistent and unchangeable efforts to do all in his power against the loyal and for the disloyal." Horace White, now editor of the *Chicago Tribune*, broke with Johnson following the veto, while John Russell Young, now writing editorials for the *New York Tribune*, declared the administration dishonored.[18]

Within the Washington press corps, the president retained only a small circle of allies—more often unscrupulous men who took advantage of Johnson's isolation after his policies alienated him from respectable reporters. William W. Warden, who corresponded principally as "Data" for the *Baltimore Sun* (and also reported for the *Boston Post, Cincinnati Enquirer, Philadelphia Ledger,* and *New York Times*), served as the president's private secretary and as a conduit between the White House and Capitol Hill. Other correspondents viewed Warden suspiciously, certain that he would not hesitate to use his inside position to scoop them. In 1867, when Johnson's Annual Message appeared in the press even before it reached Congress, Representative Robert Schenck charged that a White House lackey had sold the message. The accusation produced "significant winks" in the press gallery, and the *Washington Evening Star* confirmed that "the correspondent for the *Boston Post* peddled the message yesterday by telegraph through all the cities of the country, compelling [the other correspondents] to send the message to their papers in self-defense." William Warden was the *Boston Post*'s correspondent.[19]

Another journalist of questionable ethics, Simon Hanscom, also attached himself to Johnson's presidency. One of the few men who could enter the president's office unannounced, Hanscom developed a reputation as an office-jobber, using his influence to arrange for federal appointments, at a fee. Instead of denying the charge, he advertised it. When former Congressman James Buffington welshed on an agreement to pay for appointment as an internal revenue collector, Hanscom printed a handbill proclaiming Buffington's breach of faith. (The scandal did not prevent Buffington's reelection to the House the next year.)[20]

In his boldest use of the correspondents, Johnson enlisted the more reputable aid of Joseph McCullagh, an Associated Press reporter who also corresponded as "MACK" for Midwest papers. Between them, the president and the correspondent popularized the interview as a journalistic and political device. Interviews had long been a means of gaining information, and both James Gordon Bennett and Horace Greeley had pioneered in publishing their interviews in dialogue form. During the Civil War, Washington correspondents had persistently interviewed everyone down to the president's dinner guests, to collect bits and pieces of news. Lincoln often spoke with individual reporters, but these were informal conversations rather than formal interviews and were not quoted directly. It took a president under threat of impeachment to develop the interview into a means of carrying his case more directly to the people.

McCullagh was at his desk in the Senate press gallery when a page handed him a note that the president wished to see him. The Republican McCullagh had instructions from his Missouri papers to "do the fair thing to both sides" while covering the battle between Congress and the president, and Johnson appreciated the lack of bias in his dispatches. "The damn newspapers are as bad as the politicians in misrepresenting me," Johnson told McCullagh. "I don't want you to take my side. I can fight these fellows single-handed; but put me down correctly." McCullagh took no notes during his sessions with the president but raced back to his office afterward to write what he remembered in a first-person, question-and-answer format. The interviews revealed Johnson as a proud and reasonable man who retained his sense of humor through his ordeal, and without the violent intemperance that often slipped out when he confronted hecklers on the stump. Pleased with their collaboration, the president summoned McCullagh back. "I want to give these fellows hell," he said, gesturing toward the Capitol, "and I think I can do it better through your paper than through a message, because the people read the papers more than they do messages."[21]

Other correspondents immediately embraced the interview as a journalistic device, and politicians came to recognize the power of direct quotations. Congressmen granted interviews on the issues of the day, some going so far as to prepare their own questions as well as answers, which obliging correspondents then published as their own work. For his part, Ben: Perley Poore despised the practice. Interviewing, he complained, degenerated "into a mere catechism of question and answer," which he dismissed as "undramatic in form and style." Poore saw the interview as a "dangerous method of communicating between our public men and the people," because it diminished the correspondent's role from interpreter to mere scribe.[22]

Like Poore, Sam Clemens, a newcomer to the press galleries, also found interviewing a less than noble practice. Writing from Washington during the winter of 1867–68, he ridiculed the interview in a letter published under his pen name, Mark Twain:

> I came across one of the lions of the country today at the Senate—General Sherman. The conversation I had with this gentleman therefore ought to be reported, I suppose. I said the weather was very fine, and he said he had seen finer. Not liking to commit myself further, in the present unsettled conditions of politics, I said good morning. Understanding my little game, *he* said good morning also. This was all that passed, but it was very significant. It reveals clearly what he thinks of impeachment. I regard this manner of getting

a great man's opinions a little underhanded, but then everybody does it.[23]

The epic struggle between Congress and the president made Reconstruction an exciting but treacherous time for the Washington press corps. One correspondent later reminisced that he would "rather run all the risks of the Gettysburg campaign again than go through the stormy times of Reconstruction." Yet others recalled these tense moments as their "halcyon days." General Henry Boynton of the *Cincinnati Gazette* described Reconstruction as a "rough-and-tumble, hurly-burly time in which each day's events and each day's contests with Congress presented a mass of interesting facts which gave the press an endless variety of material from which it was free to choose the particular dish which it would daily set before its readers." The good will that bonded the press and Congress during the Civil War persisted throughout Reconstruction, until Johnson's impeachment disillusioned the Republican-leaning press corps and raised suspicions about their party's legislative motives and behavior.[24]

The constitutional crisis advanced and dashed careers both on the floor and in the press galleries. Henry J. Raymond won a seat in Congress but damaged both his political reputation and his paper's circulation by allying himself with Andrew Johnson. Above in the press galleries, journalists hustled to beat their competition. James Rankin Young, who corresponded for the *New York Tribune* under the managing editorship of his older brother John Russell Young, crowed that he had beaten the entire press corps in publishing some closed-door congressional testimony. "The Special Washington Correspondent of the *Tribune*," James Young wrote of himself, "had obtained a copy of the entire evidence on Saturday . . . and on Monday morning, simultaneous with the confession of failure on the part of the other correspondents, we published two and a half columns of testimony."[25]

The *Tribune's* senior editor, Horace Greeley, took small pleasure in such minor triumphs. Greeley found impeachment an unappetizing means of settling the differences between president and Congress, and thought it smarter politics to leave Andrew Johnson alone. "All Andy wants is rope enough and time enough, and he will save us the trouble," he argued with managing editor John Russell Young. But Greeley was traveling and out of touch with his paper in February 1868, when President Johnson fired Secretary of War Edwin Stanton in violation of the Tenure of Office Act, precipitating the final impeachment crisis. Acting on his own initiative, managing editor John Russell Young committed the *Tribune* to Johnson's impeachment. Poor Greeley returned from his lecture tour in dismay, asking: "Why hang a man who is bent on hanging himself?" Although worried over the precedents that impeachment might set, Greeley supported his paper's editorial line, and the *Tribune* joined the rising chorus of editorial impeachers.[26]

Covering impeachment produced the Washington press corps's best writing and most anxious moments. During the Civil War, there had been long lulls between action, but in the weeks of uncertainty whether Johnson would be expelled from the White House, "there was not a moment when men's passions were not hot; not a moment when rumor and rancor were not in the air; not a moment when hearts did not tremble for the Republic." For Francis Richardson of the *Baltimore Sun* it was a time when the correspondents "could scarcely steal the time to sleep or eat" as they kept abreast of events and met their deadlines.[27]

Ben: Perley Poore could handle his regular morning and afternoon dispatches, but not the many special dispatches in demand for extra editions. Observing how other Boston papers had augmented their representation at the capital, Poore hired Hiram Ramsdell, a second-string correspondent for the *New York Tribune*, to cover the news from the press galleries during his absences. Meanwhile, the correspondents who haunted the lobbies and corridors found themselves for the first time subject to search by the Capitol Police, looking for incendiary devices.[28]

"This is the place to get a poor opinion of everybody in," Mark Twain grumbled from the press gallery. Twain regarded impeachment as demeaning to both sides. When Congress debated a resolution to strip the president of his personal secretaries, Twain dismissed the measure in a letter to the *Chicago Republican:* "It does not become a Congress that has been battling with the colossal artillery of impeachment to descend to throwing mud. Such conduct is neither royal, republican, nor democratic, it is simply boy's play." At the height of impeachment tensions, Twain packed his bags and returned to California to devote himself to literary matters.[29]

Twain abandoned the galleries while others were desperately

seeking entrance. The impeachment trial attracted such great crowds that for the first time the Senate issued tickets for admission to the public galleries. The new policy did not affect the men in the press gallery but complicated the work of women correspondents in the public galleries. Since Jane Swisshelm's departure, the press gallery had remained a male bastion, while the few women reporters worked out of the Ladies Reception Room. Described by one male reporter as "an elegant apartment, magnificently furnished, and beautifully frescoed," the room was near enough to the Senate chamber for the women correspondents to buttonhole senators as they passed. There they could also mingle with Senate wives, who often interceded with their husbands to obtain interviews and information.[30]

Writing as "Olivia" in Colonel Forney's *Philadelphia Press*, Emily Edson Briggs had so much trouble obtaining tickets to the galleries that she appealed to Senator Ben Wade for help. As a newspaper correspondent she considered herself entitled to a seat in the press gallery, "but as the Senate are determined to put a different construction upon the Constitution, entirely opposite to Andy Johnson and I, it seems there is no hope for me unless I manage to creep in under your broad wings," she beseeched the senator. "I hope you will remember me as the Lord did his chosen people in the wilderness, but in place of daily bread, a daily ticket will answer every purpose."[31]

Most Washington correspondents favored removing President Johnson from office, but the longer impeachment proceedings lasted, the more their mood shifted. *Chicago Tribune* editor Horace White returned to the press galleries to cover the impeachment trial himself. Although his paper had endorsed impeachment, White strongly advocated free trade and realized that the president's removal would place Senate President Pro Tempore Ben Wade, a protectionist, in the White House. Concern that Wade's presidency might lead to higher tariffs caused White to have second thoughts on impeachment. George Alfred Townsend, who corresponded as "GATH," began under the assumption that Andrew Johnson remained the chief barrier to settling the "Southern Question." But GATH's Republican loyalties eroded when he interviewed various members of Congress who seemed less excited over Johnson's Reconstruction policies than his "abuse of party patronage." Disheartened over these petty concerns to protect postmasters, revenue officers, and brothers-in-law, GATH reversed himself on impeachment.[32]

"Impeachment drags on heavily," Perley Poore complained from the press gallery, his faith in the final result rapidly diminishing. Poore worried that the Senate's failure to remove Johnson might turn him into a "mad elephant," who would stamp down the remains of Reconstruction. But Poore grew disgusted with the behavior of congressional radicals and came to curse their "d——d impeachment squabble." The impeachment trial similarly dismayed Henry Boynton, who began to treat it more critically in the *Cincinnati Gazette.* Although a Republican himself, General Boynton concluded that the radicals were making as many corrupt deals as Johnson's defenders, "probably more!"[33]

J. B. McCullagh, the president's interviewer, divided Washington correspondents into those who opposed impeachment and those who expected an office under the new regime. Impeachment supporters seemed to him more interested in getting "the ins out and the outs in." McCullagh most likely had Uriah Hunt Painter in mind. So close an adviser to Senator Wade was Painter that fellow correspondents envisioned him as the "power behind the throne" in a Wade presidency. Painter's partisanship during the impeachment trial caused his editors no end of grief. Although the *Philadelphia Inquirer* accepted his anti-Johnson diatribes, his other major paper, the *New York Sun,* objected. "We want nothing but real news," editor Charles Dana instructed Painter (much as he had lectured James S. Pike a decade earlier). "I want to avoid the appearance of too much partiality for the Republicans in your dispatches, or in every other part of the paper." But Painter had become too involved in the events to keep his passions out of his reporting. "This is *not* a partisan paper," Dana protested. "The general rule of the *Sun* is not to attack anybody. What we want is the facts. The comments, and especially ill-natured ones, we wish to add ourselves." Still, even Dana's objectivity had its pragmatic limitations. "Please be careful in checking about Mr. Evarts," Dana cautioned after Painter filed a story on the president's lawyer, William Evarts. "He is a stockholder in the *Sun,*" Dana pointed out, "and one must not say anything unpleasant about him."[34]

President Johnson wisely left his defense to his attorneys. Despite rampant speculation in the press gallery that the president would appear in his own behalf, he remained at the White House.

Newspaper Row on the night after the vote on Andrew Johnson's impeachment.

William Warden kept Johnson informed on each day's proceedings. "Well, Warden," Johnson would ask when his secretary appeared, "what are the signs of the zodiac today?" Warden continued to file his daily newspaper dispatches, but the president was the chief customer for his news.[35]

Until the day of the vote, impeachers felt confident of victory. Wagers ran high in the press gallery, with Uriah Painter betting heavily on removal, and William Warden staking "all he could raise, beg, borrow or anticipate" on Johnson's acquittal. When the president won reprieve by a single vote, Warden collected several thousand dollars, while Painter became "a very lame duck for a long time after."[36]

The anticlimactic impeachment trial shattered the harmony between the Washington press corps and Republican leaders of Congress, leaving each side disillusioned with the other. On the eve of the breakup, a valedictory for the old era had taken place at the Washington Correspondents' Club second annual dinner. Fifty correspondents and their friends from Congress met at Welcker's restaurant near Newspaper Row, one icy night in January 1868. For an evening, they put away political cares and professional competitiveness to celebrate what club president George Adams called "the kindly brotherhood among the craft." They were bound together, said Adams, "by trials and sympathies that the outside world cannot comprehend."

Adams saluted Representative James Brooks, one of the first Washington correspondents, who had arrived in Washington as correspondent for the *Portland Advertiser* in 1832, back in the days when the "one-horse dispatch" delivered to his paper a copy of the president's annual message days after it had gone to Congress. "I need hardly add, gentlemen of the club," Adams added, "how easily the thread of civil tenure which binds some of us to our salaries would be broken if we failed, perhaps, to publish in the day and sphere in which we act, a President's message several days in *advance* of its delivery to Congress!" Among the diners were several other journalists who now sat in Congress. William E. Robinson, once "Richelieu" for the *Tribune*, represented a New York district in the House. Rhode Island Senator Henry Anthony owned the *Providence Journal*, and Representative J. Lawrence Getz edited the Reading, Pennsylvania, *Gazette and Democrat*. Representative James G. Blaine, who had succeeded Brooks as editor of the *Portland Advertiser*, responded to the toast to the "Journalists in Congress." Then House Speaker Schuyler Colfax, who still owned the *St. Joseph Valley Register*, lifted his glass to the reporters: "May they always wield the power of the club honestly, conscientiously, and wisely." Colfax could not have imagined that within a few years the press would wield its club not only against himself, but against Blaine and Brooks as well, battering their political reputations.

As the toasts proceeded, Ben: Perley Poore saluted the Boston press, not as Bohemians but as "a fitting representative of the purity, learning, and enterprise of New England journalism." In a more self-deprecating mood, presidential secretary William Warden noted that despite the Washington press corps's *esprit de corps* and their collective desire to improve the respectability of their profession, "in the estimation of many, we are a scaly set of fellows, utterly regardless of truth or moral principle." Their profession had given grounds for such a reputation, Warden went on, for "your genuine vagabondish, shiftless (and often shirtless) 'Bohemian,' is the exact type of a Washington correspondent, as viewed from a distance." Warden had no doubt that they would outgrow this unjust image. "There is no class of citizens who more than we manipulate political sentiments, and furnish the material out of which public opinion is molded, and it behooves us to be honest and sincere in our work." Having only recently come under fire for offering early copies of the president's message for sale, he concluded: "If now we can only put a stop to unauthorized or surreptitious publications of official documents we shall gain the confidence and esteem of all. [Laughter and applause.]"

The evening concluded with Mark Twain's ribald toast to women, "The Pride of the Profession and the jewel of ours" (notably George Washington's mother, "She raised a boy that could not lie—*could not lie*. But *he never had any chance*. It might have been different with him if he had belonged to a newspaper correspondent's club").[37] While the collegial dinner offered diverting relief from impeachment, it could not overcome more powerful trends. Within months, disenchantment over impeachment settled onto Newspaper Row. At the same time, rumors of corruption spread through the press corps, who both leveled charges against the politicians and became themselves targets of congressional investigation. As relations between reporters and their sources worsened, the Correspondents' Club disbanded after only one more dinner.

For Ben: Perley Poore, the most lasting dividend from the impeachment squabble was the working relationship he had developed with his assistant, Hiram Ramsdell. Although Poore worried that Ramsdell's dispatches too often flattered the impeachers, he admired Ramsdell as a skilled reporter and a shrewd Washington operator. More ominously, Zebulon White, Ramsdell's chief at the *New York Tribune*'s Washington bureau, came to suspect that the reporter was lobbying on the side "in order to live in the style he has maintained."[38]

Once William Warden sold the president's annual message to the press, the buying of news grew rampant on Newspaper Row. During the slow months of the congressional recess after the impeachment trial, reporters began to form "rings" to pool their cash and buy bureau reports, sometimes before those reports reached the desks of the cabinet members who had to sign them. Other journalists pointed to Hiram Ramsdell—who held a patronage post as special agent in the Post Office Department in addition to his newspaper correspondence—as an active member of a post office ring. Sidney Andrews of the *Boston Advertiser* fingered Ramsdell,

Warden, and a handful of other correspondents who pooled their money to buy news, "the common stock going out to all the papers represented. It gives you some of the service of a number of men, but not much exclusive news." Perley Poore hated the idea but gave Ramsdell twenty-five dollars as his share of a bid on a Treasury Department report. In normal times, Poore would not even have bothered telegraphing so long and dry a report to his paper, since not more than a paragraph might be published. But now he paid for the report to avoid being scooped. "I fear that the days of honest journalism are over," Poore dismayed.[39]

In 1871, Hiram Ramsdell became a national *cause célèbre*, when he spent $500 (a combined $325 from the *New York Tribune* and $175 from the *Cincinnati Commercial*) to purchase a copy of the still-secret Treaty of Washington that settled American Civil War claims with Great Britain.[40] Who leaked the treaty? New York Senator Roscoe Conkling and other opponents of the *Tribune* called the paper's Washington bureau chief, Zebulon White, and his assistant Hiram Ramsdell, to testify and ordered them confined until they revealed the culprit. "We know the spirit that prevails through the profession to which these young gentlemen belong," said Senator Oliver Morton in defense of the pair. "Their honor, their reputation, their pride, their word, have all been pledged that they will not make this disclosure, and they will go up to this disconsolate, gloomy dungeon and stay there before they will do it." The "gloomy dungeon" was the Pacific Railroad Committee room in the Capitol, comfortable quarters filled with the correspondents' friends and supporters. Senator Matthew Carpenter, a leader in the attack on the two journalists, reported that he had been eating lunch in the Senate restaurant when waiters whirled the largest table into the center of the room, covered it with cloth, and informed him that it was reserved for "the Washington correspondents of the *New York Tribune* with their families."[41]

The Senate eventually released White and Ramsdell without obtaining their confessions. But John Hassard, who covered for White and Ramsdell during their captivity, warned the *Tribune* that the source of their leak had nearly been exposed. "It is believed on the Row that the secret will come out pretty soon," Hassard wrote, "[Senator] Carpenter having got a clue tonight out of Tisdell." Willard Tisdell, a Senate secretary, had been at the *Tribune*'s office on the night the treaty arrived. Describing the others present in his testimony, Tisdell mentioned one name not previously identified: Major Ben: Perley Poore.[42]

Since the Senate investigators aimed primarily at embarrassing the *Tribune,* they showed no curiosity about what the Senate Printing Committee's clerk, who had access to the unreleased treaty, was doing in the offices of a rival newspaper office at precisely the time that its correspondents obtained the document. Nor did they ever call Poore to explain. As usual, Poore was in severe financial straits. Unable to publish the secret treaty in his own paper without exposing his breach of office, he possessed both motive and opportunity to sell the treaty to Hiram Ramsdell. Having once lamented that his paper would have to open an office on Newspaper Row, "and put it under the charge of some one who will go into the ring operations, and cheat and steal with the rest," Perley Poore apparently fulfilled his own expectations.[43]

Money always remained in lesser supply than could meet Poore's demands. He counted on his newspaper income for personal and family expenses, reserving what he earned at the Capitol for his Indian Hill estate. As he grew older he increasingly resented the *Journal's* policy of paying him for only the months that Congress met, and in 1883 he abruptly resigned to write a column of reminiscences for the *Cultivator,* for "a liberal *annual* salary." Even this arrangement could not pay his bills, and by 1886 he had returned to corresponding by letter again, where he had begun forty years earlier. In addition to the *Cultivator,* his weekly epistles went to a half-dozen other papers. "Think of that, bloated bond holder," Poore wrote to an old friend, "and wish that you had to work so hard for bread, butter and creditors that you could have no time to be ill." Ben: Perley Poore, the epitome of the Bohemian correspondent in Washington, labored dutifully to the end of his life. One day in May 1887, after delivering a manuscript to the Government Printing Office, he collapsed while climbing the Capitol steps. Poore never recovered and died two weeks later in his rooms at the Ebbitt Hotel, overlooking Newspaper Row.[44]

5

Uriah Hunt Painter, Lobbyist

A CORRUPT ATMOSPHERE pervaded postwar Washington, tarnishing the press as well as the politicians. Wartime correspondents like Horace White had speculated financially without jeopardizing their standing as journalists. The outside profits they earned by exploiting their inside knowledge had been their own business. But after the war, when newspaper correspondents branched into lobbying and other private business dealings, they raised the first serious questions about the ethics of Washington reporting.

Ben: Perley Poore observed that scantily paid correspondents were forced to "prostitute their pens" as lobbyists. Journalists' wheeling and dealing, buying and selling of news, and hunger for patronage created an image of corruptibility. Lobbyists and influence peddlers speculated how much it would cost to buy the loyalty of correspondents and thereby shape national news and opinion. For most reporters, such charges were unfounded, but a few of their colleagues so badly blurred the distinction between journalism and lobbying as to cast doubt on the professional ethics of the entire Washington press corps. Correspondents like the Philadelphia *Inquirer*'s Uriah Hunt Painter strained the definitions of legitimate journalism until their actions forced Newspaper Row to respond. In an era famous for corruption, it was a rare exposé that did not tar Painter's name.[1]

Painter had begun as an investigator, rather than the subject of investigation. When President Andrew Johnson sent the Alaska Purchase Treaty to the Senate in 1867, he picked up a tip from the chairman of the Senate Foreign Relations Committee, Charles Sumner, who sensed something unsavory in the precipitous way that Russia sold the Alaska territory for $7.2 million. Painter heard other rumors that the Russian minister was spreading money freely. He doubted "that all the seven millions of gold would go into the Russian coffers" but advised his readers that those lobbying in the treaty's favor were "certainly doomed to defeat." Then, unexpectedly, the Foreign Relations Committee reported the treaty out, and the Senate promptly ratified it. A stunned Uriah Painter explained that "the cry of more domination swept everything before it with such velocity that Senators asked in vain for more light or time to learn who is really to get so many millions of dollars."[2]

Having been proven wrong, Painter developed an obsessive interest in the Alaska story. A year later, when the House of Representatives appropriated the funds to pay for the territory, Painter came across a cable dispatch indicating that only $5 million in gold had passed through London on its way to Russia. He set out to find what became of the other $2.2 million, an investigation that led to a blind alley after one of the reputed lobbyists for the appropriation, former Representative Frederick Stanton, flatly denied any involvement. Painter abandoned the story until August 1868, when he spied a small item in a New York newspaper that Stanton's partner, Robert J. Walker, had his pocket picked of $20,000 in gold certificates. Certain that these were Alaska funds, Painter told congressional leaders that he had uncovered the "biggest lobby swindle ever put up in Washington," but they ignored his charges.[3]

For months, Washington correspondents traded stories about cash payments to congressmen and the press to influence the Alaska vote. At first the correspondents joked about having been cheated out of their fair share of the alleged bribery fund, but the longer the story persisted the more it called into question their personal honesty. James Rankin Young reported these rumors to the *New York Tribune,* calling for Congress to investigate. The day that his story ran, an ex-Confederate colonel named James Martin called on Young and claimed to possess a list of congressmen and correspondents who had received money from Robert Walker, including $5,000 for Young, similar amounts for other reporters, and a large sum for Secretary of the Senate John W. Forney's paper, the *Washington Chronicle.* "I do not intend to pursue you gentlemen of the press," said the colonel, "because it is perfectly legitimate for you to have the money; but I want to get those damned members of Congress and others who got this money and cheated me."

Young knew he had received no Alaska money himself, and Horace Greeley assured him that none had gone to the *Tribune*, but Martin's accusations fit too closely the rumors circulating 'on the Row. That afternoon, Young convened the dozen correspondents on Martin's list. The perplexed correspondents concluded that Walker and Stanton must have tricked the Russian minister into believing that they had bribed the press and then absconded with the money themselves. William Warden remarked that he had favored the treaty "not dreaming of any such fund out of which anybody was to be paid. If there was money to be made out of that, I am sorry I did not know it." Several newspaper articles reported Martin's allegations, but it was Richard Hinton's story in the *Worcester Spy* that caught congressional attention—because the *Spy* was owned and edited by a Massachusetts representative. When a congressman's newspaper alleged bribery of other members of Congress, it presented an issue too inflammatory to ignore. In December 1868, a House investigation called Hinton to testify, but he could give no evidence beyond the allegations he had published, attributing his story to "rumors now afloat" among newspapermen.[4]

The House committee dismissed Colonel Martin as an unreliable source. Robert Walker and Frederick Stanton appeared before the committee and admitted that they had acted as agents in behalf of the treaty. Walker had received $26,000 for his services, which included writing favorable articles for Colonel John W. Forney's *Washington Chronicle*. He also convinced the Russian minister to pay the *Chronicle* $3,000 for its support. Walker explained that since Colonel Forney had resigned as Secretary of the Senate, he had "a perfect right" to the money. But Walker insisted that he had not paid a dollar to anyone else connected with the press.[5]

Having confessed to lobbying, Walker and Stanton made their own charge against the scandal's most persistent investigator, Uriah Painter, whom they accused of trying to blackmail them for a cut of the Alaska money. Painter had sent another lobbyist, Robert Latham, as an intermediary to inform Walker and Stanton that he could influence a good many votes in Congress for a price. In his testimony, Latham explained that his friend Painter would try anything to get a story. "I do not think Mr. Painter would be very scrupulous as to the way he obtained information," he said. "I think he would 'play possum,' and appear to be one way while he was the other."[6]

Once the accuser, now the accused, Uriah Painter testified that he had instructed Latham: "When you see Stanton go right at him and ask him if there is money in it or not." Although the approach was open to misinterpretation, Painter swore that he never dreamed of taking money for himself. He could not have changed his position on the treaty because he had placed himself "fairly and squarely" against it in his dispatches. Yet the incident seriously undermined Painter's credibility. The *New York Times* commented that the investigation had revealed only that "a Mr. Painter seems to have gotten himself into trouble, but Mr. Painter is not the Government."[7]

Doubting Painter's declarations of innocence, correspondent George Alfred Townsend portrayed him in poetry as "The Striker," the term for reporters who opposed a claim or bill before Congress simply to be paid off by its supporters:

> Slouched, and surly, and sallow-faced
> With a look as if something were sore misplaced
> The young man Striker was seen to stride
> Up the Capitol stairs at high noontide,
> And as though at the head of a viewless mob—
> Who could look in his eyes and mistrust it?
> He quoth: "They must let me into that job,
>   Or I'll bust it!"
> Wonderful youth! Such power to keep
> In a land where Justice ne're is asleep;
> To stagger the councils of state with fear,
> Or stop the growth of a hemisphere;
> The time-piece of law to crush in the fob,
> Or by violence re-adjust it,
> And, lest he be "let" into this or that job,
>   He can "bust it."[8]

The House committee brought no formal charges against Uriah Painter, but its members expressed distrust of his ethics, and those of Washington reporters in general. Chairman John Broomall, who represented Painter's home district of Chester, Pennsylvania, asserted that he would believe no Washington correspondent under oath. Committee member J. Lawrence Getz, himself the owner of a Pennsylvania newspaper, retorted that a reporter's oath was "as good as that of any member of Congress." Broomall snapped back that he had no faith in the Washington press and hoped they would never praise him in their dispatches, since that would only give the public grounds to suspect his honesty.[9]

Broomall's sneer still echoed when the Correspondent's Club met for their third and final dinner. In a more somber mood than the previous year, Vice President Schuyler Colfax solemnly advised the assembled correspondents to exercise their responsibilities prudently, for in their hands lay the making and unmaking of great men. The *New York Tribune* responded archly: "We have generally found that the correspondents who are most unpopular with Congressmen are the men who do not assist in 'making' these reputations." Pointing to the angry Representative Broomall, the *Tribune* suggested that a reporter "who will tell the constituency of Mr. Broomall every other morning that he made a great speech, that the stenographers were dissolved in tears as they took down his pathetic sentences will be honored by him, and by those of his class, as an ornament to his profession."[10]

The *Cincinnati Gazette*'s Washington correspondent, Henry Boynton, congratulated editor Whitelaw Reid for the *Tribune*'s response to Broomall. "His investigation is a farce—and worse, as I believe," wrote Boynton. Sources inside the committee had told him they felt constrained against exposing fellow members of Congress, "and yet when they catch a poor customer like Painter they make the country ring with it." Boynton bemoaned that "just now when the lobby and corrupt Congressmen are joining hands to fight newspapermen who *will* expose them, we could all have wished that the Painter matter had not come up."[11]

The investigating committee's final report found no evidence to support press accusations that members of Congress had taken bribes. The committee condemned the "loose morality" of the Washington press corps, "which for sensational purposes, or to cater to a morbid curiosity, couples names of public men or private citizens with clandestine receipt of large sums of money in connection with votes or influence" on congressional actions. The Alaska investigation cast more of a pall on the press than on the lobbyists they sought to expose. On Newspaper Row, the incident left correspondents wary of street gossip, at the moment when stories of even larger scandals were being whispered about.[12]

Uriah Hunt Painter suffered the greatest loss of face in the scandal. This was a bitter blow for a proud man who until then had earned an admirable reputation as a Washington correspondent. Born in 1837, Painter was the second of nine children in an old-line Quaker family. He grew up in a white-pillared mansion on a five-hundred-acre farm along Brandywine Creek in Chester, Pennsylvania. His grandfather had published Pennsylvania's leading anti-Masonic newspaper; his father formed one of the state's first Republican clubs; and his mother was active in the antislavery movement. During the 1830s, Painter's father had opened a bookstore, and received so much of his stock through the generous support of Philadelphia publisher Uriah Hunt that he named his son for him. The senior Painter also organized the first telegraph company in West Chester County and owned a lumber mill. After Uriah attended Oberlin College, he returned home to manage the lumber mill and become superintendent of the telegraph office.[13]

At heart an entrepreneur, Uriah Painter might have devoted his life to business ventures, had he not been caught up in Republican politics during the turbulent 1850s. Young Painter attended the Republican conventions in 1856 and 1860 and campaigned strenuously for John C. Fremont and Abraham Lincoln. Wanting to see Washington politics for himself, he arranged a reporting assignment for the *Philadelphia Inquirer* and joined Lincoln's inaugural train bound for the capital. The *Inquirer* had recently acquired a new editor and style. In 1859, twenty-nine-year-old William W. Harding had assumed control of the stodgy *Pennsylvania Inquirer* upon his father's retirement. Harding changed the name and image of the paper, discarded its system of credit subscriptions, and hired a squad of newsboys to peddle the paper on the streets. He abandoned the four-page folio format for an eight-page style and expanded its coverage of both local and national news.[14]

With the outbreak of the Civil War, publisher Harding charged Uriah Painter to "go wherever you think it will advance the enterprise of the *Inquirer.*" During the first battle of Bull Run, the twenty-two-year-old Painter followed the news so far that he found himself behind enemy lines. Painter had joined other correspondents and congressmen on a Sunday outing to watch the Union victory, only to be caught in the retreat. He escaped the Confederates by mounting a bleeding artillery horse and clinging to its mane. Correspondent Henry Villard saw Painter gallop past him, urging on his horse "by merciless cudgelling." When Painter reached Washington at 2:00 A.M., he learned that the first passenger train would not leave until the next morning. Convinced that Confederate troops were marching on the capital, he boarded a freight train and spent the night sleeping on the floor of a baggage car.[15]

With government censors controlling the telegraph wires out of Washington, only Uriah Painter got a true report to his paper, by carrying the news in person. The *Philadelphia Inquirer*'s first edition on Monday proclaimed "A Glorious Day for the Union." Later that morning, publisher Harding was startled when his Washington correspondent, supposedly marching to Richmond with the Union army, burst into the office with news of the disaster. The *Inquirer*'s next edition announced the "Total Rout of Our Army." Before scooping the entire northern press, Painter had the foresight to give advance notice of his story to Philadelphia financier Jay Cooke, who unloaded his stocks before the market collapsed.[16]

During the war, Painter's astute battlefield correspondence made him important military and political friends—and sources. At the war's end, peacetime reporting seemed less challenging, and he considered going back into business. In 1866, Painter threatened to resign from the *Inquirer* because of a "weekly allowance which merely suffices to pay my expenses of subsistence and leaves me nothing to save on or hope for in the future." William Harding rushed to Washington with offers of higher salary and stock options that satisfied his foremost correspondent. For as long as Harding remained publisher, Painter's position as Washington correspondent was secure, no matter how often his dispatches deviated from the paper's editorials, or his integrity came under public scrutiny. Uriah Painter stuck to Washington journalism for another twenty years, because it offered the best opportunity to achieve his goal of making money.[17]

Painter delved into business and real estate deals, which frequently involved lobbying Congress and compromising his position as a journalist. Business interests came to appreciate Painter, not only as a member of the House and Senate press galleries but as clerk of the House Committee on Post Offices. Jay Cooke and

Company retained his services to funnel advance news on legislation. Painter also lobbied for his own publisher, to repeal a tax on newspaper advertising. "You were the first to set the ball in motion at Washington, and deserve great praise for your energetic efforts in obtaining a result so highly necessary to the railroad fraternity," Harding wrote in appreciation.[18]

Lobbying was as old as government, and yet in the post-Civil War years the press perceived lobbying as a threat to the republic. Emily Briggs, otherwise known as "Olivia" to the readers of the *Philadelphia Press*, reported in February 1869 that the distinguished magazine writer James Parton was making his way about Capitol Hill collecting material for an article on lobbying. "It is said he is going to hold up the monster in the broad light of day—this creeping, crawling thing." But after three weeks of vigilant search, Parton had found no monstrous lobby. In exasperation he turned to Ben: Perley Poore and asked: "Perley, where *is* the lobby of which the papers tell us such dreadful things?" "The Lobby?" Poore responded with a broad smile. "The Lobby is a gigantic myth."[19]

Parton's *Atlantic Monthly* article found not even a smoldering ember of lobbying danger. His conclusions contrasted sharply with the image that the regular Washington correspondents were telegraphing from the capital. Mrs. Briggs, for instance, described Collis P. Huntington of the Central Pacific Railroad as "the great, huge, devil-fish of the railroad session," who had hired female lobbyists, "fat, fair and forty," to seduce congressmen into voting land grants to the railroads. Parton, by contrast, found the female lobby "small and insignificant." Not lobbyists, he argued, but national demand for transcontinental transportation accounted for the subsidies Congress provided the railroads.[20]

Parton's commentary appeared during the early months of Ulysses Grant's administration, an era branded as the "Gilded Age" and the "Great Barbecue." Whether or not a "great myth," the lobby became the staple of novels, stage plays, and newspaper editorials. Correspondents like George Alfred Townsend wrote with distaste about the scramble in congressional cloakrooms for "franchises, lands, subsidies, and ports of tariff and taxation." He believed that lobbyists had become an integral part of Washington life because they shared similar missions with congressmen: each served small constituencies rather than the nation as a whole. At a time when

Congress faced such pressing public issues as labor unrest, railroad expansion, corporate growth, and currency fluctuation, it was devoting excessive attention to private bills. Major appropriations were squeezed into the last hours of the legislative calendar, when special amendments could slip by unnoticed. Congress, he charged, had become a market house where some three hundred congressional districts and numerous lobbying interests had their desires "satisfied, exchanged and sold."[21]

Townsend considered lobbying corrupt by definition, while others like Ben: Perley Poore accepted it as a fact of legislative life. The nation was undergoing a massive transformation after the war, spurred by the railroad building boom. The Republican party's ascendancy meant adoption of an aggressively Hamiltonian approach to government, with Congress voting land grants for railroads and protective tariffs for industry. Expansion of government responsibility placed greater demands on Congress, which had wrestled much of the federal leadership back from the executive branch after Lincoln's strong wartime presidency. The high turnover of members, and inadequacy of staff, left many congressmen unprepared to deal with these complex issues. Lobbyists filled the vacuum, providing the information, advice, and assistance Congress needed. Yet some lobbyists acted with excess and an appalling lack of ethics.[22]

Uriah Painter learned that the big money came from railroad lobbying, and he collected his share. "You did your work first rate and we are abundantly satisfied," wrote Jim Fisk of the Erie Railroad. "If we can do anything for you at *any* time, let me know and I shall be most happy to respond." Tom Scott, an executive of the Pennsylvania and the Union Pacific railroads made regular use of the correspondent. "I hope you will kill the claim bill in the House because those parties will be very useful to us in the next winter," Scott wrote in 1867. "Break their necks." On another occasion, Scott encouraged Painter to plant stories favorable to the Union Pacific, and to get Lawrence Gobright to send them out as Associated Press dispatches. In 1869, Scott wrote concerning a land grant bill: "Can't you get Senators Sherman, Cameron, Cattell, Stockton, Scott and others to help in disposing of it?" Three days later a note from Scott read: "Message received. A glorious result."[23]

One of Painter's friends asserted that "from 1862 till the close of the first Grant administration in 1873, no man in Washington had a stronger 'pull' with the Republican party leaders. It was 'see Painter' when anybody asked a favor." Such a reputation carried risks. Once, when Painter lobbied against the nomination of a candidate for Internal Revenue Collector in Philadelphia, one of the candidate's supporters accosted Painter outside his committee room in the Capitol. The assailant knocked the reporter to the ground, kicked him in the face, and beat his head against the stone floor before Capitol policemen finally intervened. The nomination was never confirmed. By contrast, Painter used his influence to have his one-time patron Ben Wade appointed as a government director of the Union Pacific Railroad in 1869.[24] He also remained close to another Union Pacific director, Representative James Wilson of Iowa. In 1872 Wilson wrote to Painter: "Tell Oakes Ames to look up Senate bill 875 and House bill 2168 (both identical) and see to it that they do not pass or even get reported from the committees. Those bills, if passed, will 'gut' the bond grant roads, U.P. and all others. Tell him not to neglect this matter one hour, and to see that all of his friends are posted. Don't show him this letter."[25]

Painter's lobbying was not lost upon other members of the press galleries. In 1870, F. C. Grey of the *Washington Chronicle* implored Representative Benjamin Butler to investigate Painter's lobbying activities. Grey detailed the distress in the House press gallery as reporters watched Painter buttonholing members on the floor, where he had access as a committee clerk. He described Painter as "a fellow with infinite 'brass' and impudent who has the credit of controlling one third of the members of the House." Other correspondents took to calling Uriah Hunt Painter "Uriah Heep," after "that crawling impersonation of meanness" in Charles Dickens's *David Copperfield*. Like Uriah Heep, Painter had an ability to winnow information out of those who had no intention of giving it, and of using it for his own advantage.[26]

Despite his Quaker upbringing, and his ability to make money, Painter was a coarse man. It was said that he never wore an overcoat or underwear. He swore profusely. The liberal reformer George W. Childs, whose round face and bushy side-whiskers bore an uncanny resemblance to Painter's, was so afraid that they would be mistaken for each other, that he begged Painter always to return the greetings of people he met on the street and never to say "damn" in public.[27]

For Uriah Painter, who lost so heavily when he bet that Andrew Johnson would be impeached, the Grant years proved highly prosperous times. His lobbying, business deals, and investments all paid off handsomely. By 1870 he could afford to send his father on a long-cherished voyage to China. In 1873, Painter constructed two elegant dwellings, containing "all the modern improvements," just blocks from Newspaper Row.[28]

The passage of time might have erased the stigma of the Alaska scandal, had Painter's name not surfaced in the revelations about Credit Mobilier. "That myth, that nondescript, that 'what-is-it,' that 'who-is-it,'" as Senator James Nye called it, Credit Mobilier was the construction company created to build the transcontinental Union Pacific Railroad. As the company's principal agent in Washington, Massachusetts Representative Oakes Ames spread its stock among friends in Congress, "where it will do the most good for us." By February 1868, the stock was worth four times its par value, but Ames offered it to congressmen at par. He assured anyone with qualms that the Union Pacific already had received all the federal land grants it needed, so there could be no conflict of interest. In several instances, Ames required no money down and simply held the stocks until the accumulated dividends covered the purchase price. The lucky owner collected his stock without paying a cent. Ames expected that key members of Congress would identify the continuing prosperity of Credit Mobilier and Union Pacific with their own interests. Among those to whom he spread the company's largess were House Speaker Colfax, Representatives James G. Blaine, James Garfield, and James Brooks, and Senators James Patterson and Henry Wilson.[29]

Uriah Painter was the first correspondent to smell out the Credit Mobilier scandal. The exchanges of stock had been kept secret, but in 1868 a company director, Henry McComb, had sued for stocks and dividends belonging to him, and some of Credit Mobilier's shady dealings came out in court. Painter picked up the story from McComb, his real estate partner, but instead of scooping Newspaper Row, he never published a word. The reporter went to the directors and demanded a cut on the deal. They promised fifty shares, but Oakes Ames had only thirty shares left. "He said he was promised more," Ames later testified, "and was quite indignant that he did not get fifty shares."[30]

The Credit Mobilier scandal remained buried for four years until it surfaced during the 1872 presidential election. Liberal Republicans had bolted from their party rather than support President Grant's reelection. Independent-minded Republican newspaper editors—among them Horace White of the *Chicago Tribune*, Murat Halstead of the *Cincinnati Commercial*, and Whitelaw Reid of the *New York Tribune*—assumed the leadership of the Liberal Republican convention. The editors were chagrined when their quixotic colleague, Horace Greeley, won the party's presidential nomination. Despite their misgivings, they closed editorial ranks around Greeley. Charles Dana, Greeley's former managing editor, handed him a golden issue by exposing the Credit Mobilier.[31]

"The King of Frauds," ran the *Sun's* headline on 4 September 1872; "How the Credit Mobilier Bought Its Way through Congress." Basing its story on Henry McComb's four-year-old testimony and other documents, the newspaper listed those who had received stock from Ames. The only nonmember of Congress on the paper's list was "Painter (rep.)." Daily throughout the election campaign the *Sun* reprinted this list, demanding that those named come forward with the truth. House Speaker James G. Blaine, facing a September election in Maine, issued the first flat denial. Blaine's statement placed pressure on the others to follow suit, which they did with varying degrees of dissembling. In South Bend, Indiana, Vice President Schuyler Colfax dissociated himself from Credit Mobilier so completely that he left no doubt in the minds of his listeners that he had never owned any of the stock. When Colfax's testimony before a House committee later contradicted his South Bend speech, no further explanations could overcome the public perception that he had lied.[32]

George Alfred Townsend, then writing a column called "Chronicles of Congress" for the *Washington Capital*, received a telegram from Horace White asking him to investigate Credit Mobilier for the *Chicago Tribune*. Culling through the old dockets of the McComb case, Townsend became convinced of McComb's truthfulness and of the congressmen's perfidy. A railroad executive told him: "What surprises me most is that the newspaper profession, with all its acuteness, did not discover this matter long ago—four years ago—it being an old subject of conversation amongst railway men and operators." With Townsend's dispatches (under his pen name GATH), the *Chicago Tribune* pursued Credit Mobilier as vigorously as any newspaper and pressed the demand for a congressional investigation.[33]

As much as possible the *Philadelphia Inquirer* avoided mention either of Credit Mobilier or its correspondent's part in the story. In a rare exception, the paper published a letter from Pennsylvania Representative William D. "Pig Iron" Kelley, who protested his treatment in the *Chicago Tribune*, denied that he had received any Credit Mobilier stocks, and asserted that Uriah Painter had been wrongfully included on the list of stock recipients. Kelley quoted Oakes Ames as saying that his only association with Painter had been a real estate transaction. Kelley's letter was wrong on both counts. Sworn testimony would later reveal that he and Painter had received shares of the profitable stock. But for the time being the *Inquirer* was satisfied. "The slanders, abuse and calumnies are not believed by the people," an *Inquirer* editorial proclaimed.[34]

Credit Mobilier had no influence on the November elections. Grant and his implicated running mate, Henry Wilson, trounced the hapless Horace Greeley. Sunk in depression, Greeley died three weeks later. All of the accused congressmen who ran for re-election won. But the allegations had been too sensational to ignore when the Forty-Second Congress reconvened in December. After paying homage to the deceased Greeley, Speaker Blaine

Reporters at the telegraph office in the House press gallery, in 1875.

stepped down from the podium to endorse an investigation of Credit Mobilier. Blaine, who said that he had turned down Ames's offer of stock, wanted to distance himself from those who had not. However, the official investigation only intensified publicity and blackened the names of all those associated with Credit Mobilier, innocent or guilty. Even Uriah Painter had to cover the story.[35]

The hearings began in secret session, but closed doors fanned rumors and on 6 January 1873 the House voted to conduct its investigation in public. At first the correspondents packed the committee room, but after the first few days their numbers dwindled. The committee released daily transcripts of the testimony, which their newspapers could reprint in full, or with partisan editing, and the correspondents knew that the Associated Press would provide their papers with summaries of the day's happenings. Still, Oakes Ames's accusations and other members' rebuttals filled the nation's front pages, leaving readers with the impression of widespread malfeasance.[36]

Uriah Painter avoided testifying, but other Washington correspondents took the stand. Among the most embarrassed was the *New York Times*'s Lorenzo Crounse. Schuyler Colfax called the *Times* correspondent to testify about a dispatch he had filed quoting Oakes Ames as saying that Colfax had been "entirely right" to deny that he had received any stock. "My recollection is not absolutely distinct," Crounse told the committee evasively; perhaps Ames had said Colfax was "probably right." Oakes Ames replied that he had said nothing of the kind and pointed to another of Crounse's dispatches that directly contradicted his testimony. "If that is the character of your statements they ought not to have any authority with anybody," Ames snapped.[37]

Correspondent Henry Boynton went before the Senate investigating committee to explain why he had sent a story to the *New York Times* in September 1872, attributing to Senator Henry Wilson a "full and absolute denial" that he had ever owned Credit Mobilier stock. In truth, Wilson had purchased the stock in his wife's name but had returned it when he became concerned about McComb's lawsuit. Boynton, who reported for the *Cincinnati Gazette*, said that he had filed the *Times* story as a favor during Crounse's absence. He told of seeking out Senator Wilson to ask if he would deny the charges against him. Wilson had given Boynton an absolute denial and knew that he would file the story that night.

Vice President Wilson did not contradict the reporter. "General Boynton is a man of character and truth," he told the committee, "and I should take his word." Although the committee later cleared the vice president of any wrongdoing in taking the stock, it concluded that the *Times* dispatch had been "calculated to convey to the public an erroneous impression."[38]

According to GATH, Credit Mobilier left Congress "so wholly demoralized by apprehension of other exposures that neither House took definite action, and Congress adjourned under a cloud, and the entire country . . . was overcast with doubt, shame, and indignation." The House absolved all but two of its members, censuring Oakes Ames and James Brooks, the House Democratic leader. Brooks had been vulnerable because he was a government director of the Union Pacific at the time he received his stocks. Within weeks, both Ames and Brooks had died in disgrace. The Senate investigating committee recommended James Patterson for censure, but his term expired before the full Senate acted against him. Of all the accused congressmen, Speaker Blaine most fully redeemed himself, wrote the *New York Tribune:* "He was born under a star as lucky as his predecessor's [Colfax's] was unlucky."[39]

Two politicos destroyed by the Credit Mobilier scandal were members of the newspaper fraternity and guests at the correspondents' dinners. James Brooks, one of the earliest Washington correspondents, and Schuyler Colfax, the first journalist elected as Speaker and vice president, ended their careers with their reputations ruined. Mary Clemmer Ames, Washington correspondent for the *New York Independent,* attributed their downfall to envy within the press corps. "We hear so much about the power of the press!" she wrote in one of her letters. "Well, it is a fiendish power so far as it presents personal enmity and private spite." Ames suggested that newspapermen had felt slighted by Colfax's successes. "Jackanapes crows to his cronies on 'Newspaper Row': He didn't invite me to dinner; but I can write him down . . . He'll feel the power of the press to his sorrow."[40]

Few in the press felt satisfied with the final congressional reports on Credit Mobilier. In his eulogy for his departed editor, former correspondent James S. Pike argued that the scandal had vindicated Horace Greeley. The editor had run for president, said Pike, because he had seen the federal government become "rotten through and through." Greeley's *Tribune* added that the failure to censure Colfax had been "another coat of whitewashing." Other papers mocked Congress for limiting its rebukes to Ames and Brooks. Even the *Philadelphia Inquirer* dismissed the House report as "plainly an effort to save the majority of offenders by making scapegoats of the two principal ones."[41]

During that same short session of Congress, Credit Mobilier shared headlines with sensational charges that Senator Samuel Pomeroy had bribed a Kansas state legislator during his campaign for reelection. And Congress voted itself a retroactive pay increase, which the press denounced as a "Salary Grab." The bad press generated around these stories caused public confidence in Congress to plummet, and in the next election Republicans lost control of the House for the first time since the Civil War.

The intensive coverage of the Credit Mobilier scandal chilled the correspondents' once intimate relations with congressional leaders. "Up to that time Newspaper Row was daily and nightly visited by the ablest and most prominent men in public affairs," wrote Henry Boynton. "Suddenly, with the Credit Mobilier outbreak, and others of its kind which followed it, these pleasant relations began to dissolve under the sharp and deserved criticism of the correspondents." Years of estrangement followed, during which time Newspaper Row remained bereft of its nightly visitors from Capitol Hill. Relations between the press and the Congress became more formal, Boynton noted, "and each assumed relations bordering upon a warlike attitude towards the other."[42]

When the Republicans lost their majority in the House, Uriah Painter lost his sinecure as a committee clerk. He continued to report on Congress, and lobby it, for another dozen years, but past scandals continued to haunt him, and new reporters spread backroom stories about his nefarious ways. In the 1880s, Frank Carpenter, writing as "Carp" for the *Cleveland Leader,* identified a man connected with the press galleries "who is charged with having something to do with the Credit Mobilier scandal, and who is suspected of being an agent of Jay Gould and of John Roach, the big shipbuilder."[43]

Painter had indeed become an agent for John Roach, whose shipyards, in Painter's home county in Pennsylvania, had constructed the two largest American steamships, the *City of Peking* and *City of Tokio,* for the Pacific Mail Company. But Pacific Mail fell behind in its mail shipments to the Orient, jeopardized its federal subsidies, and was unable to meet its payments to Roach. The aggressive financier Jay Gould made use of this crisis to drive down the price of Pacific Mail stock and take over the company, so that he could merge the transoceanic steamship line with the Union Pacific and forge a transportation empire. The front lines of his battle for control were located in the committees of Congress, notably the House Committee on Post Offices and Post Roads, where Uriah Painter served as clerk.[44]

Roach hired Painter as his Washington agent. "I think you had better use your Influence to stop all action at present with regard to P.M. bills," the shipbuilder notified Painter at one point. In numerous scribbled and misspelled notes, Roach sent Painter on missions to see committee chairmen, to plant questions, to influence committee reports, and above all to keep him posted on the latest developments. But Painter was playing a double game. When the legislative battles ended and Roach had lost, Painter wrote to collect his reward from Jay Gould: "At the request of General [Grenville M.] Dodge [Union Pacific's Washington agent], I induced some parties here to do some important work that he desired to have done effectively and in which he did not desire to appear for fear of complications in other matters of greater value to you," Painter explained. "Nothing was left undone that was possible with the exceedingly limited means at my disposal."[45]

Painter had not been the only Washington journalist lobbying in behalf of the Pacific Mail subsidies. In 1875 a House investigation revealed that the company had also paid $25,000 to the ubiquitous Colonel John W. Forney, $5,000 to Donn Piatt, publisher of the *Washington Capital,* and $15,000 to William B. Shaw, who still corresponded for the *Boston Transcript, Chicago Journal,* and *Cleveland Herald.* Shaw admitted taking money in return for information, adding: "I have been in the habit of doing it for ten or twelve years." He had collected inside news for Pacific Mail and other clients in his guise as a reporter. When asked if he had ever disclosed his business relations with New York stockbrokers when making his inquires at the congressional committees, Shaw responded: "Oh, no!" But he saw no impropriety in his behavior, since he had never been a committee clerk. The House voted to expel all journalists who lobbied for any legislation but took no action against William Shaw, Uriah Painter, or any other accused members of the press galleries.[46]

The Panic of 1873 caused the failure of Jay Cooke and Company and the resignation of Henry D. Cooke as governor of the District of Columbia, events that brought to light yet another instance of lobbying and influence peddling by a Washington correspondent. In the years after the Civil War, "Boss" Alexander Shephard had directed a monumental rebuilding of Washington through street improvement and sewer construction, and had interested a number of newspapermen in lucrative real estate deals and city contracts. When Congress looked into Boss Shephard's transactions, the name of William W. Warden floated to the surface. A local road contractor testified that he paid the correspondent a percentage of the profits he received from a city contract, in return for Warden's influence with the Board of Public Works. The correspondent had frequently boasted of having "influence with almost everybody in the District." Warden denied the charges and described himself as a practicing attorney who had not done much "newspaper business" in years. His denial might have been more credible had Warden not also been accredited to the press galleries as correspondent for the *Baltimore Gazette*, owner of the *Washington Republic*, and president of the Washington Correspondents' Association— which quietly disbanded.[47]

The public identification of journalists with lobbying prodded Washington correspondents to put their house in order. "Painter, like Shaw, another Washington Lobbyist, has a nominal connection with a newspaper," commented the *New York World*, "so that he can figure among congressmen as a newspaper correspondent, although the salary these men received for their alleged newspaper work would not pay for the postage stamps on their correspondence." Since Congress had been unable to bring itself to eject lobbyists from the press galleries, the correspondents proposed to take on the job themselves. In November 1877 George Adams, Henry Boynton, and other leaders of the press met with House Speaker Samuel Randall to discuss press gallery accreditation. Over the next two years a set of rules was devised, which the correspondents adopted at a gathering in the *New York Times* office on Newspaper Row in 1879. These rules defined accreditable correspondents as those whose primary salary came from sending telegraphic dispatches to daily newspapers; barred lobbying by any member of the press gallery; and prohibited all clerks from executive agencies (although not from congressional committees). To pass judgment on applications for admission, and to enforce the rules, they established a Standing Committee of Correspondents. The House adopted this plan in 1879, and the Senate followed in 1884.[48]

Chaired by General Boynton, the new Standing Committee set about cleaning house. Adopting a "grandfather" rule, the committee did not attempt to expel reporters whose names had already been linked to lobbying, but confined its efforts to screening new applicants. William B. Shaw remained an accredited correspondent until well into his seventies at the turn of the century. Uriah Painter held his press gallery pass until 1885, when William Harding sold the *Philadelphia Inquirer,* and he lost his special relationship with the management. Painter retired from corresponding, although as a stockholder in the *Washington Post* he contributed occasional articles to that paper.[49]

Operating under the new rules during his final years as a correspondent, Uriah Painter acted with more discretion, but his reputation as a "superserviceable" man at last made him wealthy. Painter invested in the work of a twenty-three-year-old electrical wizard who was seeking to break Western Union's monopoly on the telegraph by developing means to send multiple messages over the same lines. In 1878, the inventor came to Washington to demonstrate another of his creations, the phonograph. Uriah Painter escorted Thomas Edison around the Capitol Building and White House, and convinced President Rutherford B. Hayes and various congressmen to record their voices on Edison's wax cylinders—persuading cynics that the inventor was not a ventriloquist. As one of the earliest investors in the Edison Speaking Phonograph Company, Painter served as Edison's Washington agent, looking after his patent interests and arranging his free railroad passes.[50]

Alexander Graham Bell's new telephone also captured Painter's imagination, and he organized the first telephone company in Washington. One story indicated that Painter offered to sell an option to develop the telephone to Jay Gould—who controlled Western Union—but that Gould had dismissed Bell's machine as a toy. Years later, House Speaker Joe Cannon regretted having turned down Painter's offer to sell him stock in Bell's telephone. Investments in Edison and Bell allowed Painter to devote himself entirely to business in the years after the sale of the *Inquirer* cut him loose from newspaper reporting. Among other ventures, his con-

Uriah Hunt Painter (*left*) introduced inventors Charles Batchelor and Thomas A. Edison (*seated*) with their phonograph to the president and members of Congress in April 1878.

nection with the Pennsylvania Railroad earned him the presidency of a small subsidiary line on Maryland's Eastern Shore. Painter's business deals kept him a frequent visitor to Washington and a familiar figure in all the best hotel lobbies.[51]

Having suffered the defamation of his journalistic reputation, Painter craved respectability. In the 1890s he purchased the house on Lafayette Square, where William Seward had negotiated the Alaska treaty, and demolished it to build a grand opera house where he could entertain Washington's elite. The Painter family affixed his name to the opera house on a bronze tablet, as his own Washington monument (which lasted until the 1960s when the opera house made way for a federal office building). Not surprisingly, when Uriah Hunt Painter's end came in 1900 (he was sixty-three), the press gallery remembered him as "one of the few newspaper men of Washington who died wealthy."[52]

6

General Boynton Makes Peace

"WHY DID YOU lug me into the article, anyway?" demanded the claims agent who barged into the *Cincinnati Gazette's* Washington bureau on Newspaper Row one August afternoon in 1883. "Because you all belong to the same gang of swindlers!" snapped correspondent Henry Van Ness Boynton, drawing up his diminutive frame against the burly intruder. The claims agent landed a punch, but Boynton recovered and tossed his assailant out onto the street. For defying physically and politically powerful adversaries, General Boynton won his reputation as "the most combative of the political writers following the Civil War." Fellow reporters labeled him "brave, manly, and self-reliant," and "a man of iron character, [and] unyielding opinions." From the 1860s through the 1890s, Boynton took on claims agents, lobbyists, senators, and Speakers of the House with equal relish. Unabashedly partisan, he unhesitantly assailed his own party's officeholders whenever he suspected them of betraying the public trust. When Henry Boynton launched a crusade, he invariably won, and relished his victories. Correspondent O. O. Stealey suspected Boynton of indulging in combativeness just for sport, recalling that he once promised to put a politician "on the Gridiron for the fun of the thing and to see him wiggle."[1]

For all his fighting spirit, Boynton's ultimate achievement was that of peacemaker. During the Gilded Age, when American newspapers were breaking free from partisan dependency, and when investigatory journalism sorely discomforted politicians, General Boynton worked to rebuild the ties between the press and public men by establishing more formal rules to govern Washington journalism. Boynton became the prime mover in creating the Standing

Committee of Correspondents, which would govern the congressional press galleries. For like reason, he launched the Gridiron Club to rekindle the mutual trust and confidence essential for Washington reporting.

Henry Boynton inherited a righteous combativeness from his father. Born in West Stockbridge, Massachusetts, Henry spent his childhood following his father, the Reverend Charles Brandon Boynton, from pulpit to pulpit throughout New England and the midwest. In 1846 the Reverend Boynton moved to Cincinnati as minister of the Sixth Presbyterian Church, where he preached against slavery and made his church a stop on the Underground Railroad. Those who heard the minister's thunderous antislavery sermons, recalled that "Dr. Boynton was never afraid to do what he believed to be his duty." His outspokenness led to his break with the presbytery, and the transformation of his church into the Vine Street Congregational. A founder of the Western Tract Society, the Reverend Boynton personally toured Kansas to report on the clash between pro- and antislavery forces in that troubled territory.[2]

Son Henry graduated from Woodward College in Cincinnati, enrolled in the Kentucky Military Institute for his master's degree in civil engineering, and stayed at the institute to teach mechanics and astronomy. After the battle of Bull Run, Henry Boynton was commissioned a major in the Thirty-Fifth Ohio Infantry. He commanded a regiment at Chickamauga and Missionary Ridge and received the Congressional Medal of Honor for valor in combat. Severely wounded, he was brevetted from the army as a brigadier general in September 1864 but remained on the battlefield as a correspondent for the *Cincinnati Gazette*. In 1865, both father and son moved to Washington. Charles Boynton became chaplain of the U.S. House of Representatives, where he prayed over that body throughout the stormy years of Reconstruction and impeachment. Sitting above him in the press galleries, Henry Boynton covered the same proceedings as the *Gazette*'s Washington correspondent.[3]

Henry Boynton saw politics as an extension of the battlefield, and he covered political movements and strategies with the same precision he had devoted to wartime reportage. "He writes clean, incisive English, and thoroughly believes in what he writes," another correspondent noted with admiration. The popular impression of correspondents as writers who switched sides and worked for whomever paid their fees never applied to General Boynton. His Republican partisanship ran resolutely through his dispatches. A typical Boynton account began: "The Democrats have determined to wash their hands of any responsibility for the tariff bill which the conferees must agree upon. It remains to be seen whether the people will permit the Democrats to thus escape the responsibility." Boynton was the type of correspondent who never hesitated to use the personal pronoun; and while his articles appeared in the *Gazette* unsigned, according to the custom of the day, his authorship was no secret. Other newspapers reprinted his pieces with the preface: "General Boynton writes as follows to the *Cincinnati Gazette*."[4]

On Newspaper Row, Boynton's colleagues admired him as "dignified, upright and thoroughly loyal to the profession." Few of them held the confidence of so many public officials, or could boast of as many important visitors as came to see Boynton in his office. Nor did many members of Congress possess his width of knowledge of public affairs, which he shared with his political allies. Boynton's vast array of inside sources kept him ahead of most stories and made him skeptical of the rumors that floated daily through the Row. If General Boynton knew nothing about some item of gossip, then the other correspondents were wise to discount it. Younger reporters also testified that no Washington correspondent stood more ready to give advice and encouragement to novices in the field, or to come to their rescue in a controversy.[5]

The Republican Boynton shared an office with O. O. Stealey, correspondent for the Democratic *Louisville Courier-Journal*. Clustering several correspondents for different papers in a single office helped keep down housekeeping expenses and broadened contacts. The Democratic Stealey could tap congressional sources closed to the Republican Boynton. Younger men in the office also did much of the legwork on a story, while the older men used their better access to those in power. Even as they shared the news, each put his own slant on it. Nightly, Boynton and Stealey used the same private telegraph wire in their office. Boynton would lead off by filing "two or three thousand words booming Republican policies and roasting the Democrats." Then Stealey would take the wire to blast Republican outrages upon the people. Boynton, meanwhile, would have prepared another volley on the intentions of the Democrats "to reduce American labor to the pauper class of Europe." It was a marvel to Stealey that the wires did not burn as they carried such wildly contradictory messages.[6]

Henry Boynton demanded respect from the public men he covered. Reporting on Washington news from the impeachment of Andrew Johnson to the Progressive era, Boynton saw nine presidents and hundreds of senators, representatives, and cabinet officers come and go, in "a hurried march towards political oblivion." He was bemused by the mistakes that most politicians made in their dealings with reporters. Only a handful bothered to learn

General Henry Van Ness Boynton, Washington correspondent for the *Cincinnati Gazette*.

how the press really operated. The rest made press relations need-lessly difficult, either through arrogance or ignorance. Boynton gave the example of a senator facing a hard fight for reelection, who visited President U. S. Grant at the White House and questioned him on a major story of the day. The senator next made the rounds of newspaper bureaus, offering his information—in the strictest confidence—to one correspondent after another, and capped off his circuit by handing a copy of his account to an Associated Press reporter. Along the Row, correspondents sent off their exclusive stories, only to hear from their editors that it merely duplicated a wire service story. The senator's good press terminated posthaste.

To Boynton, it seemed only logical that the press and public men needed each other. Politicians required publicity; reporters wanted news. Each should have been able to satisfy the other's desires. But too often politicians considered the cultivation of the press beneath their notice and expected the press to cultivate *them.* Boynton never could understand why more public men failed to learn the "proper methods" of using the press to promote themselves and their issues. Not a day went by, he pointed out, when a member of Congress could not reach the public through the press corps, yet these same men sneered at the press as sensationalist. Such attitudes misread the Washington correspondents, invariably cautious men who held confidences tightly. If the Washington press really was sensationalist, a half-dozen correspondents telling all they knew could pull down "the very pillars of the temple," Boynton asserted. It irritated him how flippantly public officials treated the reporters who protected them. The slightest criticism sent members onto the floor to make "personal explanations" for the *Record,* which they prefaced by insisting that they were not in the habit of taking notice of newspaper attacks. Those who protested the loudest were the same ones who followed the press the closest, "and with more cause for apprehension than any others."[7]

Take the upright Republican senator from Iowa, James Harlan, whose daughter had married Abraham Lincoln's son. Harlan's political roots reached back into the free soil movement of the 1850s. As a senator he earnestly promoted the Homestead Act, college land grants, a Pacific railroad, and other landmarks in the Republican program. In 1865, Lincoln had appointed Harlan secretary of the interior, a post from which he later resigned in protest against Andrew Johnson's policies on Reconstruction. By the beginning of the Grant administration, the forty-eight-year-old senator was being mentioned in the press as a potential presidential candidate. Reporters further deduced Harlan's national ambitions when he purchased Colonel Forney's *Washington Chronicle*, for the day of the "official organ" had not completely passed.[8]

Despite his effort to buy his way into the newspaper world, the Iowa senator was never popular with the Washington correspondents. Harlan dated his bad press back to his days as secretary of the interior, when he had cleaned house of the "virtual pensioners" in his department, among them "many newspaper correspondents and other proteges of Congress." But railroad fraud, not patronage, prompted Henry Boynton's attack on the senator. In the 1860s the federal government parceled out millions of acres of western land to encourage railroad construction, in the process enriching those members of Congress and the cabinet who held stock in the railroad companies. "These things are in the past," Boynton wrote in January 1869. "But hundreds of similar schemes, quite as extensive, are now before Congress, and the lobby engaged in pushing them is larger and more influential than ever before."[9]

Boynton initiated his fight "against some of the rotten officials here" with a series of articles exposing past practices. Under the headline, "A Startling History of Fraud and Dishonest Legislation—How Public Lands Are Squandered," his exposé ran in the *Cincinnati Gazette* and the *New York Tribune*. Boynton accused James Harlan, as secretary of the interior, of withdrawing land from public sale for his friends, and of illegally selling Cherokee land to the railroads. When the articles appeared, the senator jumped to his feet in the Senate to call attention to the newspaper attack—the first time he had done so in his legislative career, he said. Harlan scorned those press scavengers "who live on the crumbs," and in a long, detailed defense he dismissed Boynton's charges as absurd. The senator could not fathom what had motivated the attack, since he had never treated the correspondent "except, in my humble way, with the uttermost kindness." Any reporter truly interested in exposing a public evil, Harlan declared, should have checked his facts before firing his guns.

Harlan deftly tied Boynton's attack to the recent Alaskan scandal, by lumping the correspondent in with the reputed blackmailers in the press, "hanging around Washington writing for news-papers, styling themselves correspondents, and occupying seats in that gallery by the courtesy of the Senate." As Harlan painted the picture, the Alaska scandal revealed that journalists were allied with lobbyists to plunder the Treasury. Unscrupulous reporters had managed to convince citizens with private claims that they could influence the passage of legislation for a fee. A few simple folk fell for this deception, said the senator, but not the railroads, which refused to hire them. So "this class of correspondents" retaliated by denouncing the railroads in their papers and undermining the railroads' allies in Congress. "I, however humble, must be made the target for these slanders," Harlan concluded, "because I am a declared friend of a judicious use of the public lands."[10]

After this denunciation, Senator Harlan declined to respond to any more of Boynton's accusations. Harlan relied instead on his supporters in the Iowa press to defend his name. In various Iowa newspapers, there appeared unsigned letters from Washington rebutting Boynton's charges. In his private correspondence, Harlan made it clear that politics lay at the root of his troubles. Writing to Representative William Allison, known to harbor ambitions for his Senate seat, Harlan suggested an Iowa paternity in Boynton's articles. Their publication in a Cincinnati newspaper had merely been a blind, to give it more force when reprinted in papers in Dubuque, Davenport, and Keokuk, to drive him out of the Senate.

His motives impugned, General Boynton had no intention of allowing the matter to rest. He continued a drumbeat of criticism against Harlan in the pages of the *Gazette*. No matter how often the senator defended his record, the persistent newspaper charges—in the words of a sympathetic observer—"worked like a slow poison upon the minds of many fair-minded people in Iowa." In the next election, Harlan lost his bid for renomination to William Allison. To add further injury, Senator Harlan also became implicated in the Credit Mobilier scandal. Although a Senate committee exonerated him, his political career was left in ruins. James Harlan lost all subsequent campaigns to regain public office. The senator departed from the Washington scene, while the correspondent endured.[11]

Iowa voters' abandonment of a once-popular senator demonstrated the power of the press. But what power was it? Did the press persuade through logic or emotion? Did it gain attention through investigative reporting or sensationalist writing? How could so intangible a force be measured? Lord Bryce, the British ambassador to the United States, grappled with the power of the press in his study, *The American Commonwealth*, published in 1888. Bryce dissected newspapers' power into three categories: narrator, advocate, and mirror or weather vane. For reporting events, he judged American journalists the most active in the world, trying to satisfy their readers' enormous appetite for news. As advocates, newspapers claimed power because they were "universally read," although the growing popularity of independent papers showed that American readers would no longer follow a party press mindlessly. As mirrors of public opinion, the press won deference from government officials; but with nearly every view finding expression in some paper, it was hard to tell which views truly reflected public opinion. "What struck me," Bryce wrote with characteristic insight, "was that in America a leading article carries less weight of itself . . . and is effective only when it takes hold of some fact (real or supposed), and hammers it into the public mind." Here was Henry Boynton's real strength as a correspondent—his tenacity in following a story, his refusal to allow any denial to go unanswered, his blend of self-assurance, self-righteousness, and combativeness.[12]

Although victorious in his contest with Harlan, Boynton smarted over the charges that had linked him with "blackmailers" in the press. The Washington correspondents were by and large honorable men who had achieved their positions through a combination of knowing public affairs and having the courage to report what they saw. But among them stood "a few shysters, lobbyists, and sensationalists" who made the rest vulnerable to guilt by association. Daily, Boynton felt the chilling effect of Credit Mobilier and other press-revealed scandals. His friendships with politicians cooled and his office no longer attracted its stream of congressional visitors.[13]

To improve this unfavorable climate, Boynton joined with other prominent Washington correspondents to reform the House and Senate press galleries. Congress had failed to police the membership of the galleries and had not enforced the standing rules that prohibited reporters from advocating private claims before Congress. The Speaker of the House and Senate Rules Committee nominally held this authority, but neither seemed able to differentiate between the legitimate reporters and the flocks of clerks, lobbyists, and other quasi-journalists who applied for seats in the gallery.

In 1877, Boynton's group of correspondents opened negotiations with the new Democratic Speaker of the House, Samuel Randall. They formed a five-member executive committee to draft regulations, which two years later Speaker Randall accepted. Enforcement of these press-sponsored rules fell to the Standing Committee of Correspondents, which would pass judgment on all applications for admission. The Senate followed suit in 1884, giving the Standing Committee jurisdiction over both galleries. The press corps elected General Henry Boynton as the Standing Committee's first chairman. As chairman, he policed the membership with an eye toward rooting out lobbying and improving the collective image of the congressional correspondents.[14]

Designed to bar lobbyists, the gallery rules had even more drastic impact on other groups. The rules specifically shut the press gallery doors to all those government clerks who moonlighted as "special correspondents" for small country papers, for glory, extra salary, and free railroad passes. Executive department clerkships were year-round posts that the correspondents generally could not hold because their assignments frequently moved them away from the capital. The regular correspondents considered these interlopers unfair competitors who could afford to take assignments at lower pay, and who clogged up the press galleries during dramatic moments on the floor. While barring executive clerks, the new rules exempted congressional clerks—positions often held by Washington correspondents.[15]

By barring from the press galleries any journalist who did not file telegraphic dispatches to daily newspapers, the new rules effectively denied accreditation to all women and black reporters, who either wrote for weekly papers or posted their stories by mail. During the 1870s women journalists had increasingly availed themselves of the press galleries; but by the 1880s those galleries reverted to exclusively male preserves. Similarly, in the 1870s, Frederick Douglass received access to the press galleries as editor of the *New National Era*. After Douglass departed, no black reporter occupied the press gallery until 1947.[16]

After the Republican General Boynton had achieved these new gallery rules through accommodation with Democratic Speaker

Samuel Randall, he fell out violently with Randall's Republican successor, J. Warren Keifer, an erstwhile friend and political ally from Ohio. The Boynton-Keifer confrontation began on a routine day at the end of the Forty-Seventh Congress. On 1 March 1883, Boynton arrived at the House press gallery in midafternoon. In the previous November elections, the Republicans had lost their majority in the House and were now hurriedly completing work on a tariff bill before turning control of Congress over to the Democrats in three days.

A House-Senate conference committee met to settle differences on the tariff bill that evening, and Boynton joined the lingering knot of correspondents outside the closed committee room door. As the conferees wearily departed near midnight, the correspondents cornered knowledgeable members to gather what news they could. Boynton ignored the conferees and sought out the clerk of the House Committee on Ways and Means, Major John M. Carson—who also corresponded for the *Philadelphia Ledger* and shared Boynton's office. The two men walked down Pennsylvania Avenue from the Capitol to Newspaper Row, with Major Carson detailing to General Boynton the various tariff schedules just adopted. Back at their office, each man prepared his dispatch. Carson dictated his story for the *Ledger* to Robert Wynne, a young reporter in the office, who in turn sent a copy to his own paper, the *San Francisco Examiner.* Another junior member of the office, William Barrett, took notes during Carson's dictation and filed a dispatch to the *Boston Advertiser.*[17]

Later that evening, Speaker Keifer arrived at the news bureau and went to the back room. A resident of the nearby Ebbitt Hotel, the Speaker made a habit of stopping at Boynton's office, and this evening he was anxious to learn what had happened within the conference committee. Both the Speaker and the correspondent were short, stocky, full-bearded men of about the same age, background, and temperament. Both had volunteered for Ohio regiments after Bull Run; both had been wounded in combat; both had been brevetted brigadier generals. After the war, Boynton's path had led into journalism, Keifer's into law and politics. Using the Grand Army of the Republic as his springboard, Keifer won election to the House in 1876, and in 1881 he upset James G. Blaine's candidate, Tom Reed, for the Speakership.

Inexperienced in parliamentary procedure, bullheaded in behavior, and partisan to the marrow, Warren Keifer presided over the House of Representatives for two stormy years. The Republicans' narrow majority did not suppress party factionalism. Keifer suspected Blaine and Reed of working to undermine his leadership. Blaine had expected the House to follow his dictates in choosing a Speaker and could not forgive Keifer for winning. Other disappointed aspirants to the Speaker's chair were doing whatever they could "to gain a little cheap applause" at his expense. Keifer's defensiveness swelled as he presided over the House during the last frustrating days as Speaker.[18]

Throughout his troubles, Keifer leaned on General Boynton for advice, and for the support of his paper. The *Cincinnati Gazette* circulated widely in the Speaker's central Ohio district, and he subscribed to the paper at his own home. On this evening, Boynton gave the Speaker the bad news that the conferees had slashed duties on woolen products, which would surely reverberate against Ohio Republicans in the next election. The two men poured over Boynton's copy of the House rules to plan strategy for scuttling the tariff. "Isn't this a damned queer thing, for the Speaker of the House to be giving away how he is going to defeat the tariff bill?" asked one of the younger journalists in the front room. Correspondent Robert Wynne replied, "Well, he is very well acquainted with General Boynton and knows he is perfectly safe in this office in anything that he says." As Wynne predicted, none of these strategy talks appeared in Boynton's dispatches. When the House finally adopted the tariff bill, with the Ohio Republican delegation voting in the negative, Boynton urged Ohio sheep growers not to blame either the Speaker or the Republican majority.[19]

Following the vote, the House reconvened for a noisy and rambunctious last night session. The Speaker repeatedly bellowed for order and pounded his gavel but failed to silence the chamber. Crowds jammed the public galleries, with some members' wives complaining they could find no seats. From the floor, a Representative from Kentucky spotted empty seats in the press gallery and moved that they open its doors to any guest with a pass. When no one raised an objection, the Speaker ordered the Sergeant at Arms to open the doors to the reporters' gallery. Shocked correspondents found their press gallery sanctuary invaded, in Boynton's words, by a "crowd of pushing, impudent, brazen sight-seers, male and female," who took every seat, obstructed the aisle, and "delayed the reports of the whole press of the country." Not until the early hours of the morning, when tired visitors began to drift away, did the correspondents regain their gallery. In his dispatch to the *Gazette* that night an indignant Boynton denounced the Speaker's inexcusable violation of the rules.[20]

Near 2:00 A.M., when the gallery was clear of strangers, Boynton sent reporter William Barrett from his office to see the Speaker. Standing in a corridor outside the chamber, Barrett described the press's inconvenience and requested that the Speaker reverse his order to avoid more confusion later when the House reconvened. Irritated and exhausted, Speaker Keifer felt in no mood to cooperate. If the reporters wanted seats, let them find them like anyone else. "The press has a good deal of influence and I think it will be worth while to pay some attention to it," Barrett warned. "I don't care a God damn for the press," the Speaker growled, ending the discussion.[21]

General Boynton took the Speaker's unfriendly attitude and unparliamentary language as an act of war. He marshaled a half-dozen correspondents to spend the night in the gallery and bar the doors when visitors tried to return the next morning. At 9:00 A.M., when the House reconvened, the journalists admitted only those with press gallery passes. Below in his office, Warren Keifer stormed over this insurrection but was powerless to act since his Speakership officially ended with the Forty-Seventh Congress at noon.[22]

Some fifty correspondents met later that day in the House press gallery, where they voted unanimously to condemn the Speaker's action as well as his "ungentlemanly, unprovoked, and entirely unwarranted language." Former Speaker Keifer replied that he neither considered the correspondents' rights superior to those of the ladies, nor could see how his actions had inconvenienced the press so terribly. He also denied using the vulgar language attributed to him. But the correspondents interpreted his action as a precedent that could undermine their privileged position in the House. Almost every member of the gallery pilloried the former Speaker in dispatches, none more vociferously than Henry Boynton. Keifer later wrote in his memoirs: "I was personally charged with wilfully opening the press gallery as an insult to the dignity of newspaper men, and, with this, other false statements were published, which could not be answered through the same medium, by me or my friends, which made an unfavorable impression, scarcely yet removed from the public mind."[23]

Had Keifer allowed the matter to rest, its ill-will undoubtedly would have evaporated over time. But insecurity drove Keifer to defend himself by attacking his assailants as disappointed lobbyists. He accused General Boynton of having tried to bribe him to win passage of a special claim. To bolster his charges, Keifer waved about a letter he had received on 27 February 1883:

> Dear General: McGarrahan—you have doubtless heard of him—appeals to me to ask you to give Mr. Dunnell a chance to ask for a vote on his (McG's) bill.
> It has been reported favorably from committee.
> To have a vote seems fair enough when one side is a great monopoly, and the bill seems to be a fair one to both sides. I have no interest of the remotest kind in this matter, but have always thought McG. the victim of a rich corporation, and so he has always had my sympathy.
> Truly yours.
>
> H.V. Boynton[24]

The note seemed innocent enough, but Keifer insisted that Boynton had gone to his office to press the matter in person. When the Speaker refused to support the claim, Boynton allegedly called him a fool for not having used his position to make the kind of money that Speakers Colfax and Blaine had (a double-edged charge that also assailed Keifer's adversary, James G. Blaine, then campaigning for the Republican presidential nomination). Boynton supposedly declared there were millions in the McGarrahan claim, if it passed, enough to make both of them rich. The Speaker recalled that when he rejected this corrupt proposition, the correspondent "stepped quickly to the door and went out."[25]

Keifer's story made its way back to Henry Boynton, who reacted by demanding a congressional investigation into this defamation of his character. The new Democratic majority in the House willingly arranged for a public confrontation between the Republican minority leader and eminent Republican correspondent. Appointment of a special investigating committee forced Keifer to scramble for corroborating evidence. For his part, Boynton mustered a lengthy list of journalists and Congressmen willing to speak in his defense. With the sole exception of Uriah Hunt Painter, every Washington correspondent endorsed Boynton as man of honor and integrity. By contrast, Keifer's witnesses were a sorry lot whose testimony deflated under cross-examination. The committee reported that it found Keifer's charges improbable, and the House, in a stunning rebuke to its former Speaker, voted to accept the report.[26]

The consensus on Newspaper Row, reported the *Washington Evening Star*, was that Keifer was "out of his head," and if he was not careful he would also be out of his seat. Indeed, Keifer lost his race for renomination later that year. Henry Boynton claimed victory, having politically destroyed an old friend and confidant in defense of principle and personal honor.[27]

Perhaps Boynton won a Pyrrhic victory. By disgracing a former Speaker of the House, he had not bettered the relations between Congress and the press, as the Standing Committee on Correspondents had been trying to do. There had been something ominous about this fight between two staunch Republicans. Party loyalty no longer bound together congressmen and correspondents. The day of "party papers" was quickly passing, and most correspondents considered themselves independent. The "press Congress" as the galleries were sometimes called, had tripled in size, further breaking down the old intimacy with the members. "The newspaper press of the country, without regard to party, has become, in the main, thoroughly independent in its criticisms of all public affairs and public men," wrote Boynton. He had no quarrel with such press independence, but he realized that it would deeply affect the means by which Washington correspondents cultivated their sources and collected the news.[28]

Months after the Keifer debacle, Grover Cleveland defeated James G. Blaine for the presidency, ending two decades of Republican control of the executive branch and drastically changing the patterns of Washington life for the correspondents. That same November, the now immense, three-hundred-pound, gray-bearded Major Ben: Perley Poore stopped at General Boynton's office on Newspaper Row. Ill health and the lure of an annual salary had caused Poore to resign from the *Boston Journal*, and he was making his living by writing his reminiscences and (with Hiram Ramsdell) a campaign biography of the presidential ticket of Blaine and John A. Logan. Boynton turned to his officemate, O. O. Stealey and said, "the Major has just made a suggestion I think well of." Poore explained his idea for a "club without a clubhouse," a dining club where correspondents and public officials could mingle for off-the-record evenings of good food, good drink, and good stories, to relieve some of the tensions and walls of suspicion that had grown between them.[29]

Poore had in mind the old Washington Correspondents' Association, disbanded since the Alaska scandal. Subsequent efforts to establish newspaper clubs in Washington had failed, largely because of the hostility between the national correspondents and the local Washington reporters. "Every attempt to organize a press club had proceeded on the idea of shutting out the correspondents," observed Charles T. Murray of the *New York Times;* "every correspondent's club had barred the local press." Charges of lobbying had further muddied the waters and prevented social mingling between politicians and the press. But an eating club struck Boynton as an intriguing solution, and he mulled the idea over during his walks to the Capitol with Major John Carson. Not many other correspondents showed enthusiasm for the plan, but in January 1885, when a group of reporters took the popular Judge R. C. Crowell to dinner at Chamberline's restaurant, Major Carson used the spirit of the evening to promote a regular series of dinners. They appointed a committee to draw up bylaws and tossed about several names, including "The Terrapin" and "The Skillet," before deciding upon "The Gridiron," after the rack on which chops were roasted.[30]

The Gridiron Club held its premier dinner in February 1885, and at first met monthly whenever Congress was in session. Except for an occasional "ladies' dinner," Gridiron functions were stag. Nevertheless the club adopted the rule: "No reporters are present, but the ladies always," meaning that decorum would be maintained and no coarse jokes or off-color stories would be told, as if women sat in the audience, and no remarks would appear in the next day's newspapers without the speaker's permission, as if there were no journalists within earshot. For keeping confidences, the Gridiron Club intended to rival the confessional. So seriously did they take this rule, that the correspondents banned George Alfred Townsend from attending their dinners after GATH indiscreetly quoted a dinner guest in one of his dispatches.[31]

Membership was originally limited to thirty-five, but Gridiron members could invite guests to the dinners. Editors and publishers, judges and diplomats, senators and representatives, cabinet members and presidents became regular guests. Befitting a Bohemian dining club, they feasted on menus of blue teal ducks, planked shad, Smithfield ham, stewed terrapin, Kentucky mutton,

Gridiron punch, fine wines, and pure Havana cigars. A quartet sang "Hear Dem Bells" as they rang the dinner bells, and members entertained with renditions of popular songs. Before long, clever journalists wrote their own satirical lyrics, with a political twist. It was a short step to political skits, roasting the public men of the day. "The invitations of this club to the highest in power and influence are seldom declined," General Boynton noted proudly. "This has brought about social relations which are of mutual benefit to each of these influential parties in public affairs." Boynton breathed easier now that public men were "coming to their senses again." The popularity of the dinners reached such levels that in 1890, the House of Representatives had to dispatch its Sergeant at Arms to retrieve enough members from the Gridiron Club to establish a quorum.[32]

Ben: Perley Poore served as the Gridiron's first president. At one club dinner he confessed to a sideline that had long supported him financially: "If any of you gentlemen are going to Congress I can furnish you with speeches for a reasonable consideration." Formation of the club marked the end of one era for Poore's generation. Poore died two years after his Gridiron presidency. The year that the club had held its first dinner, the *Philadelphia Inquirer* was sold and Uriah Painter lost his position as Washington correspondent. Death, retirement, and replacement removed the Civil War era correspondents one by one. The older men no longer headed the Washington bureaus, with one exception, reported a trade magazine, "and he is Gen. Boynton of the *Cincinnati Commercial-Gazette*. He conducts the editorial portion of that antiquated journal's business. A young Mr. Wynne gets the news."[33]

General Boynton persisted as a Washington correspondent until the *Gazette*, having merged with another paper, cut back its staff. Meanwhile, he promoted the presidential candidacy of his old friend William McKinley, former Ohio representative and governor, whom he urged to campaign on a single gold standard. McKinley, a cautious bimetalist, preferred to make the tariff his chief campaign theme, but Boynton—with a publicist's eye—argued that William Jennings Byran's free-silver platform had made currency the only issue. McKinley's conversion to the gold standard simplified and sharply defined the contest. In 1898, Boynton retired as a correspondent to redon his army uniform during the Spanish-American War. Later he returned to Washington as presi-

A Gridiron Club dinner in 1899.

dent of the District of Columbia school board and chairman of the Chickamauga and Chattanooga National Military Park Commission. He maintained strong enough ties with his longtime profession to be elected president of the Gridiron in 1899. Henry Boynton died in 1905, at age seventy, and was buried as a soldier at Arlington Cemetery. O. O. Stealey paid a final tribute to "the best newspaper correspondent in Washington, for the reason that he was active, industrious, and outspoken and uncontrolled by men or parties."[34]

The battling General Boynton combined the peculiar mix of adversarial and intimate relations between the politicians and the press common to his generation. Those he fought he defeated, but he left his mark as a peacemaker, having established the Standing Committee of Correspondents, to keep lobbyists from undermining the integrity of his profession, and the Gridiron Club, to perpetuate the spirit of the old Bohemian Brigade.

7

James G. Blaine, Journalist and Politician

SOME POLITICOS adjusted more readily than others to the growing professionalization of the Washington correspondents during the late nineteenth century. Despite the persistence of highly partisan newspapers, and the intensity of voters' party loyalty during the Gilded Age, shrewd politicians like Speaker of the House and U.S. Senator James G. Blaine never took the press for granted. Blaine courted correspondents for Republican and Democratic papers alike and learned how to give reporters what they wanted. Having begun as an editor and reporter rather than a lawyer, he employed his instinct for news and genius for self-advertisement to generate an immense and devoted national following. A Senate colleague, the colorful but uncharismatic Kansas Republican John J. Ingalls, puzzled over the process that elevated a politician like Blaine to political idol. "Other leaders were admired, loved, honored, revered, respected," Ingalls noted; "but the sentiment for Blaine was delirium."[1]

Blaine understood that political careers required constant replenishment of publicity, and that election to Congress by itself guaranteed neither national fame nor popularity. "A man's name may be in the *Record* every day," the *Washington Star* observed; "he may make speeches all over the country; he may have his name written in red letters on the board fences by the wayside—still he must be unknown . . . unless the newspapers take him up." Some of the ablest men, especially in the House, were scarcely known outside their districts. Some members of Congress expressed disdain for the press, some felt afraid of its power, yet most desired to see their names in print and would rather tolerate slander than accept obscurity. Journalists suspected that a few members stirred up controversies strictly to draw attention to themselves, cultivating notoriety until it became fame.[2]

Correspondent Henry Boynton had reasoned that politicians need only learn the methods of the press to win cooperation from the Washington correspondents. If so, it followed that politicians with a background in journalism would have the advantage in press relations. The increasing number of journalists entering Congress after the Civil War attested to Boynton's logic. These lapsed journalists proved more able than the typical lawyers, farmers, and businessman in Congress to grasp the abstract nature of the news: that someone had to identify, collect, condense, and explain it to the public. Elected officials who wanted to influence what their constituents read, needed to cultivate those writing it. Tips to favored reporters, leaks of confidential information, availability, and quotability all made a senator or representative popular with the Washington press corps. Astute members also realized that no matter how irreverent and irritating these "Bohemian" correspondents acted, they included some of the sharpest minds in the newspaper business. Serving as their editors' and publishers' private advisers in Washington, the correspondents molded editorial reaction to men and events at the capital. It paid ambitious congressmen to take key correspondents into their confidence—and some went a step further by taking them onto their payrolls as well, perpetuating the tradition of journalists acting as committee clerks and private secretaries.[3]

Not every journalist who won election achieved success in Congress. Horace Greeley, Joseph Pulitzer, and William Randolph Hearst all tried and failed. Each discovered that he had less influence over legislation as a freshman member of the House than as a newspaper editor. In 1880, when *American* magazine published two columns thick with the names of journalistic alumni of the House and Senate, it concluded that "many a good journalist has been spoiled in making a poor Congressman." But the magazine made an important distinction: "When a man is more a journalist than politician, he is like a fish out of water in Congress. Not so with those journalists to whom a connection with the press is only a *stepping-stone* to political preferment."[4]

Successful journalists-turned-politicians divided into several categories. Some legislators retained command of their newspapers as power bases. During his twenty-five years in the Senate, Rhode

Island's Henry Anthony never relinquished editorial control of the *Providence Journal*, which served as the organ for the state's Republican party, textile industry, and senior senator. Joseph Hawley similarly held tightly to the reigns of the *Hartford Courant* during his thirty years in the House and Senate. In contrast to these congressmenwho happened to edit newspapers, Amos Cummings exemplified the newspaperman who had a second job in Congress. An editor of the *New York Sun*, Cummings in 1886 won election to the House, where he took notes from his seat on the center aisle, much to the envy of other correspondents. "From the gallery over the Speaker's head those newspapermen who are not Congressmen look down on the Congressional reporter and his operations," noted the *Washington Star*. "The odor of news in which he revels floats faintly up to their nostrils and they sigh."[5]

Kansas Senator Preston Plumb epitomized a third variation: the politician who retained the habits of his former trade. Once editor of the *Emporia News*, Senator Plumb took subscriptions to all the New York papers, several from Chicago, Philadelphia, Kansas City, and St. Louis, as well as every local paper from Kansas. At his office near Newspaper Row, an estimated eight hundred daily and weekly papers were piled high in baskets beside the senator's desk. "By reading the local papers, I can tell just what the people of Kansas are thinking and talking about," he explained. "I get no better return for any of the money which I spend than for that which I pay out for local newspapers of my state." Plumb also supplemented his subscriptions with generous loans to Kansas editors, which they repaid in cash and in editorial endorsements.[6]

Of all the journalists in Congress, James G. Blaine pursued the press most assiduously. No other gathered the power, influence, and national reputation that he enjoyed for over thirty years in Washington. The "Plumed Knight of Maine" served as Speaker of the House, United States senator, and secretary of state. He figured as a major contender in every Republican presidential contest between 1876 and 1892. "No public man in our country, except perhaps Henry Clay, had such a devoted following," marveled Senator Chauncey Depew. His millions of passionate supporters were dubbed "Blaniacs." In an era when candidates advertised upright character, sense of duty, honor, morality, integrity, and manliness, Blaine won admiration for a magnetic and dominant personality. "The personality of James G. Blaine was the most conspicuous and remarkable of any in American life during the period immediately succeeding the Rebellion," wrote correspondent Noah Brooks. "He will always be remembered by the hosts who admired him as 'the magnetic man from Maine.'"[7]

Washington correspondents found Blaine irresistible. "I defy anyone, Republican or Democrat, to be in his company half an hour and go away from him anything else than a personal friend," wrote one reporter. Meeting privately with journalists, Blaine had "a familiar way of speaking one's name, and of placing his hand on one's knee." Another correspondent remembered him as "kindly and considerate." Even Charles Dana, whose editorials in the *New York Sun* habitually assailed Blaine, "in a way secretly loved" his nemesis. Yet Blaine evoked loathing as well as love. The private Blaine cultivated the Victorian image of devoted husband, attentive father, and kind friend, while the public Blaine was so aggressive in debate, audacious in behavior, and acquisitive of wealth and power that his supporters in the press had trouble varnishing over the roughness of his personality. Ben: Perley Poore struggled with mixed emotions. In his memoirs, Poore praised Blaine as a popular man "who exercised a fascination over all," but in personal correspondence he added: "I wish he wasn't quite so tricky."[8]

Blaine entered politics directly out of journalism. Born in western Pennsylvania in 1830, he attended Washington and Jefferson College before moving south to teach mathematics and classical languages at the Western Military Institute, near Lexington, Kentucky. There he came under the spell of the aging Henry Clay, after whom he modeled his political style. (Noah Brooks noticed how much it pleased Blaine whenever the press drew parallels between his career and Clay's.) After marrying and starting a family, Blaine abandoned teaching, briefly toyed with the law, and was drawn into journalism by a chance to purchase a share of a small Whig newspaper in Maine, his wife's home state. It was at the *Kennebec Journal*, wrote Washington correspondent Hiram Ramsdell, "that the natural bent of his mind for the career of journalism which had before been displayed only in occasional articles, showed its full force." Blaine absorbed himself in studying the paper he had bought, going through bound volumes of back issues to master its tone and the minutiae of Maine politics. He took over as editor in November, following the Whig victory in the state elections. That January, the new Whig majority in the state legislature designated the *Journal* as the state paper, with a contract to print all official notices. Years later, Blaine reminisced about his editorial days, when as State Printer he made $4,000 a year and spent $600, "a ratio between outlay and income which I have never since been able to establish and maintain."[9]

Outfitted in a blue swallow-tail coat with bright gilt buttons, James G. Blaine cut a familiar figure at the state capital in Augusta. By the age of twenty-seven he was a power in Maine politics and a founder of the state's Republican party. One Maine politico recalled Blaine having a "Western *dash* about him that took with us Down-Easters." In 1857 he became editor of Maine's most influential daily, the *Portland Advertiser* (owned by a member of Congress), dividing his time between Portland and Augusta, where he covered sessions of the state legislature. Blaine's legislative reporting became legendary. He never took notes, instead relying upon a "divine memory" to produce reasonably accurate—and in some cases improved—accounts of the debate. Rarely did speakers object to his polishing of their remarks. "No test of a man's power is more severe than the demand made by a daily newspaper," Blaine later commented. "Without the opportunity for elaborate investigation of each subject as it arises, he must have a mind well stored with knowledge; without time for leisurely composition, he must possess the power of writing off-hand with force and precision."[10]

The lure of politics eventually overpowered his commitment to journalism. Blaine won election to the state legislature in 1858; became chairman of the Republican State Committee; and by 1860 was Speaker of Maine's House of Representatives. During these years he continued to write weekly letters for the *Advertiser*, whenever the legislature met. He relinquished his editorial post in 1860, only after its new owners determined they needed a full-time editor in Portland. By then, Blaine had outgrown both the paper and state-level politics. After he won election to the U.S. House of Representatives in 1862, he made national politics his sole career.[11]

In Washington, the freshman Blaine stood out from the average Congressman. Tall, agile, bright, versatile in conversation, well-read on an endless variety of subjects, he delighted listeners whether in small groups or vast audiences. Senator Depew noted that the average politician of the era commonly had only one speech, which he divided into sections lasting anywhere from fifteen minutes to four hours, depending upon what the occasion demanded. But Blaine trusted himself to extemporaneous speaking. Instead of stately oratory, he courted interruptions, loved repartee and off-the-cuff responses. In debate, he searched for an opponent's weak point and attacked it incessantly until he brought his adversary "to the verge of desperation." He had an editor's instinct for never letting a charge go unanswered, but this sometimes proved a liability for a politician. Sometimes when it might have been wiser to keep silent and allow public furor to subside, Blaine simply could not resist a caustic response, further provoking the opposition. He worked hard to win his enemies over, but too often enraged them even more.[12]

Politically and financially a risk-taking gambler, Blaine could catch his political opponents off guard and attract headlines with his boldness and unpredictability. Knowing that he made wonderful copy, the correspondents filled the press galleries whenever he sought recognition on the floor. His explosive temper was "capable of great gusts of anger, but incapable of prolonged resentment." Not so the targets of his barbs, who often bore long grudges. Early in his congressional career, Blaine launched his most celebrated verbal assault on a vainglorious fellow Republican, Roscoe Conkling of New York. Although sharing the same age and ambitions, Blaine and Conkling were men of vastly different temperament and style. Conkling's arrogant demeanor caused lesser men to shy from encounters, but it only provoked Blaine's defiance. Correspondent David Barry thought the two men "as jealous of each other as two woman rivals in love."[13]

In the spring of 1866, a New York correspondent published a glowing paean to Conkling, placing upon his shoulders the mantle of the recently deceased Republican leader Henry Winter Davis. The tribute must have grated on Blaine, for a few days later it came to mind while he was sparring with Conkling in a House debate. "The haughty contempt of that large-minded gentleman is so wilting; his haughty disdain, his grandiloquent swell, his majestic, supereminent, overpowering, turkey-gobbler strut has been so crushing to myself and all the members of the House that I know it was an act of the greatest temerity for me to venture upon a controversy with him," Blaine mocked. Recognizing Conkling as a potential obstacle to his rise to party leadership, Blaine sought to diminish him by ridiculing his obvious pomposity. Conkling had taken the comparison between himself and the mighty Davis far too seriously, Blaine concluded, since the resemblance between the two men was more like "Hyperion to a satyr . . . dunghill to diamond . . . a whining puppy to a roaring lion."[14]

Political cartoonists seized upon the turkey strut and Hyperion curl and exploited them unmercifully. The New Yorker never lived down the allusions nor forgave his assailant. Conkling never again spoke to Blaine, although they served together in the same party in the House and Senate and attended the same functions for years. The personal feud prevented either man from winning the White House, since each devoted himself to denying that honor to his rival. Blaine made repeated attempts to heal the rift, always unsuccessfully. In 1884, when Blaine ran for president, Republicans begged for Conkling's endorsement to sway the pivotal state of New York. Although Conkling by then had left public office for a law practice, he remained unmovable. "No thank you," he replied. "I don't engage in criminal practice."[15]

Although the Blaine-Conkling feud generated abundant press coverage, it represented only a fraction of Blaine's allure to the Washington correspondents. "No man in America better understood the ways and means of reaching the public ear through the newspaper press than Blaine," wrote correspondent David Barry. Blaine actively befriended and aided reporters, regardless of their party, but "if a reporter wrote critically of Blaine he found himself cut off from this important source." Blaine possessed an editor's "keen sense of the public's wants," and an editorial eye for the leading topics of the day. He also knew how to present his ideas and opinions in a newsworthy manner. "None knew better than he how to use the channels of the newspapers for creating impressions upon the public mind."[16]

Washington's resident critic, Henry Adams, used Blaine as the model for the corrupt, immoral, and compelling Senator Silas Ratcliffe in his novel *Democracy*. Adams drew this portrait of his fictional senator's dealings with the press: "Several newspaper correspondents, eager to barter their news for Ratcliffe's hints or suggestions, appeared from time to time on the scene, and dropping into a chair by Ratcliffe's desk, whispered with him in mysterious tones." What Ratcliffe/Blaine whispered back to the press was his inside knowledge of Washington affairs. Because of the high offices he held, Blaine had ready access to the kind of news that reporters wanted. On the few occasions that he turned down their requests, he somehow did it in a way that made him seem to be doing them a favor. Members of the press gallery joked that Blaine could tell them "what the weather was yesterday morning in Dakota; what the Emperor's policy will be touching Mexico; or what day the 16th of December, proximo, will fall; who is chairman of the school committee on Kennebunk; what is the best way of managing the national debt; together with all the other interests of today, which anybody else would stagger under."[17]

One reporter recalled that he never found it necessary to interview Blaine, because if he had any news to impart "there would be no human possibility of [Blaine's] missing the chance." Blaine invented the Sunday news release, recognizing that anything distributed on that slow news day would get prominent display in the Monday papers. He experimented with the semipublic letter, intended more for the press than for its nominal recipient. He floated trial balloons to test public sentiment, and disavowed them if they burst. He never hesitated to write editorials for friendly newspapers to publish anonymously.[18]

Blaine especially wooed the *New York Tribune*, on the grounds that so many Republican papers followed its editorial lead. When the *Tribune* arrived each day, he dropped whatever else he was doing to devour its contents. He had courted Horace Greeley's favor with lavish praise but without success. During the Credit Mobilier scandal in 1872, the *Tribune* treated Blaine more roughly than others. Following Greeley's death, the paper took a marked turn in its editorial tone. A Blaine supporter, Whitelaw Reid, assumed the paper's management with the aid of loans from another Blaine enthusiast, financier Jay Gould. With Reid in control, the *Tribune* became almost a personal organ for Blaine and gave him an outlet for his unsigned editorials. "Do me a favor to insert the enclosed in the *Tribune* of Saturday morning if possible," he wrote to Reid. "Of course, *my* sending this to you is private and confidential." He suggested that "the publication of the enclosed as an 'editorial' in the *Tribune* would do no harm to any one, but a great deal of good to many—myself among others." He might send an item "for your political column, a statement which I hope you may think worth making." Another item came from what he called an exceedingly reliable source. "I want you to publish it . . . prominently—from an 'unknown correspondent.'" Or, "I send you to be published the enclosed as 'the other shoe'—and I have sent it out to distant papers saying it would appear in the *Tribune* by Monday."[19]

Similar items went to other sympathetic editors. To the publisher of the *Boston Journal* he forwarded a letter from "a special friend in Ohio," with specific instructions: *"Please put it under the head of your Washington dispatches."* Of course the Washington correspondents objected to being bypassed. Ben: Perley Poore alerted his publisher that Blaine had "twice gotten me into scrapes by giving me paragraphs which he would not father"—that is, he disavowed authorship of a story after it was challenged. "Only a week or two [ago] I saw an editorial in your paper denying that he had retired to the cloakroom when the third-term vote was taken, which had his ear-marks," Poore referred to a vote in the House of Representatives disapproving a third-term for President Grant. Since this vote would help clear the way for Blaine's presidential candidacy, he supposedly had absented himself from the chamber. Neither Poore nor his assistant, E. B. Wight, agreed with the editorial since they both saw him go to the cloakroom and then stand in the doorway, neither fully present nor fully gone. "But no man is perfect."[20]

Blaine applied his instincts for publicity to make himself the center of press attention during his first bid for the presidency in 1876, but at the same time he demonstrated the dangers inherent in such attention. During a House debate over the pardoning of former Confederates, the usually moderate Blaine unexpectedly waved the bloody shirt by demanding that former Confederate President Jefferson Davis be excluded from the list for his complicity in the "gigantic murders and crimes" at the notorious Andersonville prisoner-of-war camp. Blaine's masterstroke electrified Republicans and once again saddled Democrats with the rebellion by forcing them to rally to Davis's defense. Writing to the *Boston Journal*, Ben: Perley Poore credited Blaine's words with having "a magical effect, and the loyal men of the Union are again rallying around the old flag." The *New York Tribune*'s Hiram Ramsdell pictured Blaine standing in the House chamber "like a gladiator in the midst of an arena," an image that Colonel Robert Ingersoll converted to a "plumed knight" when he nominated Blaine for president at the Republican convention.[21]

"Mr. Blaine's Contest with the Democratic Majority" read the headlines, confirming how completely Blaine had personalized the contest. "After the Andersonville debate," judged Senator Ingalls, "Blaine developed phenomenal strength both in New England and the West." Washington correspondents agreed that publicity from the amnesty issue catapulted Blaine to front-runner for the Republican presidential nomination. Editors pledged their support for Blaine's "brilliant fight." The retired editor James Watson Webb congratulated Blaine for so dramatically grasping the initiative and escaping the condition "which was always fatal to Webster and Clay . . . the absence of an exciting cause or excuse for every man's feeling that they were called upon to fight a battle in your behalf."[22]

Having seized the spotlight, however, Blaine suffered from its scrutiny. Suspicious Washington correspondents began collecting rumors about Blaine's private finances. Some correspondents already knew about his problems but had withheld the story in deference to party loyalty. Correspondent E. B. Wight reminded his publisher how "last summer we spoke about certain curious features in Blaine's personal record which are not publicly known." Wight warned that the stories had now fallen into the hands of Democrats who planned to release them after Blaine won the nomination.[23]

A small group of reform-minded Republican journalists met in Cincinnati to discuss the Blaine rumors. General Henry Boynton of the *Cincinnati Gazette* and Joseph Medill of the *Chicago Tribune* were among those who had heard that Blaine had been bribed with railroad stock before becoming Speaker. Before publishing their story, the journalists sent word to Blaine, privately confronting him with the charges. Although he never responded to their letter, Blaine was prepared when the story broke in the *New York Herald* (editorially sympathetic to Roscoe Conkling). Blaine rose in the House to correct "certain errors" that had appeared in the press and read into the record testimonials from railroad executives and financiers who absolved him of guilt. This denial seemed to satisfy Congress and most of the press, but General Boynton still harbored doubts. If Blaine was innocent, why was he afraid of a congressional investigation of the charges? Boynton dug until he uncovered additional evidence of unethical stock and bond trading on Blaine's part. His stories reopened the controversy and handed House Democrats an opportunity to investigate, and they soon produced the bookkeeper for Blaine's broker, James Mulligan, who held letters Blaine had written about his railroad deals.[24]

Headlines that read "Mr. Blaine's Desperation," and "Blaine on the Defensive" described his deteriorating position. "Whose rep-

The Two Blaines.

utation is ruined this morning?" Ben: Perley Poore bemoaned the negative press coverage. "Each zealous newsgatherer . . . regards a Presidential aspirant not favored by the journal which he represents as his personal foe, in whose armor he knows the vulnerable points." But Blaine, in a stunning gamble, went to Mulligan's hotel room and spirited away the incriminating letters, which he proceeded to read—selectively—to the full House of Representatives. General Boynton complained that only five of the nineteen Mulligan letters had gone out over the Associated Press wires, and in fact Blaine had censored even those five letters, rearranging their sequence and leaving out the most embarrassing items when he read them on the House floor, and later when he corrected the proofs of the *Congressional Record*.[25]

"Blaine's Enemies Disarmed, A Complete Victory in the House," Hiram Ramsdell proclaimed. Uriah Painter cabled the *Philadelphia Inquirer*, "The Democracy was utterly routed, their column was broken, their leaders utterly demoralized." Rarely had such a rapid transformation of political fortunes taken place. The Republican press admired Blaine's nerve and sympathized with his fight against desperate odds. Even Democratic correspondents like Theron Crawford of the *Chicago Times* saw partisan vindictiveness behind the congressional inquiries. Crawford gave Blaine the benefit of the doubt in his dispatches, and in return for such fairness (and access to Democratic readers), Blaine took Crawford into a confidence that was "more than frank." All of his publicity, however, was insufficient for Blaine to overcome a coalition of party stalwarts, led by Roscoe Conkling, and party reformers, who handed the nomination to the bland, noncontroversial Ohio governor Rutherford B. Hayes.[26]

"I don't mind being abused so long as I am not forgotten," Blaine once remarked, testifying to his belief in publicity, good or bad. Yet he had miscalculated the effect that the constant repetition of stories, rumors, and vague suspicions could have in undermining his credibility. As Lord Bryce had noted, American newspapers were most effective when hammering home some fact into the public mind through continuous repetition. Bryce doubted that the majority of Blaine's supporters ever believed the charges of corruption they read against him. "They could not be at the trouble of sifting the evidence, against which their own newspapers offered counterarguments," he noted, "so they quietly ignored them."[27]

Never leave an accusation unanswered; always give your supporters some reason to doubt the evidence against you; confuse the issue if you must; do whatever is necessary to present yourself in the best possible light: these were the operating assumptions that politicians like Blaine employed to cope with new trends in the press. Having trained in the partisan journalism of the 1850s, Blaine spent his later political career contending with a steady erosion of the partisan press, with editors and reporters who saw themselves as professionals and identified with journalism rather than party politics, and with more balanced, "objective" reporting as the goal of the news. As a partisan, he despised the independent editors of the "Respectable Dailies." By the 1870s, newspapers were "*made to sell*," the elderly James Watson Webb lamented in a letter to Blaine. "When you and I were editors we did not follow, but made, public sentiment; and we also made presidents. But things have changed now."[28]

No matter how genial his press dealings, Blaine's attempts to manipulate the correspondents and their editors revealed his contempt for them. In the short run he succeeded, but over time his behavior raised deep suspicions and distrust among the Washington correspondents, who regarded him as devious and untrustworthy. Like James Brooks and Schuyler Colfax, Blaine's former profession turned against him. He owed much of his success to his knowledge of the press, and much of his failure to the fact that the press knew him only too well.

Excessive newspaper attention to such flamboyant types as Blaine and Conkling troubled more traditional and reserved politicians. Massachusetts Senator George F. Hoar worried over how frequently one Senate colleague's buffoonery and quarrels got his name in the newspaper headlines, and speculated that he was likely to wind up president. "Never," snapped Representative Nathaniel Banks. "Why, don't you see that papers all over the country are full of him every morning?" asked Hoar. "People seem to be reading nothing else." "Mr. Hoar," Banks replied, "when I came down to the House this morning, there was a fight between two monkeys on Pennsylvania Avenue. There was an enormous crowd, shouting and laughing and cheering. They would have paid very little attention to you and me. But when they come to elect a President of the United States, they won't take either monkey."[29]

Nor did voters take James G. Blaine. In 1884 he at last won the Republican presidential nomination, only to lose the race narrowly to a man who kept the press at the farthest distance possible. One of Grover Cleveland's few newspaper friends described him charitably as "shy of correspondents and reporters." Privately, Cleveland raged against the press "ghouls" who invaded his privacy and misrepresented his programs. Cleveland was the only president to decline to attend a single Gridiron dinner. He was also the last president to deny correspondents any working space within the White House. In contrast to their comfortable press galleries at the Capitol, reporters stood in the elements outside the North Portico of the White House to interview presidential visitors on the street.[30]

During Cleveland's presidency, the White House maintained extraordinary secrecy. Cabinet officers refrained from discussing policies in the making, and reporters had to await formal announcements. The president so hated leaks that a cabinet secretary once asked a reporter not to walk with him across the White House lawn, for fear that Cleveland might see them together. President Cleveland regularly left the capital without informing the press and completely eluded their net when he underwent cancer surgery on board a yacht in New York harbor, keeping the full story obscure for years.[31] One of the few officials in his administration sympathetic to the Washington correspondents was the president's secretary, Daniel Lamont, a former journalist. When Cleveland appointed Lamont to the cabinet in his second term, a Washington correspondent approached the president to discuss Lamont's successor. "We are hoping that you will appoint a man who will be good to us newspaper men," said the journalist. "I have a notion," Cleveland replied, "of appointing a man who will be good to me."[32]

Grover Cleveland's "meager publicity sense" restricted his presidency. Unlike Blaine, he rarely tested public opinion in advance, and he expressed annoyance whenever correspondents speculated about his intentions. Facing a largely Republican press, the first Democratic president since the Civil War assumed that the best he could do was to act in a dignified and honorable manner. He gave interviews only occasionally and then to just a few trusted correspondents. Otherwise he paid little attention to the press.

Had James G. Blaine rather than Grover Cleveland won the election of 1884, Washington correspondents could have expected substantially more sophisticated treatment. Instead, Cleveland's aloof attitude helped explain why the White House remained such poor competition against Congress for press coverage. Not until Theodore Roosevelt entered the White House in 1901 would a president seriously attempt to harness the press to influence public opinion—using many of the methods that Blaine had pioneered—and begin to tilt the scales of press attention toward the other end of Pennsylvania Avenue.[33]

8

—

Emily Briggs and the Women Correspondents

"IMMEDIATELY OVER the speaker's desk, railed off like the others, rose a succession of rigid-looking boxes, ink-bottles sunken in the top and ink-stains mapping the cloth surfaces, indicating the exclusive domain of the newspaper reporter," correspondent Charles Murray sketched the press galleries in his novel *Sub Rosa,* published in 1880. "This is where Events move with such astonishing rapidity and prolific Cause is helped along, pricked and goaded by twenty to forty young men and a trifle of women, for the entertainment and bedevilment of the outside world."[1]

That same year, the "trifle" of women correspondents, always few in number by comparison to the men, disappeared entirely from the press galleries. Just a year earlier, 20 women such as Emily Edson Briggs, who wrote social and political news from Washington under the pen name "Olivia," were accredited to the House and Senate press galleries, along with 147 men (only a fraction of whom attended on any given day). Once the new rules of the Standing Committee of Correspondents went into effect, the 1880 edition of the *Congressional Directory* listed not a single accredited woman correspondent, and for the remainder of the nineteenth century women's names rarely surfaced among the burgeoning lists of congressional correspondents.[2]

Press gallery rules never specifically prohibited women but instead tied accreditation to reporting for daily newspapers and sending dispatches by telegraph. Women writers failed to qualify under these provisions because they worked for weeklies or posted their columns of Washington society news through the mail. Since editors neither believed women could report political news nor considered their pieces worth the price of the telegraph tolls, their hiring procedures guaranteed that the press galleries would remain exclusively male.

Banishment of women journalists from the press galleries reflected the larger exclusion of women from Gilded Age politics. Except in a few frontier states, women could neither vote nor hold office. Yet women's interest in national politics was reflected in the vigorous women's suffrage movement, which convened national meetings in Washington and lobbied Congress for women's rights, temperance, and other social issues. Like Madeline Lee, the fictional heroine in Henry Adams's novel *Democracy,* women were drawn to Washington "bent upon getting to the heart of the great American mystery of democracy and government." Senate speeches had bored Madeline's sister, Sybil, who "naively assumed that the speeches were useful and had a purpose," and who ceased attending after a single tedious day in the galleries, but Madeline continued to visit whenever a "splendid orator" was due to speak. "She wanted to learn how the machinery of government worked, and what was the quality of the men who controlled it." In reality as well as in literature, women visitors found the congressional galleries the most accessible of government arenas and took advantage of Congress's open doors. "The work of this government being the work of legislation," one male commentator instructed in 1890, "the woman who proposes to be a force in politics must master the questions before Congress."[3]

Women spectators had accounted for the largest share of the crowds that packed the old Senate chamber's galleries in the days of Daniel Webster, Henry Clay, and John C. Calhoun. When the spectators' places became filled, gallant senators would vote to admit the overflow of women onto the floor, where they might be seated at the senators' desks. In 1859, when the Senate opened its new chamber with more spacious galleries, it provided a "Ladies' Robing Room" and a "Ladies' Gallery," reserved exclusively for women visitors. Within a few years a "Ladies' Retiring Room" served the wives of members, women reporters and lobbyists, and other female visitors to the Capitol. Disparaged as "gallery goddesses" by the men of the press, women often constituted the majority of the audience in the Senate and House galleries. From front row seats they watched the proceedings intently. Male reporters deduced that these women were looking for an "intellectual treat" in the debates, or merely passing time on their way to the

Congressional Library. In contrast to the plentiful women visitors to the galleries, women rarely served on the congressional staff. The first, Isabel Barrows, was hired as a House committee stenographer in 1871.[4]

Joining the women in the gallery were female lobbyists, a group much exaggerated in number and influence. Professional and corporate lobbyists like Sam Ward and Collis P. Huntington hired women to entertain members of Congress, and newspapers reported that "some of the prettiest women in the United States" haunted the Capitol. "You may see them any day about the Congress—gay, well-dressed and youthful in appearance at all events; off-hand and coquettish with the doorkeepers, but always with the sharpest imaginable eye to the business they are there for." Eventually, House Speaker Tom Reed found it necessary to abolish the Ladies' Waiting Room adjacent to the House chamber, ostensibly to convert it into a committee room, but in fact because he considered it "an atrocious source of scandal."[5]

Mark Twain's novel *The Gilded Age* and its stage adaptation made popular the beautiful and scheming female lobbyist in the

The ladies' gallery of the Senate during President Johnson's impeachment trial.

character of Laura Hawkins. Many a curious visitor toured the Capitol in the hope of spotting one of these spiders of the lobby. "The rural newspapers are full of descriptions of her, and these descriptions not only appeal to the imagination, but are drawn from the imagination," wrote the *Washington Star* in 1891. Such a woman, living and entertaining in great splendor, with unlimited financial resources to influence votes in Congress, might have existed in the past, but the *Star* "strongly suspected that the lady is a myth." More typically, the female lobbyist turned out to be a poorly clad, nervous woman seeking a small private claim.[6]

Among the gallery crowd of congressional wives, lobbyists, dilettantes, and students of government, women journalists constituted a small but notable band. Like their male counterparts, women correspondents' origins dated back to the days of the editor-journalist. Mrs. A. S. Colvin had edited the *Washington Weekly Messenger* sporadically between 1817 and 1828. In 1829, Anne Royall settled in Washington and two years later launched a small weekly paper, *Paul Pry,* eventually renamed the *Huntress,* both names suggesting a contentious and intrusive nature. The widow of a Revolutionary War veteran, for years she lobbied Congress with a claim for her late husband's pension. Royall eked out her living by writing travel books before turning to newspaper publishing. *Paul Pry* depended upon cheap paper, cast-off type, and young orphans to set the type. In the face of all these adversities, Anne Royall published the paper until her death in 1854.

Eccentric in dress and manner, Royall was once convicted as a "common scold," as a result of her rancorous dispute with the Presbyterian Church but was saved from a public dunking in the Potomac River when two newspapermen paid her ten-dollar fine. "She was homely in person, careless in dress, poor in purse and vulgar in manners," as Senate Doorkeeper Isaac Bassett described her years later. "When the Senate was in session, she would send for me to call the Senators out to see her . . . You either had to take a copy of her book or subscribe for her paper or give her money. If you refused, you were called all the ugly names in and out of the dictionary." Congressmen subscribed, at a higher rate than for others, simply to keep their names out of her paper. Bassett recalled an occasion when Henry Clay was preparing to speak and the galleries were crowded in anticipation. Royall marched out onto the Senate floor and demanded Clay's subscription. "Certainly madam,

I will take your paper," the senator responded. Reaching into her basket, she produced a roll of paper on which she added his name, and then took his money. When the gallery burst into applause, Royall "shook her head and left the Senate."[7]

Anne Royall had few pretensions of serious journalism, and her satirical style and unusual behavior merely served to confirm the prejudices of male reporters. As her source of livelihood, her paper concentrated largely on gossip and polemics on corruption and religion. "As to politics, I have never made it my study," she explained. "I think no woman has any business with politics; there is something so masculine and opposed to female delicacy in meddling with the affairs of state that I view it with sovereign abhorrence."[8]

Ideology rather than personal economics motivated the first woman political correspondent, Jane Swisshelm, to come to Washington. The passionately antislavery Swisshelm was a more serious journalist than Anne Royall, but she too reinforced stereotypes of women journalists as eccentric and unprofessional. Having gained entry as the first woman in the press gallery in 1850, Swisshelm lost her gallery accreditation when she published an exposé of Senator Daniel Webster's private life. Her banishment from the press galleries made it all the more difficult for other women who followed. Even Swisshelm, when she returned to Washington in 1865 to publish a weekly paper, *The Reconstructionist*, had to operate out of the public galleries.[9]

During the turbulent 1850s, Gamaliel Bailey published an abolitionist paper, the *National Era*, at the capital in competition with the slavery-tolerating *National Intelligencer.* Bailey hired two women journalists on his staff, Sara Jane Clarke, who wrote as "Grace Greenwood," and Abigail Dodge, who signed herself "Gail Hamilton." Clarke came to Washington in 1850 from Pompey, New York, as assistant editor of the *National Era* and as a correspondent for the *Saturday Evening Post*. At first she wrote poetry and literary essays, and then branched into character sketches of congressional personalities, interwoven with essays advocating abolition and women's suffrage. As Grace Greenwood she wrote in a mostly light and humorous vein but was capable of criticizing the politicians she covered. "We are told that a Congress of women would be shockingly unruly, passionate and slanderous," Greenwood commented; "but it would take women of forty Billingsgate power to surpass the late displays of honorable gentlemen of both honorable houses."[10]

Abigail Dodge, or "sunny, laughing Gail Hamilton," as Emily Briggs described her, a school teacher and writer from Hamilton, Massachusetts, joined the *National Era*'s staff in 1856. She also corresponded for a Boston religious weekly, covering political and social issues from an antislavery perspective. Dodge eventually returned home to care for her ailing mother and did not resume her career in journalism until the 1870s. By then her major objective had changed from abolition to promoting the career of her cousin's husband, James G. Blaine, as his publicist, speechwriter, and biographer.[11]

The typical woman journalist of nineteenth-century Washington tended to be widowed (like Royall and Swisshelm), unmarried (like Dodge), or untangling herself from an insufferable marriage. Sara Jane Clarke's ne'er-do-well husband, Leander Lippincott, flaunted his infidelity while living off her income. Clarke found him a job in the federal government, but in 1878 he was caught filing false Indian claims and fled to Europe. Correspondent Mary Clemmer Ames had separated from her husband, a minor federal official, in 1865. An occasional newspaper writer in the past, Ames began a "Woman's Letter from Washington" for the *New York Independent* the following year. She continued the column for the next twenty years, covering a range of subjects from women's rights to political corruption. Ames wrote in "stately, solemn prose," said fellow correspondent Emily Briggs. "Sometimes it is bitter and pungent, as many of our public men know."[12]

Content to take a seat in the Ladies' Gallery, Ames expressed disdain for women who applied for membership in the press gallery. "Because a woman is a public correspondent it does not make it at all necessary that she as an individual should be conspicuously public," wrote the inherently shy Mrs. Ames, "—that she should run about with pencils in her mouth and pens in her ears; that she should invade the Reporters' Galleries, crowded with men; that she should go anywhere as a mere reporter where she would not be received as a lady." Her view was that those who acted loudly and intrusively brought reproach upon all women journalists. She wanted women reporters to set higher standards than men and to apply those standards to reform Gilded Age politics. Mary Clemmer Ames's letter writing and ideas reached a receptive audience, making her the highest paid woman journalist of the 1870s.[13]

Regardless of what drew them into journalism, women reporters faced common barriers of discrimination. They constituted a minority not only within the galleries and the Washington press corps, but within the journalism profession and among writing women as a whole. With so many other occupational doors shut to women, professional writing fell somewhere between socially acceptable and unsuitable behavior. Women who wrote well enough could nurture literary ambitions. "The number of writing women is simply incalculable," wrote Fannie Mathews, "but of literary women incredibly small." Mathews's mother's maid intended to write her memoirs, her family cook talked about publishing a recipe book, and her milliner begged her to read the manuscript of her first play. Newspapers, because they published everything from daily news to theater and book reviews and social commentary, provided another outlet for writing women. But Mathews warned that journalism might make women "de-feminized" and unattractive as wives. Men would never propose to "the woman to whom they can tell the least bit of scandal; the woman who is ready to write up the latest horror for their columns; the woman whom they can send to jails to interview the freshest murderess; the woman whom they may jostle at midnight, or after, as each is hurrying alone down the elevated staircase to their homes."[14]

Journalism offered nineteenth-century women wider opportunities than any other profession except the stage. A few women reporters earned salaries comparable to men's, and special writers commanded comfortable incomes. Beyond economics, newspaper writing expanded a woman's horizons. "The newspaper woman soon learns that the world is bigger than a tea-cup, and in her absorbing work she finds no place for the tittle-tattle of the drawing-room or the gossip of the boudoir," wrote Edith Tupper in 1894. Liberated from "tiresome conventionalities," reporters gained a freedom of action denied most other women. "Her goings and coming are not so sharply inspected, her sayings and doings not so harshly criticized." A single day for a newspaper woman, crowded with events, was worth "a year of the monotony and stagnation" that was the typical woman's lot.[15]

Ambitious and persistent women could enter journalism, but they faced resistance at every step. Male colleagues treated one woman reporter as if she had "a sort of upper grade chicken pox or measles." They assumed that she would eventually get married and leave the newspaper. Women writers encountered hostility and indifference as they applied for jobs. "The principal objection raised whenever I applied was that I was a woman, and consequently disqualified for reportorial work," recalled one writer. Editors considered the women who wrote book reviews and other back-of-the-paper items "too impractical" for daily reporting. One editor explained that "people with literary tastes are too fanciful for plain news gathering." Another male editor, who employed women reporters "with considerable satisfaction," reasoned that their chief drawback was their lack of contact with public men, "and this simply because their sex prevents them from gathering in hotels, clubs, cafés and places of like character, where men find it convenient to sit and discuss all sorts of topics."[16]

Women reporters invariably covered society news, and not always by choice. "I think there is no class of employment in the world which I would have liked less than professional intrusion upon the august movements of the *elite*," wrote a woman who had reluctantly agreed to society reporting after her editor had insisted that nothing else existed around a newspaper office for a woman to do. Society reporting forced women reporters to spend much of their income on their wardrobes, to dress properly for social events. They needed to gain entrance to functions where reporters might not be welcome, and they had to fend off milliners and dressmakers who pressed them to mention their wares. "Eternal vigilance is the watchword of the society reporter," commented a woman correspondent who found political assignments less taxing.[17]

Writers of fiction often portrayed woman journalists as meddling, tactless, blunt-spoken harpies—the type Henry James satirized as Henrietta Stackpole in *The Portrait of a Lady*. "My poor Henrietta," his heroine protested the woman journalist's intrusiveness, "you have no sense of privacy." "You do me great injustice," Henrietta rejoined, "I have never written a word about myself!" A more sympathetic appraisal of women reporters came from Washington author Frances Hodgson Burnett, famous for writing *Little Lord Fauntleroy*. "Do you see that little woman on the sofa?" asked a character from Burnett's 1883 novel, *Through One Administration*. "She is 'our Washington correspondent' for a half-a-dozen Western papers, and 'does the social column' in one of our principal dailies, and tomorrow you will read in it that 'one of the most brilliant receptions of the season was held last night at the charming house of Mrs. Winter Gardner, on K Street.'" To earn her ten dollars a column, the society reporter "goes to receptions, and literary and art clubs, and to the White House, and the Capitol, and knows everybody and just what adjectives they like, and how many; and is never ill-natured at all, though it really seems to me that such an existence offers a premium to spitefulness."[18]

Although more independent than other women, the nineteenth-century woman journalist was ultimately dependent on male editors. She competed in a man's profession and yet was assigned to cover women's news. Such incongruities blended through the career of Emily Edson Briggs. The daughter of an Ohio blacksmith, Emily Edson taught school before marrying the young politician and editor, John R. Briggs, Jr., in 1854. The couple moved to Keokuk, Iowa, where Briggs bought the *Daily Gate City* and took an active role in state Republican politics. But crop failures depressed Iowa's economy on the eve of the Civil War, and the *Gate City* went bankrupt. John Briggs appealed to an Iowa representative whose career his paper had promoted, and secured appointment as assistant clerk of the House of Representatives, under Colonel John W. Forney.

John and Emily Briggs arrived in Washington in 1861, just as the city was swelling with soldiers and civilian federal employees. When the Treasury Department hired women clerks to replace the men going off to war, newspaper articles scorned the women as incapable of handling the job. In defense of women workers, Emily Briggs penned an indignant letter to the *Washington Chronicle*. Her style caught Colonel Forney's eye. When he learned that the wife of one of his clerks had written it, he summoned her to his office. Struck with terror, Emily Briggs was sure that she had offended her husband's chief. But instead of anger, Forney expressed delight with the opinionated nineteen-year-old and hired her to write for his *Philadelphia Press*. At first she wrote book reviews and then advanced to writing four to six letters each week on Washington government and society. Not until she saw her first piece in the *Press*, did Emily Briggs learn that Colonel Forney had given her the pen name "Olivia," the identity she kept for her entire journalistic career.[19]

Unlike the many widowed or unhappily married women journalists, Emily Briggs enjoyed a harmonious marriage. She accompanied her husband on his many travels, which provided material for her letters. His government post and political connections opened doors for her at the Capitol and the White House. After John Briggs died of tuberculosis in 1872, she continued reporting for another decade. Briggs became one of the first women correspondents to use the telegraph for "spot news," a sudden flash of important and late-breaking information. Yet, since telegraphing "cost a fortune," she generally corresponded by letter, writing long and detailed accounts of the people and events she observed from the reporters' galleries or at an evening's social gathering. She wrote at night in her rooms at the National Hotel. Hearing the cry, "Manuscript!" she would hurry downstairs and hand her letter to a horseback rider, who then raced to catch the evening train. In Philadelphia, another rider met the train and delivered the package to the *Press*.[20]

Emily Briggs never hesitated to write about politics or to express strong opinions on issues, but her real talents lay in her colorful descriptions, her keen eye for social and fashion trends, and her witty style of writing. She compared sitting in the galleries of the House of Representatives to being "hermetically sealed up in a huge can." She described the ladies of the gallery as "beautiful human butterflies in glaring hoops and gig-top bonnets, curls and perfumery." Reporting on the arrival of senatorial and cabinet wives, along with other gallery visitors, she observed that "The carriages bring the cream, and the street cars the skim milk."[21]

Openly partisan, Briggs defended favored Republicans from newspaper attacks. When General Boynton castigated Senator James Harlan for illicit business dealings, Emily Briggs pointedly covered the social receptions at Harlan's elegant mansions and testified to his noble character. "A thrust at Senator Harlan is a stab at every man, woman and child who knows him best," she asserted, suggesting that his press assailants "be broiled like St. Lawrence on a gridiron." She implored the press gallery to "have a care for the reputation of the men whom we have trusted in war and in peace."

Throughout Andrew Johnson's impeachment trial, Emily Briggs sat in the galleries providing "pen-and-ink" portraits of the congressmen who most fascinated her. The coarse Ben Butler, a leader of the House impeachment effort, won her comparison to a chestnut burr: "If we could only open the burr we might forget our bloody fingers and find ample reward for our pains." She defended

Emily Edson Briggs, better known as "Olivia."

the Senate's president pro tempore, Ben Wade, who stood next in line to succeed President Johnson (and who furnished her with tickets to the proceedings), as "one of the kindest men in Congress, also woman's best and truest friend," identifying him as "the coming man . . . whom destiny has called to be the leader."[22]

Briggs saved her harshest criticism for the railroad lobby, a "huge, scaly serpent," which she pictured "winding in and out through the long, devious basement passage, crawling through the corridors, trailing its slimy length from gallery to committee room, at last it lies stretched at full length on the floor of Congress." She despised the railroad financier Jay Gould, accusing him of keeping "one of the most beautiful women in Washington busily employed on the Congressmen, and astonishing to relate, the Senators seem rather to enjoy it than otherwise." But even Gould paled in her estimate by comparison to the Central Pacific's Collis P. Huntington, "the great, huge devil-fish of the railroad combination."

In lurid prose, Briggs depicted how with every congressional session Collis Huntington would establish himself in a suite at the Willard Hotel, soon swarming "with his recruits, both male and female, until scattered in the proper direction by order of the commander-in-chief." Huntington's "camp-followers" included former senators and representatives, discharged Capitol employees, and others who knew the ropes and had access to the congressional chambers. By contrast to the loathsome Huntington, the Union Pacific's Sidney Dillon appeared to Briggs as handsome as a Greek statue, but deceptively dangerous: "As he stands mentally playing with a Senator, he might easily be mistaken for something more than human, yet neither horns nor tail are visible."[23]

Emily Briggs regarded Roscoe Conkling as the most alluring of all politicians, designating him "the Apollo of the Senate." If Senator Conkling was a planet, she wrote, he should be Mars; "not because of his rapid revolution around the great central power, but owing to that precious high-colored ingredient which was used so lavishly in his physical construction." Watching the senator during another's speech, Briggs commented that Conkling "sniffs him from afar, as one mastiff does another."[24]

Although not a feminist, Emily Briggs covered the National Woman Suffrage conventions in Washington. At her first convention she heard Mrs. Lippincott, better known as "Grace Greenwood," deliver the keynote address and learned that not all women

reporters were treated equally. Those who supported women's suffrage received far better care from the convention managers.
Briggs spied Miss Nellie Hutchinson, the "spicy little reporter of
the *Tribune*," getting papers directly from Susan B. Anthony on
the speakers' platform, "whilst your correspondent was left in the
cold." Covering later conventions she learned to soften her criticism of the women's movement.[25]

Briggs defended her fellow women journalists. She wrote admir-
ingly of Mary Clemmer Ames, whose style and interests as a political correspondent contrasted so starkly with her own. She praised
"Shirley Dare," social reporter for the *New York World,* "the true
woman journalist, who accepts the situation, and is willing to fight
the battle of life on the woman's platform." Of her coverage of society news, Briggs observed that "the New York *World* has sent her
here upon as delicate and difficult a mission as the females of olden
times undertook when they were sent out by their sovereigns to
distant courts to take charge of certain branches of diplomacy." A
male reporter could slip relatively unnoticed through a social reception, but not so a woman: "She must be able to bear inspec-
tion." Briggs considered men wholly unsuited for writing a respectable society story. "The great New York dailies have tried man after
man at the capital, and have finally concluded there are some
things which men cannot do."[26]

Editors had long since discovered their readers' appetite for society news, and Washington's social elite had a political significance
that made their parties and receptions national news. Male correspondents from James Gordon Bennett to Ben: Perley Poore had
sent social news along with their political reporting. Some newspapermen had also discovered that covering receptions meant free
meals, and that milliners and dressmakers would pay them to mention their fashions in their social reporting. "Of all the nauseating,
disgusting characters around Washington," wrote Rollin Kirk, a
failed and angry ex-correspondent, the worst were "the shallow-
pated sycophants who 'write up' the society columns for the Washington papers. In return for a dinner, or even a glass of wine, these
'society writers' will make mention of the lowest men and
women."[27]

Society reporting meant recording the guest lists and describing
in minute detail what the women guests wore, naming materials,
styles of lace, and other ornamentation of the gowns. Mark Twain

once lampooned the practice in his Washington dispatches, describing one belle in "a pink satin dress, plain in front, but with a good deal of rake to it—to the train, I mean; it was said to be two or three yards long. One could see it creeping along the floor some little time after the woman was gone." Since most male reporters could not tell brocade from broadcloth, they tended to dismiss social reporting as too trivial for their attention. Both by default and by design, the task fell to women.[28]

Gilded Age Washington kept society writers busily employed. To head the district government, President U. S. Grant appointed former journalist Henry Cooke as territorial governor and Alexander Shepherd to the board of public works. Together, Cooke and Shepherd instigated a massive rebuilding of the city, grading and paving streets, removing old buildings, ripping up railroad tracks, and providing new parks. The city became a magnet for the newly rich, otherwise shunned by the established social elites of Boston, New York, Philadelphia, and Chicago. Millionaire miners from western states purchased Senate seats, built lavish châteaus along Washington's newly paved avenues, and introduced their marriageable daughters into society. "The social side of Washington was to be taken for granted as three-quarters of existence," Henry Adams commented. "Politics and reform became the detail, and waltzing the profession."[29]

The Grants brought to the surface a new generation of political and social leadership, heady victors of the Civil War eager for prominence and advancement. The press reported lavish receptions at the Washington homes of Vice President Schuyler Colfax and House Speaker James G. Blaine, or such flamboyant cabinet officers as W. W. Belknap and George Williams, in extravagant detail. Congressmen, who before the war had left wives and children at home and lived bachelor existences in boardinghouses around the capital, now squired their families to the capital and installed them in rented houses or hotel suites. Ben: Perley Poore's *Congressional Directory* listed the female family members who accompanied members of Congress, with symbols to designate unmarried daughters. Nevada Senator William Stewart abandoned his boardinghouse and built a "castle" in the fashionable West End. Senator James G. Blaine constructed an imposing mansion on Dupont Circle. High-style entertaining brought forth a spate of etiquette books to tutor congressmen from the hinterlands. "Society is the handmaiden of politics," one guide advised, and "personal influence is a mighty power to conjure with."[30]

Washington society at first courted the press and gloried when the newspapers reported on their receptions. Then press coverage turned critical, especially after members of Congress attempted a "Salary Grab" to support their higher standards of living. (At the close of the Forty-Second Congress, members voted to raise their salaries and made the pay hike retroactive, giving even the lame ducks a healthy bonus; following a public outcry, the next Congress repealed the salary increase.) Scandal plagued the most prominent social leaders: Vice President Colfax was implicated in Credit Mobilier; and cabinet members Belknap and Williams were accused of having misused government funds. Senator Stewart, having eroded his finances through lavish entertaining, decided against running for reelection. James G. Blaine was forced to rent out his too-costly mansion. Henry Cooke was ruined in a financial panic. Boss Shepherd, who replaced Cooke as territorial governor, himself later fled to Mexico under charges that he and his associates profited from the capital's rebuilding.

After this wave of scandals, the Blaine family tried to play down their reported entertaining. "Gail Hamilton"—Mrs. Blaine's cousin and James G. Blaine's publicist—wrote articles rejecting the popular image that Washington was "dominated by wealth or corrupted by extravagance." Social reporting followed official society into decline. Washington society would always be news, but its reporting no longer commanded the same avid attention or generous payment. When the Standing Committee of Correspondents barred women reporters from the press galleries, the indignity hastened their decline in number.[31]

Although Emily Briggs lost her press gallery pass, she had rarely used the privilege. She never had felt welcome among the men of the press gallery, and during her husband's clerkship she had worked out of his office in the Capitol. After his death, and the closing of the press galleries to women, she wrote less frequently. She retired to a spacious home, the Maples, on Capitol Hill, which she occupied until her death in 1910.[32]

After 1880, Washington became a less hospitable town for women journalists. By 1890, when the American press reported on the exclusion of women from the reporters' gallery in the British parliament, an American feminist reminded readers that the Capitol press galleries also belonged to the men. "Where did they get this right?" asked Laura Jones. "Male reporters have a gallery and comfortable seats overlooking the House and Senate at the points where they can best see and hear; they have writing-rooms, tables, stationery, pages, and the conveniences, and a door-keeper guards these sacred precincts and perquisites, and keeps them for masculine use." By contrast, women reporters, whatever their merit, and whatever newspaper they represented, had to contend for seats outside the press gallery, "without a ghost of any convenience for writing."[33]

An unexpected denial of Jones's charges came from a woman claiming to be the sole female member of the press galleries. Margaret Sullivan Burke argued that the press galleries at the Capitol belonged to no one. Congress made them available for the correspondents of the daily papers, "and each paper is alone responsible for the style of representative sent here by its management, whether male or female, old or young, black or white." The problem, she insisted, was not that the press galleries excluded women, but that editors and publishers preferred to hire male reporters. Absolving the correspondents and the Congress, Burke pointed to a bench outside the gallery that had been reserved for women writers and yet stood empty no matter how crowded the rest of the galleries became. True, there was no writing desk at the bench, but "the ladies who occupy the seats do society work" and wrote their letters at home. Opera glasses were the only equipment they needed to cover Congress.

Margaret Burke placed herself in a different category. A middle-aged woman with grown children, she had a "considerable taste for politics and none in the world of society." In 1887 she began reporting on congressional proceedings. Lacking a regular newspaper, she could not claim a seat in the press gallery and recorded what she could from the ladies gallery. But the other "ladies of the press" around her talked throughout the proceedings, causing her "to bungle my copy horribly." From the male reporters she encountered no hostility, but rather "the natural chivalry of cultivated men." Colonel John Carson of the *Philadelphia Times* took an interest in Burke's work and sent it to some of his papers with the neutral signature "M. S. Burke." She soon drew the same per column rate as the men in the gallery.

No matter how kindly, the male correspondents would open the press gallery to Margaret Burke only after she conformed to their rule of reporting by telegraph for a daily paper of her own. Burke feared that she could not handle that job alone. She watched how the "boys" on Newspaper Row took care of each other by exchanging news and covering for colleagues during their absence or illness, and knew she needed similar support. Eventually she found it from Perry Heath of the Associated Press. "Take whatever engagements you can, Mrs. Burke, and I will see that your papers are served whenever you are ill, or absent for any cause," Heath promised. He also gave her copies of any of his stories that might appeal to her local papers. With these assurances, Burke set up her own Washington bureau. "It was not so easy a task," she wrote, "for the world of newspapers had been informed by my friends that I could have no facilities on account of my sex, and the world did not know that I many times did work for the gentlemen of the press that they could not do for themselves; but at last, when the session was half over, I received the magical endorsement that opened the 'sacred precincts' to a woman."[34]

After scrutinizing her telegraph dispatches to the *Philadelphia Item*, the Standing Committee of Correspondence approved Margaret Burke's application. "Other women who have applied are engaged in social work," said correspondent F. A. G. Handy, "for which they need no such advantage at this building, their work being mostly at the White House." Burke concluded from her experiences that while women journalists were handicapped by their sex, the men of the congressional press galleries had not discriminated against her because she was a woman. But Margaret Burke's triumph was short-lived. After only a year she lost her daily paper, and although she continued to write about politics, and lived until 1917, her name disappeared permanently from among the accredited correspondents after 1890.[35]

Barred from the press galleries, women reporters were also excluded from the Gridiron Club and other networks of the trade. The Gridiron's operating rule that "the ladies are always present" meant only that members were to refrain from vulgar language and off-color stories as if ladies were present. On rare occasions, the gentlemen of the club held "ladies' dinners," inviting their wives, daughters, and female correspondents. Of the forty-nine monthly dinners the Gridiron held when Congress was in session between 1885 and 1898, women were invited to only three. The women correspondents banded together to form the National Women's Press Association in 1882. They elected Emily Edson Briggs as their first president.[36]

Despite their aloofness, male journalists never hesitated to buy news from women reporters. As reporting from Washington became an increasingly complex and time-consuming chore, a single correspondent could no longer cover the Congress, the courts, and all of the executive departments himself. Instead correspondents became "news-brokers," purchasing information from a swarm of stringers, who reported for smaller weeklies or were unconnected with any newspaper. Stringers—male and female—collected news on fashion, dress, society, hotel arrivals, and other bits of Washingtoniana that the correspondents sent on to their papers. Women journalists who may have aspired to higher status and more steady employment took what they could as stringers. Yet for decades longer, rules made by men ensured that Washington correspondence contained no more than a trifle of women.[37]

9

The Senate Fires
James Rankin Young

RECURRING PRESS violations of Senate secrecy created a paradox of nineteenth-century Washington reporting. Leaks depended upon close cooperation between senators and newspaper reporters, yet the friction these leaks caused disrupted efforts to improve relations between the correspondents and Congress. Throughout the nineteenth century, the Senate debated almost all nominations and treaties in closed executive sessions, but these were little more than a charade since the press so easily uncovered and reported their substance, quoted their speeches, and reprinted tallies of votes cast. In 1886, Senator Orville Platt pointed to the obvious when he told the Senate that there was "no secrecy possible," but senators were loath to abandon an old and comfortable tradition that suited their purposes. They reacted with irritation over the numerous leaks and applied various strategies to halt them. In 1892, one of their periodic crusades cost Washington correspondent James Rankin Young his post as the Senate's executive clerk.[1]

Secrecy fit the ambience of the late nineteenth-century Senate, which resembled something of a private gentleman's club. Through seniority and increased party regularity, a handful of committee chairmen controlled its proceedings and exercised enormous influence over the workings of the federal government. Senators insisted upon the necessity of secret sessions to protect national interests during treaty debates and to preserve the reputations of presidential nominees; but secrecy also strengthened the Senate's power over treaties. Closed doors fostered an atmosphere that encouraged the Senate to amend, revise, and reject treaties at will. Between 1869 and 1890 the Senate did not approve a single major treaty. During the 1880s it defeated four treaties for lack of a two-thirds majority, while others emerged from closed session debate significantly altered. By the 1890s, Secretary of State John Hay compared a treaty entering the Senate to a bull entering the arena. "The only thing certain is that neither will leave alive."[2]

Whenever the Senate shifted from legislative to executive business, it cleared spectators from the galleries—including the press gallery—and bolted the doors behind them. In the informality of their executive sessions, senators unbuttoned their vests, lit up cigars, and stretched out on the chamber's leather couches. Some senators felt that the relaxed nature of the closed-door sessions reduced friction and avoided the posturing that slowed down their public proceedings. Reporters passed the hours of waiting in the press gallery lobby, writing their dispatches, playing cards, and talking politics. In 1889, the *Washington Evening Star* reported that some correspondents used this time to burlesque the congressional debates, mimic the debaters, and shred many a legislative reputation. After a secret session ended, newspaper reporters were barred from the chamber for an additional ten minutes to discourage prying secrets from the members. Despite this precaution, reporters had little trouble finding senators who would talk.[3]

Senate rules prohibited members from divulging information from executive sessions, but it was common knowledge that each Washington correspondent "had his own senator" who leaked details of secret sessions. Some newspaper reporters became so successful at uncovering secrets that the senators came to them to find out what had happened. Senators quipped that correspondents might refuse to give them confidential information because they were "so leaky."[4]

The leaking of secrets was a mutual act in which both the politician and the reporter participated. Washington correspondents took care to hide the identities of their senatorial sources. Reporters for northern papers sought out southerners or westerners and avoided compromising home state senators. Wire service reporters, having no regional base, could collect information from any member. As a price for leaking information, senators expected favorable treatment, "in order that they and their political friends may be placed advantageously before the country," as Ben: Perley Poore explained in 1883. Poore further detected that a senator's willingness to cooperate with the press warmed in direct proportion to his presidential aspirations.[5]

A *New York Times* correspondent who transferred from Albany to Washington during the winter of 1892 regretted giving up the complete access to the legislature's chambers and all of its committee rooms that he enjoyed at the state capital. In Washington, doorkeepers barred his way onto the Senate floor and limited him to a bird's eye view of the proceedings from the press gallery. Imperious senators made it clear "that their will comes as near to being the law as anything can in this world of uncertainties." Even the Senate elevator changed direction instantly in response to a senator's buzz, regardless of other passengers' destinations. "After one has become seasoned to the work here he is supposed to lose sight of the obstacles which torment him at the onset of his Washington career," the *Times* correspondent concluded. "He discovers, however, that there is a well-defined feeling of resentment toward the Senate which he cannot help ascribing to the exclusiveness with which that body is hedged about." Nowhere was press resentment more apparent than in the treatment of the Senate's "un-American executive session."[6]

The Constitution neither prohibited nor required Senate secrecy, and it barely spelled out the Senate's right of advice and consent on treaties. During the First Congress, senators had goaded President George Washington into conducting business with them in person, until Washington came to the Senate chamber with a series of questions regarding negotiations with Indian tribes. The experiment failed miserably when the Senate refused to debate the questions in Washington's presence and instead referred them to a committee. "This defeats every purpose of my coming here!" Washington muttered in frustration. Washington's successors remained content with seeking the Senate's consent rather than its advice. Even so, the Senate assumed an ever larger share in treaty making through its amendment powers. At times, presidents encouraged senators to make changes, hoping to win concessions from treaty partners that they had failed to achieve at the negotiating tables. However, for most presidents treaty debates offered a vexing display of senatorial muscle.[7]

Treaties made important news, affecting both domestic and international affairs, yet the Senate's treaty debates took place entirely secluded from public view. Washington correspondents therefore mounted vigorous efforts to penetrate the veil of secrecy, including a persistent mocking of the process. Shortly after the

Senate had moved into its new chamber in 1859, senators heard noises coming from the empty galleries during a closed session. Sent up to investigate, a doorkeeper discovered two black cats locked below a trapdoor to the crawl space beneath the galleries. The *New York Tribune* suggested that the cats, when rescued, "bore evidence, in their insane demeanor, of the secrets they had over-heard during Executive session."[8]

Correspondents learned to avoid those senators who would not bend the rules. In the press gallery they said it would be easier to open an oyster with a needle than pry a secret from Senator George Edmunds. The Vermonter believed "the less the people know about the affairs of government the better," wrote one reporter. "His committee-room is a sealed box to the correspondents, and the moment any matter is referred to the Judiciary Committee the 'boys' content their souls with patience and simply wait until it is reported to the Senate."[9]

For Connecticut's Orville Platt, the secret sessions had become an exercise in futility. A respected member of the Senate's Republican establishment, Platt urged senators to abandon the pretense of secrecy during nomination debates. "Mixed they may be with untruth, mixed they may be with the fertile imagination of the newspaper reporter, nevertheless no Senator will deny me in saying that more or less what occurs in executive session is disclosed," Platt insisted. Obviously, the leaks came from within, which put all members under a cloud of suspicion. "What farce it is, Mr. President," Platt concluded. "The whole community, the world, are laughing at us that we pretend to have secret sessions."[10]

Yet few senators objected to withholding their debates and votes from public scrutiny. Rather, they resented reporters who flaunted the dignity of the Senate by unauthorized publication of their remarks and votes. North Carolina Democratic Senator Zebulon Vance defined executive sessions as the private business of the Senate and urged expulsion from the press gallery of any newsman who reported on them. "I would treat him as I would a man who would print conversations he might hear while a guest at my dinner table," said Vance. The senator advocated that reporters who violated Senate secrecy be imprisoned "till they rotted."[11]

Senatorial indignation over executive session leaks spurred periodic investigations, dubbed "smelling committees" by the press. They first applied the name to a special inquiry chaired by Oregon

PUCK.

"They hate the light, but they can't escape it."

Republican James Dolph, in 1890. Angered over the publication in the *Washington Post* and *New York Tribune* of a still-secret extradition treaty with Great Britain, Dolph set out resolutely to uncover the source of the leak. His committee inspected the gallery doors for cracks through which reporters might listen and examined the chamber's ventilation system. When the Senate went into executive session, the committee posted men on the gallery level to drive away anyone who might try to linger outside its thick doors and solid walls. Dolph's committee also instructed elevator operators not to take passengers above the first floor during closed sessions, precautions that both amused and irritated the correspondents.[12]

"There is no enterprising newspaperman here who cares whether the secret sessions are abandoned or not," wrote Frank DePuy in the *New York Times*. "If they are abandoned the interest in them will be less than it is now when the proceedings are forbidden property." Since some senators received better coverage of their speeches in closed session, *New York Tribune* correspondent Max Seckendorf recommended that for better publicity the Senate conduct all of its business in secret. Yet press mockery hid the ways that secrecy actually benefited the Washington correspondents.

They received more notice from their editors and newspaper space whenever they dispatched "secret" information. Closed sessions were reported, one journalist noted, "even more fully than the open debates." Secrets thus became a commodity that politicians could barter, and another link in the chain of intimate relationships between Congress and the press.[13]

Reporters stood to lose both credibility and sources if they divulged the sources of their secrets. Senator Dolph's "smelling committee" summoned correspondents Seckendorf, DePuy, George G. Bain of the United Press, A. J. Halford of the Associated Press, and Jules Guthrie of the *New York Herald* to testify. When not one would divulge who gave him the treaty, the ordinarily amiable Dolph accused the correspondents of sedition. Emotions grew so heated that Senator Platt again proposed abolishing closed sessions. Tennessee Senator Isham Harris countered that he would rather have no open sessions. Kentucky's Joseph Blackburn leaned toward abolishing the press gallery. "You occupants of the press gallery are our guests, and we have never been anything but liberal in our dealings with you," said a senator who asked to remain anonymous. "We have given you a private gallery from which every one except yourselves is excluded by rigid rules. You are furnished with all necessary accommodations, and you are not even called upon to pay your stationery bills." Senator Joseph Hawley, owner of the *Hartford Courant,* rose to defend the correspondents as "gentlemen who did their duty and did it well." Colorado's Henry Teller advised the Senate that the only practical way to guard against misrepresentation would be to open its doors. Senator George Vest proposed that every senator and staff member swear an oath that they had never revealed Senate secrets, an idea that brought protests from other senators, who accused Vest of impugning their honor.[14]

Senator Vest had offered his suggestion to make light of the matter, but James Dolph naively embraced the concept. Armed with an alphabetical list of senators, Dolph summoned the influential Nelson W. Aldrich of Rhode Island to answer questions in his committee room. Not only did Aldrich comply, but with some wry amusement he also remained to listen to his astute colleague, Senator William Allison, profess how little he knew about the news sources of Washington correspondents. Dolph circulated systematically through the chamber and cloakrooms, inviting senators to his inquisition. Pages and messengers searched the Capitol for senators, none of whom would admit to violating the sanctity of the secret session. But senatorial testimony revealed broad differences of opinion as to what constituted "secret" information. Senator Aldrich did not considered it a violation to tell the press whether a nominee had been accepted or rejected. Senator Isham Harris, a "smelling committee" member and critic of the press, confessed that he had once telegraphed friends the results of a secret session affecting their interests.[15]

Dolph's committee could not accept the obvious conclusion that senators released secret information when it suited their purposes. Continuing its search for a specific culprit, the committee took testimony from Senate clerks, Department of State officials, and the president's secretary, none of whom admitted divulging anything to anyone. Acting on a tip from the Senate Sergeant at Arms, the committee grilled David Barry, a correspondent who served as secretary to several senators. Barry shrugged off the charges, and years later offered his own explanation of secret sources: "Members of Congress, of course, have their own particular fortunes to consider, and, finding it necessary to use the newspapers for the purpose of reaching the ears of their constituents and the voters generally, frequently give reliable information of a confidential nature and in advance of general publicity to correspondents with whom they desire to be on friendly terms."[16]

Dolph's "smelling committee" disbanded without uncovering the source of a single leak. Adding further insult, the Senate discovered that it owed the hefty sum of $153 to each of the journalists who testified. Even though they had appeared before the committee only briefly, their subpoenas had been in effect for the entire five-month investigation, entitling them to full payment.[17]

Two years after the ill-fated "smelling committee," the controversy over secret session leaks erupted again, this time identifying and punishing a culprit: the Senate's own executive clerk. The dismissal of James Rankin Young resulted partly from politics but more from mounting frustration over the Senate's inability to control the Washington press corps. A popular, trusted member of the Senate staff, Young had put in a quarter of a century of service as a Washington correspondent and also published a Philadelphia newspaper. James Young had been born near Philadelphia in 1847, six years after his Presbyterian parents emigrated from Ireland.

When his mother died, and his father returned to Ireland for his health, a Philadelphia printer and book publisher took in and reared their children, eventually leading two of the brothers into journalism. ·Older brother John Russell Young had become secretary to Colonel John W. Forney in 1857, a job that ultimately led him to Washington as correspondent for Forney's *Philadelphia Press*. James remained in school until June 1863, when he enlisted in the Thirty-Second Pennsylvania Infantry before the battle of Gettysburg. Upon learning this news, brother John caught a train to Harrisburg and obtained James's discharge on the grounds that he was only sixteen years old. Finding "Jimmy himself" encamped in a field with his regiment, the older brother humiliated the boy by taking him home.[18]

As John Russell Young rose to the highest ranks in journalism, he carried his younger brother with him. In 1866, John Young became managing editor of the prestigious *New York Tribune*. He assigned nineteen-year-old James to tour the defeated Southern states as a *Tribune* correspondent, and later installed him as head of the *Tribune*'s Washington bureau. Together the brothers also founded the *Philadelphia Evening Star.* Despite his youth, or because of it, James Rankin Young fit comfortably into the Washington correspondents' Bohemian style of living and working. He settled into Newspaper Row and became a mainstay of the press galleries and hotel lobbies. Having risen to premature eminence through his older brother's connections, James eventually lost his post for the same reasons. In 1869, John Russell Young was caught funneling Associated Press dispatches from the *Tribune* to his family's paper in Philadelphia. Young argued against the Associated Press's tightly restricted membership, asserting that news was a public necessity that should be made available to any responsible paper able to pay for it. But he had violated Associated Press rules when he supplied its stories to a nonparticipating paper. Although the practice was not uncommon, the infraction gave an opening to Young's rivals within the faction-ridden *Tribune* staff. With his authority as editor undermined, Young resigned. His successor, Whitelaw Reid, sent Zebulon White to replace James Rankin Young in Washington. The new Washington correspondent reported that Young "took his discharge very pleasantly," and that his assistant, Hiram Ramsdell, had agreed to stay in his post.[19]

Bounced from the *Tribune*, James Young demonstrated even

James Rankin Young, "S.M." of the *Philadelphia Evening Star*.

more talent for collecting patronage than news. He corresponded for the *Philadelphia Star*, as "S. M." (the initials stood for "Sour Mash"), and for the *New York Standard* and the *Philadelphia Post*, before the Senate elected him chief executive clerk in 1873. Young held that post for six years until the Republicans lost their majority in the Senate. During the Democratic interregnum, he served as a Justice Department clerk. The Republican victory in 1882 brought reelection to his old post as executive clerk.[20]

Even during the closing decades of the century, an active newspaper correspondent on the Senate staff was hardly exceptional. In 1891, the Senate's chief clerk, Charles Wesley Johnson, had been city editor of the *Minneapolis Tribune* and owner of the *Minneapolis Evening Mail*. Senate printing clerk Joel W. Bartlett, a native of Maine, had worked as a printer and reporter under the editorship of James G. Blaine and later served on the editorial staffs of the *Bangor Whig*, *New York Evening Post*, and *Boston Traveler*. Bartlett continued to send occasional correspondence for the *New York Tribune* and other papers, while acting as printing clerk.[21]

The list of committee clerks and members' secretaries during the 1880s and 1890s duplicated many names accredited to the press galleries. The United Press was "pretty well taken care of," with Perry Heath, P. V. DeGraw, and Watson Boyle all serving as House committee clerks. Correspondents O. O. Stealey and Francis Richardson also held House committee posts. Charles B. Reade, clerk to Senator Frye, sent "specials" to the *Concord Monitor* (of New Hampshire), owned by Senator William E. Chandler. R. M. Larner of the *Baltimore Sun* also worked as secretary to Senator Arthur Pue Gorman of Maryland. David S. Barry of the *Detroit Post* and *Tribune* was private secretary to Michigan Senator Conger. J. R. Randall, the correspondent for Georgia's *Augusta Chronicle*, who in his days as a Confederate sympathizer wrote "Maryland, My Maryland," was private secretary to Georgia Senator Joseph Brown. Both correspondents and clerks were still paid only during the months that Congress was in session, so they held their newspaper and congressional positions simultaneously. Since the "money committees" (Appropriations, Finance, and Ways and Means) employed year-round clerks, Major John M. Carson resigned as correspondent of the *New York Times* to take the full-time clerkship of the House Committee on Ways and Means, but he continued to send news reports to the *Philadelphia Ledger.*[22]

The executive clerkship was by far the most sensitive post. The position existed solely in the Senate, because of its exclusive authority to advise and consent on treaties and nominations. In an office off the Senate floor, the executive clerk worked behind an elaborate screen of interwoven bronzed wire that gave the room a bank-like appearance. Instead of bank notes, its three massive safes held treaties and nominations. The air of mystery was dissipated when one realized that the details of most of these secret documents had long since appeared in the newspapers, but James Young and his staff protected their information regardless. One reporter described Young as "continually full of what cannot be otherwise than the most interesting sort of information . . . and although still actively interested in the newspaper business . . . he never allows one of the executive secrets to get away from his official self."[23]

When the senators turned their attention to executive matters, they excluded everyone, including their reporters of debate and legislative clerks, leaving the executive clerk and doorkeepers as the only staff members in the chamber. During these sessions,

Young sat at the front desk, read aloud all papers being considered, took the minutes for the *Executive Journal,* and did "everything in his jovial power to drive dull care away and make the executive sessions informal and sociable in their nature." An entertaining man, storyteller, and popular toastmaster, who regularly sang and danced at Gridiron Club dinners, Young fit perfectly into the club-like atmosphere of the closed executive sessions.[24]

When in March 1892, newspapers published the still-secret Senate debates on a Bering Sea treaty with Great Britain, senatorial suspicion fell upon the two members of the staff who had been present during the debate: the white-bearded doorkeeper Isaac Bassett, a fixture of the Senate since the days of Webster and Clay; and the executive clerk, James Rankin Young, who still wrote regularly for his newspaper. Although Young had held his position of trust for more than a decade, in recent years his paper, the *Philadelphia Star,* had quarreled editorially with Pennsylvania's two senators, Matthew Quay and Don Cameron. The Pennsylvanians may well have taken advantage of the senatorial mood "to make an example of somebody" for the leaks.[25]

As the doors were being locked at the next executive session, Senator John Sherman moved to exclude the executive clerk and doorkeeper. The attack on Young then commenced in his absence. His accusers argued that because of all the precautions taken to prevent leakage of executive session secrets, it was impossible for the newspapers to report senators' remarks so accurately unless a skillful writer put them into shape. A few senators denied this reasoning, but Young's opponents "were wild for blood," in the words of the *New York Times's* correspondent, who accused them of sacrificing "an employee for the offenses that the punishing body itself had committed." James Rankin Young was fired from his position without an opportunity to present a defense and without having the charges against him made public.[26]

Reporters in the press gallery reacted protectively to the assault on Young. Max Seckendorf of the *New York Tribune* wrote that "the general public here knows, as Senators themselves know, that employees of the Senate have been most discreet and guarded in their talk about secret sessions." He pointed out how many senators had allowed themselves to be interviewed and quoted by name in newspaper articles about the supposedly secret treaty. The veteran correspondent Henry Van Ness Boynton, never one to avoid a fight, waded in with an angry public letter to the *Washington Post*. Boynton declared that the Washington correspondents as a body knew that James Young had never leaked an executive session secret, and would so testify under oath. The leaks had come from no other sources "than senators themselves." Boynton recalled how it once took him only thirty minutes to get an accurate account of a treaty voted upon in secret. He spent twenty minutes trying to find a blank tally sheet of the senators' names and ten minutes walking to a certain senator's room to have him mark on the tally how each member had voted. "Every correspondent knows that such news comes primarily from senators, and from no other source," fumed Boynton, wondering how senators could "keep their faces straight" while charging Young with violating their rules.[27]

The correspondents could not absolve James Young without risking future sources. Elbridge Gerry Dunnell, chief of the *New York Times*'s Washington bureau, had nothing but contempt for correspondents who breached a confidence. Dunnell most likely wrote the unsigned commentary that appeared in the *Times*, suggesting that the senators release the 150 accredited correspondents from their own oaths of secrecy: "these Senators know that nothing but their demand . . . will unlock the lips of the correspondents to tell from whom they obtained, here a little and there a little, to be woven into a reasonable whole, the accounts of the discussions . . . on the Bering Sea question." But the *Times* correspondent knew this would never happen. Dunnell speculated that the Senate's attack on Young had actually been intended to throttle the Washington press corps.[28]

Young's friends in the press gallery rallied to his side. At a special meeting of the Gridiron Club, Dunnell offered a resolution declaring the journalists' "total disbelief" of the charges and their "abhorrence of the unmanly and discreditable method in which he was treated in a body from which he was entitled to expect fair play and full justice." Writing from Philadelphia, Young thanked the club for its "generous and manly" action, and reported feeling terribly homesick for Washington and the Senate chamber. When the Senate next convened in secret session, the correspondents proved James Young innocent by redoubling their efforts to reveal its proceedings. They clearly demonstrated that they had not needed the executive clerk to leak secrets. "The proof of his innocence was a more full and accurate report of its proceedings than usual being published the following morning," correspondent O. O. Stealey recalled a decade later, "and the leak has since continued."[29]

James Young's ultimate vindication came in November 1896, when the voters of Philadelphia's fourth district elected him to a seat in the U.S. House of Representatives. To celebrate his triumph, the Gridiron Club threw a dinner in his honor, at which the representative-elect entertained in song as he had for so many years as a correspondent. After three terms in Congress, Young was redistricted out of office, but he never lost his talent for collecting patronage. He gained appointment as superintendent of dead letters in the Post Office Department from 1905 to 1913, and superintendent of postage savings deposits, in Philadelphia, from 1913 to 1915. James Rankin Young died in December 1924, at age seventy-eight, five years before the Senate finally abandoned the practice of secret sessions that cost him the executive clerkship.[30]

A front-page headline in May 1929 shattered the last pretenses of executive session secrecy: "Senate's Secret Vote on Lenroot Revealed; Nine Democrats Bolt—Breaking of Party Ties Gives Former Senator Majority of 42 to 27." Under the byline of the United Press's chief Senate correspondent, Paul R. Mallon, the article ran nationally in UP's client papers. Although the vote had not been released to the press, pulling the story together had posed only a minor challenge for Mallon. The majority of votes had been predictably partisan, and the few "bolters" stood out easily enough for identification by the correspondent's senatorial sources. Yet Mallon's tally was slightly in error; the actual vote had been 42 to 26. Three senators, including one of the alleged "bolters," had not voted at all, while another two that he listed as absent had in fact voted for Lenroot.[31]

The story involved more than simply the appointment of former Senator Irvine Lenroot to the U.S. Court of Customs and Patent Appeals. Once a Wisconsin progressive, by 1926 Lenroot had fallen out of favor with Wisconsin's influential La Follette family and lost his seat in the Senate. He retired from politics and practiced law for three years until Herbert Hoover nominated him for the Court of Customs. Accusing Lenroot of having lobbied for power companies, progressive Republicans fought unsuccessfully against his confirmation. When they lost that battle, they seized upon the Lenroot leak to bring the ancient controversy to resolution. By the 1920s, reformers from both parties were crusading against Senate secrecy. Democratic minority leader Joseph Robinson and Alabama Senator Hugo Black had introduced resolutions to restrict or abolish secret debates. Nebraska's progressive Republican George Norris believed that secrecy enabled the White House to maintain party discipline, while it concealed from constituents the speeches and votes of their own senators. Norris and other reform-minded senators routinely announced in advance how they intended to vote in executive session and asserted their right to keep their constituents informed. When Mallon's story on Lenroot appeared, reformers cited its inaccuracies as proof that only open sessions would ensure accuracy and fairness in the press.[32]

Senator John J. Blaine (who had defeated Lenroot for reelection), attempted to read Mallon's story into the *Record,* only to be called to order by Pennsylvania Senator David Reed, leader of Lenroot's supporters. Quoting Senate rules, Reed warned that any senator who divulged the secret business of the Senate—even on the Senate floor—was liable to expulsion, no matter how many Americans had read the story at their breakfast tables that day. "We all know, to face the facts, that the newspapers flaunt the rule of secrecy and brag about it," said Senator Reed. He contemptuously dismissed the "so-called ethics of this so-called profession," and he found it particularly offensive that Paul Mallon was one of the four wire service reporters who had access to the Senate floor. Mallon had showed his ingratitude for this privilege by signing his name to an article that defied Senate rules. Reed called upon the Senate Rules Committee to investigate the matter further.[33]

The Rules Committee heard from the twenty-eight-year-old Mallon, who predictably refused to reveal his Senate sources (the *Washington Post* estimated their number to be "ten or more"). The conservative committee reacted by unanimously voting to remove United Press's floor privileges. To UP's defense came "Young Bob" La Follette, inheritor of his late father's Senate seat and Progressive mantle. Robert La Follette, Jr., argued in a Senate speech that newspaper reporters had taken no oath to uphold the rules of the Senate, nor were they under any obligation to respect its secrecy. Wire service reporters were not officers of the Senate, despite their privileged position on the floor. At that moment, when another wire service reporter walked onto the floor, La Follette pointed out that no provision existed in the Senate rules allowing floor access for any journalists. The practice was not a rule but a courtesy, he explained, dating back to a Senate resolution adopted in 1873—and even before that to Samuel Smith's petition in 1802. Prompted by La Follette, Vice President Charles Curtis ordered Sergeant at Arms David Barry to exclude all wire service reporters from the floor. They had already slipped away to the press gallery, and in fact the wire services never regained their floor privileges.[34]

Noting that Paul Mallon had not been the only journalist to publish Senate secrets, Senator La Follette cited the widely respected Richard V. Oulahan, chief Washington correspondent for the *New York Times*, as one whose bureau routinely reported on executive sessions. He named also Charles Michelson, correspondent for the *New York World*, and M. Farmer Murphy of the *Baltimore Sun*. But La Follette scored his most effective point when he read an article from the 17 March 1928 edition of the *Pittsburgh Post-Gazette*, in which correspondent Theodore Huntley had quoted Senator David Reed during an executive session debate and provided a tally of the vote. As he read Huntley's article aloud, La Follette stopped repeatedly to ask: "Where did the correspondent get that information?" and "Who gave that out, Mr. President?" Huntley was "an able, intelligent, ethical, conscientious newspaperman" just doing his job, but why had his breach of secrecy not raised Senator Reed's ire, as had Paul Mallon's? La Follette then divulged that correspondent Huntley was at that time on the Senate payroll as Senator Reed's secretary, and suggested that Reed begin his investigation in his own office.[35]

Such sarcasm exposed the vulnerability of every member to charges of violating Senate rules and held up to ridicule the attempts to conduct public business in secret. Senator La Follette echoed the earlier sentiments of Philip Freneau in his defense of the right of the press to publish public information and of the right of the people to hold their representatives responsible for their votes in Congress. "The conflict between secrecy and publicity has gone forward through the ages," La Follette declared, with the last vestiges of legislative secrecy to be found in the rules of the Senate. Now was the time to open the Senate's doors for good.[36]

Although Alabama's irascible Senator Thomas Heflin urged that the entire press gallery be abolished, the tide of public sentiment ran solidly in favor of full disclosure of Senate proceedings. On 18

June 1929, the Senate amended its rules and agreed to transact all future executive business in open session, unless it specifically voted for a closed meeting. On the closing day of the session, senators debated several of President Hoover's nominations in open session. Thereafter, only on rare occasions, involving the most classified information, would the Senate close its gallery doors. More than a century of struggle between the Senate and the correspondents ended with a verdict in favor of the press and the public's right to know. The outcome made it clear that legislative secrecy was a contradiction in terms.[37]

10

David Barry and the Loyalty of the Senate

BY THE TURN of the century, Congress and the correspondents had achieved a state of equilibrium in their relations. Except for occasional lapses, both sides recognized the unwritten rules of behavior that provided mutual benefit. Correspondents cultivated sources that brought them news and increased their value to their papers; politicians dispensed information and patronage in return for publicity to bolster their public images. Their intimate relationship survived sweeping changes in the press, from the rise of yellow journalism to the spread of newspaper chains. But new forms of competition made American journalism so fluid and dynamic that no form of equilibrium could long survive. The Washington correspondents' bonds with the leaders of Congress eventually broke down under the challenge of the new national magazines writers, who captured the public's imagination with their muckraking and rule-breaking style.

"No matter how preposterous a story," wrote an angry David Barry in 1906, "let it be given circulation in one of the popular magazines and the public will rise to it like a black bass to a gaudy fly." Barry raised his complaint in a series of articles headlined "The Loyalty of the Senate," a rebuttal to David Graham Phillips's series, "The Treason of the Senate," then running in monthly installments in William Randolph Hearst's *Cosmopolitan* magazine. Phillips's series caused a national sensation that would help turn public opinion against the conservative leadership of the Senate, strengthen President Theodore Roosevelt's hand in enacting his legislative program, and contribute to the movement for direct election of senators. Phillips's muckraking journalism also shook profoundly the comfortable world and work habits of David Barry and his fellow Washington correspondents.[1]

It was an era of contradictions. As historian George Haynes observed at the time Phillips's series appeared, never before had the Senate been "at once so berated and extolled." The berating came largely from the magazines. During the year prior to the "Treason of the Senate," the *Independent* had published "Unworthy Senators," the *Nation* had posted "The Senate's Role of Dishonor," and the *Arena* had asked: "Is the United States Senate the Corrupt Tool of the Standard Oil Company?" Surveying this scene, newspaper correspondent Barry charged: "It is the recklessness and ignorance of the magazine critics as a class that is responsible for the poisoning of the public mind."[2]

The hostile tones of the popular magazines and yellow press contrasted sharply with the deferential treatment that the Senate received in the daily correspondents' dispatches. The magazines portrayed the Senate as the stronghold of corporate interests, while many newspapers defended the Senate as a safeguard against radical change. When newspaper reporters criticized the Senate and its individual members, they wrote from predictably partisan perspectives, acclaiming their party's leaders, attacking the opposition, and accepting the basic structure of party organization and control within the legislative branch. Newspaper readers knew exactly where their papers stood. The magazines, by contrast, broke from the newspapers' partisan and parochial limitations and confronted national audiences with new questions and startlingly new answers. David Barry's lament reflected the intense competition between newspapers and magazines for advertisers, circulation, and general attention—a competition that undermined the rules by which Barry and other Washington correspondents had long operated.[3]

The evolution of working conditions in Washington over the forty years since the Civil War had created a set of restraints for the newspaper correspondents that separated them from the new class of magazine writers. When the "Treason" series first appeared, newspaper correspondents enjoyed close working relations with the leaders of Congress, after years of estrangement. Old General Henry Boynton reminisced about how the union of the press and public men during the Civil War had broken during the Credit Mobilier investigation and other press exposés, and how each side assumed "a warlike attitude" toward the other. The beleaguered correspondents had established the Standing Committee of Correspondents to clean the lobbyists out of their press galleries, and had created the Gridiron Club to bring politicians and the press together under more relaxed circumstances. By the 1890s, their efforts had restored cordial relations, but the relaxed atmosphere masked some of the subtle forms of press control that accompanied it. A system of interlocking loyalties and unofficial codes of behavior evolved that for all intents and purposes made Capitol Hill newspaper correspondents a part of the legislative establishment. The continued financial lure of patronage, the necessity of acquiring and maintaining sources, and even the ownership of newspapers by members of Congress compromised the independence of the newspaper correspondents and shaped the news they reported.[4]

David Barry, defender of the "Loyalty of the Senate," had profited handsomely from this system. Born in Detroit, Barry was really a child of the Senate, having gone there in 1875 as a sixteen-year-old page. As a page he studied stenography in the offices of the Senate's official reporters of debate, and he later served as secretary to a number of Republican senators and representatives, most prominently to Senator Nelson W. Aldrich of Rhode Island. At the same time, Barry worked as Washington correspondent for newspapers in Detroit, Chicago, St. Louis, Cleveland, and Cincinnati. In 1889 he joined the Washington staff of the *New York Sun*, which he built into one of the most influential bureaus in Washington. In 1904, Barry became editor of the *Providence Journal* but returned to Capitol Hill two years later as that paper's chief Washington correspondent.[5]

As a member of the Senate and House press galleries, Barry belonged to the tightly knit, homogeneous fraternity of correspondents. Washington correspondence attracted the best and the most ambitious journalists in the nation. In 1902 the *Washington Star's* editor and former correspondent, Crosby Noyes, gloried that "the Capitol press gallery has been a training school for the production of able editors, statesmen, financiers, railroad magnates, generals, governors, poets, novelists, magazinists, and men of mark in all lines." Although most reporters still wrote for openly partisan papers, and reflected their editorial views, good reporters made contact with leaders of both parties. Similarly, Republican and Democratic correspondents developed strong friendships while sending out vastly different versions of the same story.[6]

Decades after the demise of official organs and the party press, partisanship remained a fact of life among Washington reporters. David Barry was a Republican, heart and soul. He reported for Republican papers, staffed for Republican congressmen, and directed publicity for the Republican National Committee. Barry also owed his job with the *Providence Journal*, the leading paper in Rhode Island, to its clandestine owner. The letter appointing him editor was marked "approved" by Nelson W. Aldrich.[7]

Senator Aldrich's ownership of the *Providence Journal*—for "campaign purposes," as his authorized biographer explained—gave him considerable advantage in controlling the political situation back home, as well as leverage over that paper's political reporters. Before Aldrich bought the *Journal* it had long been published by his state's senior senator, Henry Anthony, who had come to politics from journalism. But Senator Anthony made no secret of his control of the paper. He stood among editors from Horace Greeley to William Randolph Hearst who served in Congress while exercising editorial control over their papers. By 1906, however, a far larger number of senators and representatives had gone into the newspaper business than the twenty-one who so identified themselves in the *Congressional Directory*.[8] Aldrich, for instance, also controlled the *Pawtucket Times* and was rumored to have a large interest in the *New York Sun*. As a conduit for Republican campaign contributions, Aldrich also provided funds for senatorial aspirants to buy interests in newspapers. Other surreptitious owners included Senator Isaac Stephenson, who bought the *Milwaukee Free Press*, "copper king" William Clark, who collected a string of newspapers across Montana, and Clark's colleague, Thomas Carter, who owned newspapers in all but three of Montana's counties.[9]

Newspaper ownership understandably depended upon a senator's personal wealth. Democratic Senator Joseph Bailey of Texas invested large portions of his more modest savings in the three Texas newspapers that supported him most consistently, and he owned ten percent of the stock of his strongest advocate, the *Fort Worth Record*. By contrast, Indiana Republican Senator Charles Fairbanks used his considerable fortune to purchase secretly a three-quarters interest in the *Indianapolis News* and four-fifths of the capital stock of the *Indianapolis Journal*. Fairbanks's ownership of these papers became public knowledge only after the reading of his will.[10]

Washington correspondents for papers owned by senators could hardly write critical or embarrassing stories about their employers. These correspondents gained entrance to political meetings where independent journalists would be unwelcome, but at the price of suppressing whatever they heard. David Barry attended a meeting of senators who chose a western colleague with ties to the copper industry as a new member of the Senate Finance Committee. Could they be sure of his vote? someone asked. "We do not have to ask him," Finance Committee Chairman Nelson Aldrich responded. "We know what the Amalgamated Copper Co. wants, and that is sufficient." Barry waited twenty years before publishing that insight.[11]

The benefactor system spread further to include patronage dispersed by congressmen who had no direct interest in newspaper management. Washington correspondents, although better paid than other American reporters, complained that their expenses were higher. Publishers were parsimonious in funding Washington bureaus, particularly for paying telegraph and telephone tolls. The *Louisville Courier-Journal* allowed O. O. Stealey 1,200 telephone calls a year and charged him for any additional calls. Stealey estimated that extra calls cost him $150 a year, or three weeks' salary.[12] Some newspapers still refused to pay correspondents when Congress was out of session, or called them back to the paper to "read copy" at the telegraph desk, to cover political campaigns, and to write general news stories. As they had since the Civil War, correspondents turned to Congress for supplemental incomes. Reporters talked about those of their colleagues who were willing "to ignore the peccadillos of certain senators and tickle the fancy of others" to get on the payroll as a personal secretary or committee clerk. One reporter was listed as the assistant horseshoer for congressional messengers' horses. Other correspondents appeared at the Senate Folding Room with orders, signed by senators, to fold 100,000 documents for $100 in payment. "Of course," wrote correspondent T. T. Williams, "they never folded any documents, but that did not make any difference, except to make their allegiance to the giver of good things absolutely secure."[13]

The correspondents of the *Boston Journal* had long followed Ben: Perley Poore's example in collecting patronage. Poore's assistant and successor, E. B. Wight, had been disdainful of the limits Poore's patronage placed on his freedom to report, but Wight himself served as clerk of a committee chaired by a Massachusetts senator. Wight's successor on the *Journal,* Louis A. Coolidge, clerked for a House committee and served as personal secretary to Henry Cabot Lodge. As Congress moved into the twentieth century, it carried over the past century's patronage system. When August Bacon, a Georgia Democrat, chaired the Senate Select Committee on Women's Suffrage (a sinecure committee created with less intention to give votes to women than to give a committee room and clerk to its chairman), he hired as his clerk the Washington correspondent for the *Atlanta Journal.* Republican Charles Fulton of Oregon, chairman of the Committee on Claims, made the correspondent of the *Portland Oregonian* the assistant clerk of his committee. All of these journalist/clerks continued to file their dispatches and to report on the public figures who hired them.[14]

Close association with a particularly powerful senator enhanced a correspondent's reputation and increased his value to his papers. Robert Larner covered Congress from the *Baltimore Sun* and other newspapers in New York and Georgia. He owed his success largely to his role as private secretary and confidant to Senate Democratic leader Arthur Pue Gorman of Maryland. Gorman's sudden death in 1906 affected the reporter grievously, and two months later Larner died at age fifty, of a "nervous and physical breakdown."[15]

Publisher Henry Watterson, himself a former Washington correspondent, doubted that any congressman could be a statesman in the eyes of a reporter. "And yet," Watterson wrote, "what loyal friendships spring into existence between them, what perfect confidence, what sympathy and appreciation!" New reporters came to Washington suspicious of politicians and desiring to root out corruption in national politics. But the daily pressure of their jobs, their need to get the story and make the deadline, and their growing appreciation of how the mechanisms of Congress actually worked, caused the correspondents to "believe in the high-minded views and upright aims of public men who [they] first thought were arrant knaves," observed *New York Tribune* correspondent Theron Crawford. Louis Ludlow, a Washington correspondent before becoming a member of Congress, noted: "In my younger days I vowed that I would never trust a politician any further than I could throw an elephant by the tail, but I have revised my opinion." Whether out of admiration or cynicism, the longer a correspondent remained in Washington the less likely he was to become outraged over what Watterson called the "shams and pretenses of parties, the sordid aims, or the base ambitions of leaders, the littleness of the great."[16]

A Washington correspondent's success depended upon his cultivation of powerful sources. But the cultivation of those sources often meant surrendering to the "Washington point of view." In his critique of Progressive era newspaper journalism, Will Irvin wrote: "So Washington correspondence, viewed in bulk, tends toward the side of the powerful." An insurgent congressman once complained to Irvin that within six months after their arrival in Washington the most fire-breathing correspondents could be found "eating out of every official hand between the White House and the Capitol." Even William Randolph Hearst reportedly had difficulty keeping his Washington correspondents militant enough to suit his papers.[17]

The higher placed the source, the more valuable the news. Committee chairmen and party leaders made the best sources for inside stories, to confirm a rumor or leak important information. A correspondent once stopped Senator Nelson Aldrich to ask why he was going abroad just when the Senate seemed ready to take up an important railroad bill. "Oh, I will be back in plenty of time for that," Aldrich replied, "the question goes over until next winter." The reporter raced for the telegraph, assured that this tip came from the Senate's most powerful leader. "It was information such as this, and easily obtained, if you are in the confidence of knowing ones, that makes the life of the newspaper correspondent in Washington these days a comparatively easy one," wrote Stealey.[18]

In practice, Nelson Aldrich was a "sphinx" when it came to giving attributed news. The senator maintained a strict rule against being quoted. David Barry's successor as chief Washington correspondent of the *New York Sun*, Richard Oulahan, recalled how a new staff reporter, unaware of this rule, had interviewed Aldrich and then quoted him in a dispatch. When Oulahan visited the senator to placate him, Aldrich indignantly explained that "he would not be able to speak freely if he was to be quoted directly." Senator Aldrich cared little for national publicity and operated most comfortably in closed committee meetings, away from public view. Many of the correspondents viewed the senator as "cold-blooded and unapproachable," capable of giving out misinformation. But the half-dozen reporters who dared approach Aldrich found him a wellspring of information on the Senate's business. Correspondent Louis Coolidge labeled Aldrich among the Senate's best "news-gatherers" because he seemed so much better informed than other senators about when things were likely to happen. Junior senators, always ready to be interviewed, never seemed to know what was going on until the matter had "passed the point of being news." Reporters sensed that most House members were so far removed from the House leadership that they learned what was happening only by reading the newspapers.[19]

Secret sessions continued throughout the first decades of the twentieth century, as did their regular leaks, even without James Rankin Young sitting as executive clerk. "I will bet a million dollars," Louis Ludlow boasted, "that within three hours after the adjournment of any executive session, I can give a full and accurate account of everything that has taken place behind closed doors. I would simply go to some Senator of my acquaintance and he would tell me." Cultivation of such sources required trust and confidentiality. "All confidences of public men were regarded as inviolate," asserted *Baltimore Sun* correspondent Francis Richardson in 1903. Elbridge Gerry Dunnell, for twenty years Washington correspondent for the *New York Times* and head of the Standing Committee of Correspondents, was famous for his close friendships with political leaders. "Public men could confide all sorts of secrets to Dunnell without the slightest danger of ever seeing them in print, if they were given under the seal of confidence," commented his assistant, Charles Thompson. Any reporter who broke his word and published remarks made in confidence would find himself shut out of Washington news sources and ruined in his profession. Correspondents like Dunnell regarded those who broke the rule with a "bitter, burning hatred."[20]

Pacts of confidentiality turned a correspondent into a "graveyard of secrets." Some politicians confessed the truth to the reporters in confidence before they could uncover the facts for themselves. Louis Ludlow wondered whether he had collected so many unpublishable stories because of his dependability or his gullibility. Correspondents went out of their way to avoid certain politicians who furnished them material only in confidence. On occasion, when they feared being scooped by a rival paper, correspondents might send confidential items back to their newspapers with instructions to publish it as a local story, without a Washington dateline, hoping in that way to cover their breach of ethics.[21]

Correspondents who abided by these unwritten rules and standards prospered. Those who disregarded a confidence, delved too deeply into a public man's life, or in some way upset the established relations between the press and the politicians, found doors shut, sources cut off, patronage unavailable, and advancement in their profession stalled.

Yet these strictures did not apply to the new breed of magazine journalists. Magazine writers developed national reputations because their names appeared on their articles. In 1885, Theron Crawford became the first Washington correspondent to sign his own name rather than a nom de plume on his dispatches, but the practice remained uncommon among newspaper reporters in 1900. Meanwhile magazine writers traveled widely, wrote on a variety of subjects, faced lengthier deadlines, and had less of a need to cultivate a regular set of influential sources. As magazine writer Lincoln Steffens moved from city to city, his most useful and reliable suppliers of information were local newspaper reporters. They could not print what they knew, for fear of triggering libel suits, alienating their sources, or losing their jobs. The same situation existed at the capital, on a national scale.[22]

Magazine writer David Graham Phillips had no need to know when Senator Aldrich might be absent from Washington or how that would affect the progress of a bill, nor did he need to cultivate regular sources willing to leak executive session secrets. Phillips could probe to an unprecedented degree into the private lives of senators, tying their wealth, mansions, and opulent life styles to their allegiance to corporate powers. When given the assignment to write an exposé of the Senate, Phillips spent little time in Washington. His only contact within the Senate was his old college roommate, Albert Beveridge, who willingly offered critical opinions of his political opponents. For the most part, Phillips based his articles on charges that were already part of the public record or common gossip in Washington. The first installment of his "Treason of the Senate" series was so strident in tone and short on facts that *Cosmopolitan* delayed its publication for a month and assigned two other reporters to unearth more evidence. When it appeared, the series made its national impact less from the newness of its revelations than from its passionate prose, its systematic and relentless exposition of its theme of corporate control and corruption of the Senate, and its lavish photographic documentation of senatorial affluence.[23]

The cover of the March issue of *Cosmopolitan* presented a sinister likeness of Senator Chauncey Depew. Unlike Nelson Aldrich, William Allison, John Spooner, Eugene Hale, and other senators whom Washington correspondents recognized as real powers, Depew was an elderly, long-winded, and peripheral solon. His ties with the railroad industry had never been secret. But Depew served as Republican senator from New York, where *Cosmopolitan's* publisher William Randolph Hearst was a Democratic congressman with higher political ambitions. Depew had also been a frequent target of Joseph Pulitzer's *New York World*, back in the days when Phillips served as a *World* editorial writers. Phillips's attack on Depew raised the ire of the Washington correspondents, who regarded the senator with affection. Just a few months earlier, the *Journalist*, a trade paper, had lionized Depew for his "warm and loyal friendships to newspaper men." The senator always received reporters cordially and made sure they got a good story—if not always the one their editors had sent them after. "He would be a scurvy newspaper man, indeed," the *Journalist* decreed, "who would not look upon the brightest and most favorable side of any story affecting 'Our Chauncey.'"[24]

The attack on "poor old Chauncey Depew" infuriated Theodore Roosevelt. The president stood to gain by the public furor that the magazines were raising in support of his program, and he had actively encouraged exactly such press support. But Roosevelt also held a strong party allegiance and feared the political repercussions of such virulent attacks on Republican members of Congress. When the "Treason" series appeared, Roosevelt was locked in a struggle over passage of the Hepburn bill to regulate railroad rates, in which he found himself in temporary alliance with Senate Democrats against his own party's leadership. Yet while Roosevelt could count on Democrats to support much of his domestic program, he knew they opposed his major foreign policy objectives. In the long run, he still needed the support of Aldrich and other senatorial targets of Phillips's series. Roosevelt also interpreted the "Treason" series as part of a campaign to promote publisher Hearst for president. As far as the Republican Roosevelt was concerned, more harm came from the "narrow, rancorous, partisan (i.e., Democrat),

MARCH

COSMOPOLITAN

TEN CEN

The Treason of the Senate

by

David Graham Phillips

Senator Chauncey Depew appeared on the cover of the first installment of "The Treason of the Senate."

from the uncouth, unlicked demagogue, and from the more puzzle-minded obstructionist than from the man who is improperly sensitive to the influence of great corporations." The conservatism of the Senate often hindered his reform programs, but it had "very distinct uses in as purely democratic a country as ours," he believed, as a check on the power of the mob.[25]

Roosevelt feared that "lurid sensationalists" like Phillips would foment a revolutionary spirit by their implications that the political system had so degenerated as to make reform useless. On the day after the second installment of the series reached the newsstands, Roosevelt warned William Howard Taft that they must do something to combat "the great amount of evil which, mixed with a little good, a little truth, is contained in the outpouring of the *Cosmopolitan*," before it too deeply shaped public opinion.[26]

While only one member rose in the Senate chamber to reply to Phillips's charges, the president of the United States delivered the chief rebuttal—and gave it twice. The first occasion for his "Man with the Muck-Rake" speech came on 17 March 1906, appropriately to a private gathering of the Gridiron Club. The previous January the club had inducted new members by making them solemnly promise "to denounce the Senate as a traitorous cabal of corporate hirelings," as a cuckoo clock signaled behind them—a sign of the lightness with which correspondents took the magazine charges. Technically, the March meeting was not an official Gridiron function, but a dinner that House Speaker Joseph Cannon gave for Gridiron members, along with cabinet secretaries, some twenty senators and sixty representatives. In accordance with Gridiron rules, correspondents could not publish Roosevelt's speech, but those who heard it later described it as one of the most vigorous of his presidency. David Barry recalled the private performance of the muckraker speech as delivered with tremendous vehemence and theatrical effect. The remarks met with overwhelming approval from the audience, and many of the newspaper correspondents present urged the president to go public with his attack on their magazine rivals.[27]

A month later, when Roosevelt laid the cornerstone for the new House Office Building, it was an open secret that he would repeat his attack on the muckrakers. Newspaper correspondents joined the crowd in anticipation of at last being able to report on the speech they heard at the Gridiron dinner. But Roosevelt played a "delicious practical joke" on them, as one magazine writer put it. Not only did he mute his attack and theatrical effects, but he balanced his denunciation of the muckrakers with a call for a progressive inheritance tax. Newspapers that hailed the anti-muckraker aspects of the speech spent their furor denouncing its "radical" confiscatory tax proposals. Roosevelt's image as a reformer survived intact. "The speech was almost the opposite of the one he delivered at the Gridiron Club and which was received with such enthusiasm by certain men," Senator Beveridge comforted David Graham Phillips. "His speech the other day bitterly disappointed a great many people here."[28]

Roosevelt's speech did not deter Phillips, whose articles continued in *Cosmopolitan* for another seven months, savaging the Senate's leadership in both parties. Although Phillips worried that the series had failed, it clearly made its impact felt. For *Cosmopolitan* the series resulted in a dramatic surge in circulation. For the magazine's publisher, Hearst, its publicity contributed to his momentum in capturing the Democratic nomination for governor of New York that year, although he failed to win the election. For Theodore Roosevelt, his attack on Phillips and the muckrakers helped him demonstrate his party loyalty and resolved some of his differences with the Senate's Republican leadership, enabling them to reach a compromise on the Hepburn bill that avoided splitting the Republican ranks. This political tour de force won Roosevelt the applause of the Washington correspondents and at the same time preserved his mantle as a progressive leader.[29]

For the Senate's leadership, publication of "The Treason of the Senate" was a dispiriting experience. Senator Spooner complained to a sympathetic newspaper editor that "the eagerness with which so many people seem to believe ill of public men, the general suspicion of everybody's character and motives, comes pretty near taking away all inspiration for public service." The following year, Spooner resigned from the Senate. Senator Aldrich, in the estimation of *New York Times* Washington bureau chief Charles Thompson, had won the kind of notoriety "that a man pays dearly for." He had become "fixed indelibly in the minds of his countrymen as the representative of certain interests that the majority would like to see curbed." Thompson doubted whether Aldrich regarded the "unrivaled admiration for his genius as a politician . . . as balancing the account." Senator Aldrich, who claimed never to have read any of the muckraking attacks upon him, also declined to run for reelection. Chauncey Depew was defeated in 1910. Arthur Pue Gorman died shortly after Phillips's attack on him appeared. The "Treason" series also gave new impetus to the movement for a constitutional amendment to allow direct, popular election of senators. The Senate reluctantly accepted the amendment in 1912, and the states ratified it speedily.[30]

For the Washington correspondents, Phillips's articles stimulated renewed pressure from editors and publishers to meet the competition of the muckraking magazines. Newspapers escalated their rhetoric, even as some magazines were cooling theirs. Public suspicion of Congress became so aroused that the correspondents could no longer extol the political skills and organizational ability of the congressional leadership without revealing how that same machinery served to block progressive legislation. This shift in newspapers' emphasis worked to the advantage of congressional insurgents, who fostered reforms within Congress, but the negative press treatment of national politics also alienated many citizens, who viewed politics as inherently corrupt and turned out to vote in steadily decreasing numbers.[31]

The cynicism of the muckraking magazines put the Washington press corps on the defensive, forcing its members to prove the independence of its judgments. In October 1906, when Lincoln Steffens, Mark Twain, and other prominent citizens announced plans to form a "People's Lobby," to watch over Congress, Charles Thompson, responded indignantly that the press gallery already constituted a people's lobby of one hundred and fifty "professional observers," who were "weighing, doubting, scrutinizing, suspecting" every congressional action. By implication, the press would appear gullible if it gave the appearance of trusting members of Congress.[32]

Although the need to cultivate high-ranking sources remained constant for the correspondents, other working conditions were changing. The steady spread of newspaper chains bolstered the business aspects rather than the political orientation of newspapers and reduced politicians' opportunities for direct control of the press. Salaries of Washington correspondents improved, diminishing the need to pad incomes with patronage. Reporters still crossed the line to take official positions on Capitol Hill, including appointments as congressional press secretaries, but generally only

David S. Barry at the time of his dismissal as Senate Sergeant at Arms.

after they had severed their ties with their papers. Patronage no longer bought the loyalty of the correspondents.[33]

As for David Barry, long and faithful service to his party earned its reward in 1919. When the Republicans regained the majority in the Senate, they elected him Sergeant at Arms. Barry held the post for the next fourteen years, until he belatedly discovered the hazards of political patronage. In February 1933, a month before the Democrats were due to take back control of the Senate and Barry was to retire from his post, an article of his appeared in *New Outlook* magazine. Barry wrote the piece as his parting shot at the reformers and insurgents whom he blamed for changing the Senate since direct elections had begun. Unfortunately for him, an over-zealous editor dropped his lead paragraph, shifted the article's focus, and published it a month ahead of schedule. The opening sentences now read: "Contrary perhaps to the popular belief, there are not many crooks in Congress. There are not many Senators and Representatives who sell their votes for money, and it is pretty well known who those few are."[34]

Outraged senators hauled their Sergeant at Arms into the Senate chamber and denounced him for this slander. Barry attempted to defend himself during later hearings before the Senate Judiciary Committee. "I have at many times in my career as a newspaper correspondent written publicly and professed my sincere belief that Congress, as a body, is composed of honest men," he professed. "Many years ago I published in *New England* magazine an article entitled "The Loyalty of the Senate" in an attempt to reply to a series of articles written by the late David Graham Phillips . . . I was at that time, as I was in the *New Outlook* article, endeavoring to represent it as the true situation that the isolated case of misconduct of individuals in office offered no basis for the loose public condemnation of the Senate we so often hear." But as an elected officer of the Senate, Barry had confused his roles and written with an autonomy his position did not offer, no matter how vague his criticisms. Barry's fall from grace, when the Senate removed him from office, revealed the perils of the patronage system, which his generation of Washington correspondents for so long had risked.[35]

11

Richard V. Oulahan, Bureau Chief

THE PASSING OF Richard Victor Oulahan on 30 December 1931 summoned public eulogies unmatched for any Washington journalist since Ben: Perley Poore a half century earlier. The *New York Times*, whose Washington bureau Oulahan headed at the time of his death, made the story front-page news and reprinted an outpouring of newspaper editorials and political testimonials in his honor. The president of the United States, cabinet secretaries, and members of Congress attended the funeral services, where they were serenaded by the Gridiron quartet. The proceedings had all the trappings of a state funeral. It was a fitting ceremony to mark the end of an era in the relationship between the press and the politicians.

Richard Oulahan represented the last of the breed of correspondents who had entered journalism during its Bohemian heyday. A protégé of David Barry, under whom he had served in the Washington bureau of the *New York Sun*, Oulahan exhibited a Bohemian bonhomie, dressed in dapper style—down to the walking stick he sometimes carried—and defended "interpretive" news writing. Yet the modern "objective" writers also claimed him as one of their own. "There was not about him the glamour of the older reporters, those adventurous crusaders, those brilliant Bohemians, those bold, reckless, charming, romantic reporters and reformers who were so very interesting and so very unreliable," wrote Walter Lippmann. Oulahan's prosaic style attracted a readership that wanted "first of all to have a record, before it desires to be entertained, excited or advised."[1]

For practical-minded journalists in Washington after World War I, "Newspaper Row" conjured up a vaguely romantic past long ex-

tinct, but for Richard Oulahan the old days seemed vastly freer
and more satisfying. He remembered the "superior beings" on
whose words he had hung when he visited the Row in the 1880s.
"What fascinated me most was the familiar way in which they referred to great men," Oulahan later recalled. "They were an uncon-
ventional and irreverent lot, full of what we have come to call pep,
but then generally honest and sincere, hating cant and hypocrisy."[2]

The green reporter of the 1880s matured into the urbane, sophisticated dean of Washington correspondents. Oulahan's English
style of dress and southern manners, his polished master-of-
ceremonies charm, and his genuine care for young reporters just
starting out made him the beau ideal of the Washington press
corps. Yet both the man and his style were self-made. Unlike most
Washington correspondents, Richard Oulahan had been born in
Washington, in 1867, and resided there almost his entire life. A
high proportion of Washington journalists were college graduates,
whereas Oulahan's formal education never went beyond the city's
public schools. Born an Irish Catholic, he entered a profession
dominated by Anglo-Saxon Protestants. But as Oulahan worked his
way up from a five-dollar-a-week cub reporter to one of the
highest-paid journalists in the business, his personal experiences
gave him a heightened sense of professional dignity. Once, when
the chairman of the Republican National Committee called Washington reporters together to promise that he would always be
ready to help the "newspaper boys," Oulahan responded frigidly:
"Would it be too much to ask what you expect to do for the newspaper men?"[3]

Oulahan's memories of Newspaper Row dated back to his teen-
age years. While he was attending high school, he wrote a school
essay about his ambition to become an editor. His father, a Civil
War army captain and Pension Bureau clerk, tried to encourage
these leanings by arranging an interview with a Washington correspondent, but the cynical correspondent warned Oulahan that
editors had no souls. He also dismissed the job of a Washington
correspondent as consisting "largely in abstracting official reports
and addresses and whipping them into shape for publication." Un-
deterred, young Oulahan apprenticed himself to another Washington correspondent for a dollar a week in carfare. His mentor reported for a string of southern and western papers, which
individually offered little remuneration, but when combined pro-

vided a comfortable income. Oulahan collected routine, regional news, like the appointment of a postmaster or the approval of a patent, then condensed it and telegraphed it to the appropriate home-state paper. It was not high-class journalism, but seeing his small items in print thrilled him.

On Capitol Hill, the correspondent sent his apprentice on the rounds of committee rooms to hunt for items of regional news for his local papers, an experience that Oulahan later described as his higher education in the workings of the government. From the press galleries, Oulahan focused his attention on the peculiarities of the individuals below, most memorably the bullet path visible across the bald head of an ex-Confederate brigadier general. He came to know the members of Congress so well that he could stand with the photographers and identify for them every senator and representative entering the Capitol. Oulahan's years of apprenticeship brought home to him the value of personal acquaintances for a career in Washington journalism.

When Congress adjourned, Oulahan's mentor secured him a reporting job at the *Washington Critic,* a small, afternoon paper, where he could learn the newspaper business while smelling the printer's ink. "Writing about Governmental affairs was journalism of an abstract, passive character," he decided; "there was no human action in it." General news reporting better tested his ingenuity and sharpened his style. Most of all he learned to work under deadline. The *Critic* operated under the adage: "Man dies, time flies, and the afternoon newspapers go to press at three o'clock." Since all "the best people" read the *Washington Evening Star,* the *Critic* competed for subscriptions and advertising with its lively style and features, and pressed upon its small staff a multitude of tasks. Oulahan rose speedily from covering neighborhood news to reporting on the "uptown beat," which included the White House and the State, War, Navy, Treasury, and Justice departments. It required tedious legwork to cover this territory, but the assignment offered a lucrative dividend: he multiplied his income by reporting on the same agencies for the press associations.

A cub reporter could cover the White House and executive agencies in the 1880s because they produced so much less regular news than did the Congress. No newspaper at that time stationed a reporter on an exclusive assignment at the White House. Reporters dropped by irregularly, in search of some specific piece of

Two original cartoons (*above and facing*) of the press gallery from the scrapbook of James D. Preston, first superintendent of the Senate Press Gallery.

information. By contrast, senior correspondents dwelt daily in the congressional press galleries. Behind the galleries' swinging doors were spacious lobbies, handsomely furnished and well supplied to meet any journalistic need. On the walls of the press lobby in the House hung paintings and sketches of prominent editors, while the Senate lobby boasted Brussels carpets, maroon leather couches, and easy chairs, gilt-framed mirrors, chilled water coolers, and "any reasonable quantity of very red liquor." In the center of each stood large, oval tables covered with green baize and stocked with writing pads, pencils, pen racks, and ink stands, compliments of Congress. Telegraph operators were on duty just steps away.[4]

Correspondents preferred the House press gallery because of the greater commotion on the House floor. During dull stretches they played cards or wrote dispatches, waiting for the doorkeepers to alert them whenever a worthwhile debate or angry exchange erupted in the chamber. Capitol tour guides advised visitors that the only way to tell whether something important was taking place on the floor was to check whether the correspondents were in their seats in the press gallery. Empty seats meant "you can be sure that nothing is going to happen." Over at the Senate, with its more sedate debates and formal speeches, correspondents used the lobby for afternoon naps.[5]

The Press in action

by Young

Jan / 2 — 1915

The old Bohemians despised didactic writing and rarely played teacher. No one went out of his way to give the young Dick Oulahan lessons in journalism, but the older correspondents never hesitated to share their knowledge whenever he asked for help. He repaid the older men and won entry for himself into their fraternity by sharing bits of news he picked up in the committee rooms. It was the era of the "blacksheet," when reporters traded carbon copies of their stories and covered for absent, inebriated, or otherwise indisposed colleagues. Favorite stories recounted times when an editor received two or three dispatches on the same story from one correspondent, each submitted by a different friend. A half century later, Oulahan still tolerated blacksheeting in the *Times's* Washington bureau.[6]

When Oulahan started reporting, the "Bohemian" label still fit the correspondents' image. Many reported for morning papers, and their late-night deadlines drew them into the hard-drinking, poker-playing night life of the capital. At night, Oulahan would walk down Fourteenth Street and peer into the lit windows at newswriters grinding out their evening dispatches. Even if they filed their copy early, they stayed near their offices in case something turned up, or their "active-minded editors" sent another of their "queries." Leaving word with their office boys where they could be found, the correspondents joined the politicians, lobbyists, and office seekers at restaurants known for the best food and gossip. They dined on steamed oysters at Harvey's restaurant and stood at the bar at Shoemaker's to gather the latest political intelligence.

The Row had its fringe of talented but intemperate "hangers-on," whose unreliability caused them to drift in and out of jobs. These men usually worked as assistants to the regular correspondents, until dismissed for some new dereliction of duty. Stories of some besotted reporter's literary brilliance and fall from grace often floated through the Row, but Oulahan (who himself drank little) considered them exaggerations. "Hard work and steady habits," he insisted, "were the chief attributes of genius even in those convivial days." In fact, Newspaper Row had been a "sand-papered" and well-varnished Bohemia. Its inhabitants made their rounds in top hats and frock coats, rather than in shabby genteel dress. For years, the reporters traditionally dressed in formal attire to sit in the press galleries on the opening day of a session. The dilapidated exteriors and "picturesque confusion" of their offices on the Row masked the middle-class values and habits of the correspondents. "As a rule," Oulahan remembered, "the chief correspondents were men of steady habits, not inclined to Bohemian diversion."[7]

By the turn of the century, the old Bohemians had retired from journalism, although for a transient, hotel-living generation—who had long complained about the city's weather and high cost of living—a remarkable number of them remained in Washington. The venerable General Henry Van Ness Boynton served on the District of Columbia School Board; Uriah Painter managed his opera house on Lafayette Square; Major John Carson held appointment in the administration of Theodore Roosevelt. Worn out, as correspondent Robert Simpson wrote, by "the work of diffusing myself over the whole field of Washington for a seven day paper," others relocated to a more comfortable editorial desk or government clerkship. When O. O. Stealey retired in 1911, he estimated that the ten or fifteen members of the Gridiron Club who held "rich Federal jobs" were all Republicans. Ironically, the Democrats were on the verge of resurgence just as it was too late for him to collect their patronage. "Boys, I am going just as my party is coming," he lamented at his Gridiron farewell.[8]

Younger journalists, with their modern notions of professional respectability, rejected the "Bohemian" label as dredging up images of unshaven reporters smelling of beer. "I do not believe in the Bohemian," sniffed one correspondent, "I cannot see that dandruff on the collar is an evidence of brains." The new men abandoned Newspaper Row and moved into more fashionable business districts and operated out of bureaus that to the old-timers looked more like lawyers' offices. In 1905, the *Washington Post* memorialized the Row, "now so broken and scattered into new buildings of several neighborhoods." When used in conversation, "Newspaper Row" came to refer to the press corps in general, rather than their specific location. When the National Press Club constructed their new headquarters in 1926, however, they did so on the site of the old Ebbitt Hotel, bringing the Washington correspondents back to their traditional haunts on Fourteenth Street. The new breed of correspondents who occupied the building tended to represent mass circulation newspapers, editorially allied to the urban reform movement. They prided themselves on their objective reporting and their avoidance of overt partisanship in their dispatches.[9]

Initiated at the *Critic*, Oulahan moved up the rungs by becoming news editor of Virginia's *Roanoke Daily Tribune* in 1887. After two years in the countryside, he returned to Washington as a United Press reporter. In 1897, Oulahan joined the Washington bureau of the *New York Sun*, headed by David Barry. He found his new chief wise, witty, and resourceful, and served as Barry's right-hand man for eight years. Barry's departure to become editor of the *Providence Journal* opened the way for Oulahan's promotion to bureau chief for the "very Republican" *Sun*. Two years as the *Sun's* London correspondent gave Oulahan a Continental polish and an English wardrobe. Although well-received as a foreign correspondent, Oulahan missed Washington reporting. He returned to the capital in 1912 (after delaying his scheduled sailing on the *Titanic* because of the illness of a newspaper friend in London) to become bureau chief for the *New York Times*. He gloried in the role of chief for twenty years until his death.[10]

Square-jawed Richard Oulahan, president of the Gridiron Club and chairman of the Standing Committee of Correspondents, became "the undisputed premier of the corps of Washington correspondents." Others admired him as a reporter who always knew "the power of strong 'copy.'" His keen memory and lively sense of humor made him a storehouse of information and delightful storyteller. He excelled in writing and performing in the satirical political skits that became standard fare at Gridiron dinners. Reporters said he could turn out a readable story even on a dull session of Congress. He produced poetry, particularly limericks, and many magazine articles, but he could never write a publishable memoir. His writing style had been too crimped by daily deadlines to sustain a book-length manuscript, and the fragments of his autobiography, unfinished at his death, never attracted a publisher.[11]

Over the course of his half century in Washington journalism, Oulahan watched press attention shift steadily from Congress to the presidency. The White House had not been a congenial place for news when he began reporting in 1886. He had spent "many unhappy hours" trying to cover President Grover Cleveland, who had a penchant for privacy. In the 1890s, the genial former Representative William McKinley better appreciated the correspondents' needs and usefulness. One of President McKinley's secretaries conducted a press briefing every night at ten o'clock, and the McKinley administration expanded its clerical staff to produce a far larger supply of press releases. McKinley also invited reporters to come inside and use a large table and plenty of chairs in a reception room outside the president's office—their first official foot inside the White House door. Unlike Cleveland, McKinley attended Gridiron dinners and let the reporters know that they could call upon him or his cabinet for information. By 1900, the president had moved to "the front of affairs," wrote a political scientist named Woodrow Wilson. "There is no trouble now about getting the President's speeches printed and read, every word."[12]

The stiff and self-conscious McKinley attracted a respectful press, but it was his youthful, more dynamic successor who first made the presidency the preoccupation of the press. Richard Oulahan met Theodore Roosevelt when he was assistant secretary of the navy; and it was Oulahan who originated the term "Rough Riders." According to press gallery legend, Roosevelt objected to the first draft of Oulahan's story. "Don't call them rough riders," he insisted, "and don't call them cowboys. Call them mounted riflemen." But Roosevelt failed to blue-pencil one reference to the term, and headline writers immediately seized upon it. "Rough Riders" won a place in the public consciousness and cemented Roosevelt's relationship with the reporter he called "Dickie."[13]

Theodore Roosevelt treated the press corps as professionals whom he could trust, and use. Presidential messages, once fiercely guarded against premature release, were now made available days ahead of schedule, with embargoes for later publication. Correspondents could telegraph the entire text back to their papers and prepare their analyses, so that their stories would appear simultaneously with the message's delivery to Congress. Roosevelt also invited Oulahan and other favored correspondents (known as the "fair-haired") to interview him during his daily shave, although he maintained a firm rule that he should not be directly quoted without his consent. This enabled him to float trial balloons and avoid "back-fires." James G. Blaine had pioneered these devices, but Roosevelt was the first to employ them as president. When the new West Wing opened in 1902, Roosevelt made sure it contained the White House's first official press room.[14]

The Rough Rider, the Big Stick, and the Teddy Bear made Theodore Roosevelt the dream of every correspondent and editorial cartoonist. From watching Roosevelt, Oulahan understood how easily the press and public could visualize the figure of the presidency by comparison to Congress, which presented "no identifying human characteristics." People simply could not see Congress "as a thing of flesh and blood, a real living personality, as something to follow or to incite affectionate admiration." Roosevelt was the first chief executive to perceive that the "aggregation of humanity" under the Capitol dome could not match a colorful presidential personality. He acted to create public opinion that Congress would be obliged to follow.[15]

Theodore Roosevelt learned he could attack both Congress and its individual members without giving the impression that he was fighting his own party, which held the majority in both houses during his entire presidency. Members of Congress similarly campaigned against Congress. They ran for reelection against Congress as a whole, against their parties, their leadership, and their programs. Constituents came to respect their own senators and representatives but not the collective, impersonal mass of the legislature. All the while, the White House worked to alert people to what the president was doing daily to advance their well-being, to show his character, and to create public sympathy for his policies. "Broadly speaking," Oulahan concluded, "the people visualize the President of the United States as the Government." So, in fact, did Richard Oulahan. In 1908 he took a leave of absence as Washington correspondent for the *New York Sun* to work for William Howard Taft's presidential campaign. Oulahan headed the "Literary Bureau" of the Republican National Committee, directing publicity for Roosevelt's chosen successor. After the election, President-elect Taft encouraged Oulahan to resume his reporting: "I shall be very sorry if you are not to continue in journalistic work in Washington where I shall see you often." Oulahan then headed the Washington staff of the new president's favorite paper. "You will never learn what the other side is doing if you only read the *Sun* and the *Tribune*," Mrs. Taft once chided her husband. "I don't care what the other side is doing," Taft responded irritably. Like Mrs. Taft, Washington correspondents attributed the president's inept politics to his failure to read their newspaper accounts more regularly.[16]

Taft tried unsuccessfully to work with the press. He was the first president to invite all accredited Washington correspondents to formal press conferences. But his press relations resembled less Theodore Roosevelt's activism than nineteenth-century presidential aloofness. *New York Times* correspondent Charles Thompson once advised Taft that he was injuring himself by speaking so positively about the archconservative Senator Nelson Aldrich. "If I have to think, every time I say a thing, what effect it is going to have on the public mind," snapped Taft, beating his fist on his knee, "—I had rather not be President of the United States." Taft's stubborn inaccessibility turned the correspondents attention back to Capitol Hill, where members were quick to divulge whatever White House news the president neglected to release to the press. At one Gridiron dinner, where he sat beside the club's president, Richard Oulahan, President Taft was dismayed when so many of the skits dealt with Theodore Roosevelt. But he never appreciated how much his own inattentiveness to the press undermined his public image.[17]

Taft lost the election of 1912 to a shrewd scholar of public opinion. Woodrow Wilson's personal demeanor, his activist program, and his decision to break tradition to deliver his State of the Union message to Congress in person, won approval from the predominantly Republican Washington press corps. Correspondent Charles Thompson, "as red hot a Bull Moose as ever," took an immense liking to Wilson; and Richard Oulahan reported that press relations with the White House were "working out first rate." Oulahan, who succeeded Thompson as head of the *New York Times's* Washington bureau in 1912, became such an admirer of Wilson that his editors in New York complained about the Wilsonian propaganda he was sending them—a remarkable turnabout for the former Republican party publicity director. Oulahan's conversion reflected the tendency of Washington correspondents to identify with strong and assertive presidents, regardless of party, particularly those who seized the initiative in promoting their legislative programs. As Walter Lippmann observed: "Nothing affects more the balance of power between Congress and the President than whether the one or the other is the principal source of news and explanation and policy."[18]

Yet Wilson's press relations had their downside. At his first news conference, Wilson shocked the correspondents when he told them it was their duty to hold back information from their readers in the national interest, and when he defined their job as informing Washington what the country was thinking, rather than the country what Washington was thinking. Seeing their role as the exact opposite, the correspondents considered his reasoning "amazing, even fantastic." Five months later Wilson threatened to suspend his press conferences altogether after newspapers quoted his critical remarks about Mexico. To appease the president, Richard Oulahan, acting as chairman of the Standing Committee of Correspondents, proposed formal rules that both the president and reporters could accept. It became their "distinct understanding" that reporters would never quote the president directly or even indirectly without his consent.[19]

Oulahan found Wilson to be "courteous in the extreme" at his press conferences but sharp and rebuking if he detected hostility in a question. President Wilson alternately courted the correspondents with humor, idealism, and keen intellect, and repelled them with cool, aloof, and condescending attitudes. At worst he lectured them like schoolboys. He gave Oulahan the impression of "matching wits against ours," sometimes answering questions without giving out any new information. Louis Ludlow, one of the minority of Democratic correspondents, confirmed that reporters never felt as personally close to Wilson as they had to Theodore Roosevelt.[20]

The saving grace for Wilson was his press secretary, Joseph Tumulty, who patched the president's often frayed relations with reporters. Having worked as a reporter himself, Tumulty held daily press briefings and extended innumerable favors and courtesies to the correspondents. When Richard Oulahan's first wife died in 1916, Tumulty saw to it that Wilson sent flowers and a warm letter of condolence. Tumulty later noted that while he disagreed politically with the *New York Times*'s Washington correspondent, he felt the highest regard for Dick Oulahan's "decency and uprightness."[21]

The White House was not alone in its quest for better publicity; much to Congress's chagrin the various executive agencies began hiring public relations specialists, who were buried deep inside agency budgets under misleading titles. In an amendment to an agricultural appropriations bill in 1908, Congress stipulated that no federal money should go for "the preparation of any newspaper or magazine articles." Two years later congressmen were startled to discover a public relations man in the Census Bureau, under the title "Expert Special Agent." Despite another law enacted in 1913 that no publicity agents be hired without congressional approval, the tide continued.[22]

By the Wilson administration, some Washington reporters were living off executive department handouts, barely rewriting government press releases for their papers. No daily handout could adequately cover the hundreds of congressmen and dozens of committees. When United Press reporter Sevellon Brown was transferred from covering the executive departments to the House of Representatives, he had to pay an experienced Hill reporter five dollars a week to teach him how to cover the House and keep him from missing a story.[23] Slowly, members began to experiment with press secretaries and publicity agents. Democrat Frank O'Hair, who upset Speaker Joseph Cannon for a House seat in 1912, hired an Illinois correspondent for the Associated Press, Lambert St. Clair, "officially as his secretary but in reality as his publicity man." When O'Hair tried to dictate correspondence to his secretary, St. Clair had to remind him that he knew no shorthand. The congressman and his secretary therefore each contributed twenty-five dollars a month to employ "a real secretary."[24] In 1918, a young San Francisco Bay Area reporter, Franc Havenner, went to work as secretary to California Senator Hiram Johnson. Havenner handled the senator's correspondence and publicity while writing a weekly newsletter to California newspapers about the activities of the California delegation, "and of course a great deal about Johnson."[25]

Government press control bloomed fullest when the nation entered World War I. Washington correspondents accepted unprecedented restraints as a wartime expediency. When Wilson suspended his press conferences, and Tumulty ended his daily briefings, public relations became the exclusive domain of the Committee on Public Information, under former editor George Creel. The Creel committee fostered a publicity campaign that dramatized President Wilson beyond that of any previous president in war or peace. It littered Washington with press releases, planted stories, and sent Boy Scouts out to distribute Wilson's patriotic speeches to the folks back home. Congress deeply resented such presidential glorification; and the Standing Committee of Correspondents forced one correspondent to resign from the Creel committee if he wished to keep his press gallery accreditation.[26]

The war turned Washington into a world news capital, and the peace negotiations made many Washington correspondents diplomatic reporters. In 1919, Richard Oulahan followed President Wilson to the Paris peace negotiations and became spokesman for the entire American press delegation. When Wilson agreed to meet with other Allied leaders in secret negotiations, and not to brief reporters on their progress, Oulahan led the press attack on keeping "the people of the world in the dark," in violation of Wilson's pledge of "open covenants." When the president decided to leak information to the press to rouse public opinion against recalcitrant parties in the negotiation, Oulahan got the leak. When Wilson's party, traveling by train through Italy, received word that Theodore Roosevelt had unexpectedly died, Oulahan "rose fitly, as always, to the occasion," as Arthur Krock recalled. "We followed him to a little *boîte* across the way from the railway station and there proposed and drank a toast to the memory of a great American."[27]

The correspondents returned from Europe troubled by Wilson's furtive behavior and suspicious of the treaty he had negotiated. Sitting in the press gallery on the day Wilson delivered the treaty to the Senate, Oulahan rated the performance not the president's best. During the monumental contest that followed, Republican senators Henry Cabot Lodge and William E. Borah seemed to exert the greatest influence over the Washington press. Oulahan found Lodge "simple and kindly, if prejudiced; strong in his dislikes and bitter toward those whose political and personal motives he questioned," and a man who willingly shared information with the press. He described Borah as "communicative, helpful, understanding, illuminative."[28]

Press gallery members betrayed their attitude in August 1919, when they joined in cheering Senator Lodge's attack on the Treaty of Versailles. It seemed obvious to Oulahan that press gallery sentiments, opposing both the treaty and the League of Nations, would enormously influence public opinion. When the British newspaper publisher Lord Northcliffe, an old friend of Oulahan's, visited Washington in 1921, he attended a luncheon of American "Overseas Writers" who had covered the Paris negotiations, and then visited the Senate press gallery. "You have just been the guest of the men who make treaties," said the chairman of the Standing Committee of Correspondents; "let me present those who unmake treaties."[29]

In losing his fight over the League of Nations, Wilson tipped the balance of press attention back in favor of Congress, particularly toward the Senate. During the debates, Senator William Borah launched the daily press conferences that helped him dominate news from Capitol Hill during the 1920s. Reporters had been congregating outside Senator Borah's office each afternoon in search of some newsworthy quote. The senator obliged by inviting them inside for informal news conferences. "Shortly after three o'clock each afternoon," the *Christian Science Monitor* reported, "all press trails lead to the office of Senator Borah." The senator asked as many questions as he answered, often inviting reporters to stay behind to talk matters over more thoroughly. Borah made a point never to criticize a reporter or a newspaper, no matter how hostile their coverage, and he cultivated friendships with reporters from Democratic as well as Republican papers.[30]

No other senator generated publicity so well, in large part because Borah was willing to make himself available for reporters at any hour. Mary Borah recalled that hardly an evening passed when some journalist did not call her husband at their apartment, and the senator invariably took the call. To the dismay of presidents and senators alike, Borah captured the correspondents' affection. Congress might recess, President Coolidge noted icily, but Senator Borah was "always in session." Senator Hiram Johnson sneered at Borah's so-called many mistresses among the press, most notably Richard Oulahan's *New York Times*. Because Borah took part in any movement in which the *Times* was engaged, Johnson complained, "it treats him with the most distinguished consideration, and gives him fullest publicity." Johnson fulminated over Borah's "ability as a publicity agent, and the ease with which he directs the moronic members of the press," but conceded that Borah was the last progressive in Congress who could get regular publicity in the conservative twenties.[31]

Columnist Raymond Clapper judged Borah's press relations "on a parity with the White House." In terms of press coverage, Congress and the White House reached a standoff during the 1920s, with the correspondents divided over which branch made the better story. United Press reporter Thomas Stokes argued that "Congress was only a sideshow" during the 1920s, although he admitted that when Congress left town, the correspondents had trouble getting Washington news back on the front pages. (The United Press still dropped its youngest reporters from its Washington payroll during congressional recesses.) "We never covered Washington in the twenties. We covered the Senate," recalled Raymond Brandt of the *St. Louis Post-Dispatch*. "You wasted your time downtown."[32]

The Teapot Dome investigation into government irregularities gave Capitol Hill correspondents an abundance of stories during the 1920s. Some reporters cooperated with Senate investigations through their own sleuthing and by preparing the questions with which senators impaled witnesses. The liberal Paul Anderson won the Pulitzer Prize for prodding senators to investigate missing bonds associated with Teapot Dome and feeding questions to Chairman Tom Walsh. But the conservative-leaning correspondent for the *Baltimore Sun,* Fred Essary, ridiculed investigations as showmanship. "Nothing is so easy as to start a congressional investigation," Essary scoffed. "A resolution, a brief but violent speech, a few newspaper interviews—and the game is on."[33]

Despite a resurgence in press attention, members of Congress detected sharp changes in press attitudes and behavior. Before World War I, Associated Press reporters had sat on the House and Senate floor and filed long chronological accounts of the proceedings—not unlike the accounts published by Gales and Seaton a century earlier. "Strangely, papers published it," commented one journalist. But the practice virtually disappeared after the war. Bourke Cockran, a New York Democrat observed the dissimilarity in press coverage when he first served in the House from 1891 to 1895, compared to his return from 1904 to 1909, and again in 1921: "When I came to this House in the Fiftieth Congress reports and descriptions of our proceedings occupied the front page of every newspaper in America," said the congressman. "When I returned to the Fifty-Eighth Congress, after an absence of eight years, I found the space allotted to us in the newspapers had shrunk to about a column. I return now, after an absence of twelve years, and find we have no place at all."[34]

If Congress could no longer count on automatic coverage of its activities, the White House could. Infused by the dynamic leadership of Theodore Roosevelt and Woodrow Wilson, the presidency grew so central to the federal government and Washington reporting that not even the lesser personalities of Warren Harding or Calvin Coolidge could diminish it. Writing in 1926, political scientist Lindsay Rogers estimated that President Coolidge's twice-weekly press conferences attracted fifty to a hundred correspondents. Ground rules required reporters to submit their questions in writing in advance, which permitted the president to decide what to answer, and prohibited the correspondents from directly quoting the president (whom they identified in news stories as a "White House Spokesman"). Rogers noted cynically that reporters had news if they could persuade the president to venture an opinion on college students' wide-bottomed trousers. The next day's editions devoted extensive space to presidential opinions, no matter how trivial.

Press conference rules, created and enforced by Richard Oulahan and his fellow Washington correspondents, allowed President Coolidge to answer questions "without danger of being held responsible, and with no fear of embarrassing contradiction." The "White House Spokesman" would denounce congressional speeches as being made strictly for political effect and predict that the people would side with the president. When congressmen complained, Coolidge simply detached himself from the offending remarks, in a manner "neither straightforward nor sincere." Frank Kent, Washington correspondent for the *Baltimore Sun*, contrasted the "weak and watery utterances" of Coolidge's press conferences with the "forceful and vigorous" news dispatches they produced. Reporters turned the passive, indecisive chief executive into "a red-blooded, resolute, two-fisted, fighting executive, thoroughly aroused and determined." The resulting presidential portrait served the reporters' own interests by appealing to the illusions of their editors and readers.[35]

Richard Oulahan never quarreled with favorable trends in presidential press treatment. He recognized that publicity had replaced patronage as a president's chief weapon for enacting his programs. As Oulahan described this process, nineteenth-century congressmen had been creatures of their home-district political machines, which were hungry for federal patronage and anxious for their representatives to maintain close ties with the administration. The direct primaries of the twentieth century had liberated members from both party machines and presidential patronage. Once the crack of the patronage whip began to sound less menacing than the voice of a congressman's own constituency, presidents with a national program would be forced to court public opinion.[36]

Since the press often served as the field on which Congress and the president contested, reporters came under fire from both sides. In an NBC radio address in 1929, Oulahan commented that it was an old story for Washington correspondents to be blasted within the legislative halls, citing the senator who referred to "these little squirrel heads in the Press Gallery." He emphasized that because of their increasing specialization, concentrating solely on Congress or the White House or the courts, "the Washington correspondents of today have no axes to grind, no favors to ask." For Oulahan, objective reporting meant the avoidance of narrow partisanship, rather than rigid neutrality. After World War I, correspondents had sought primarily to give the news, but their presence on the spot where the news originated gave them the chance to furnish their readers with "the whys and wherefores" of what they recorded. In Oulahan's definition, a reporter's interpretations represented an honest effort "to tell one's readers what is likely to happen," rather than "what one wishes to happen."[37]

As a former London correspondent, Oulahan observed that Washington reporters had grown closer to those who ran the government than had journalists in any other capital city. The press gathered news through "intimate, personal contact" with political leaders, and therefore ran the danger of being used. Oulahan doubted that many correspondents willingly allowed themselves to be exploited for political purposes, but he confessed there had been times when he took information "designed to accomplish a purpose." And he had not hesitated in sending that information to his newspaper.[38]

Richard Oulahan's personal contacts with national leaders defined his preeminence as a correspondent. At the *Times* bureau he once mentioned that to get a story, "I had to see the President, the Secretary of State, the Secretary of War and the Speaker of the House." His ability to interview all four allowed him to write the most completely authoritative account of the story. Oulahan's successor as the *New York Times*'s Washington bureau chief, Arthur Krock, ranked him among the three top leaders of the Washington

Richard V. Oulahan, Washington bureau chief of the *New York Times*.

press, with Frank Kent of the *Baltimore Sun*, and J. C. O'Laughlin of the *Chicago Tribune*, "not only in their coverage of the general news, but in producing news of special depth and authority due to the fact that they had quick access to Presidents, Cabinet members, and the leaders of Congress." Entrée to important news sources lifted them above the rest of the pack.[39]

Of all the presidents he covered, Oulahan felt personally closest to the one with the worst press relations. His friendship with Herbert Hoover dated back to the Wilson administration. During Hoover's term as secretary of commerce, the reporter had gone out of his way to assist his friend with favorable publicity. Later he joined the elite band of journalists who tossed a medicine ball around with the president each morning on the White House lawn, as part of the "medicine ball cabinet." Oddly introverted for a public man, Hoover anguished between a desire for privacy and a craving for recognition. In the Commerce Department he had presided over a well-lubricated public relations apparatus, but his courtship of influential journalists did not transfer well to the White House, where as president he needed to reach a broader spectrum of the press. Charles Michelson, the Washington correspondent who led an anti-Hoover campaign as publicity director for the Democratic National Committee, asserted that Hoover came to office "with perhaps the largest clientele among the newspaper correspondents of any president in our history, but within three months he was quarreling with them."[40]

Not a politician by training or inclination, President Hoover showed little tolerance for press criticism. His news conferences grew progressively restrictive, and "more innocuous and futile" than Coolidge's. When Hoover lectured to the correspondents, they treated him even more sarcastically in their dispatches and especially in the magazine articles that many wrote on the side. Indignant over uncomplimentary stories, Hoover tried to have some reporters barred from government offices. As relations between the White House and the press deteriorated, reporters sensed that various executive department publicity offices were taking their cues from the president and volunteering less information; government handouts diminished in number and usefulness. By contrast, *New York Times* correspondent Delbert Clark found that while Congress had no press agents, "it always has been and probably always will be the best source of uncanned news in Washington."[41]

Hoover's alienation of the Washington press corps spawned resentment for the journalists of the "medicine ball cabinet." In 1931 this hostility went public in an anonymous best-seller, *Washington Merry-Go-Round,* which accused some Washington correspondents of writing "not what they know but what the viciously partisan and reactionary policy of their employer dictates." The nameless authors charged the press with taking the side of the Hoover administration and accusing Congress of obstructionism whenever it opposed the president. The book promised to tell what newspapers would not, and what Washington correspondents could only write between the lines.[42]

Washington Merry-Go-Round was the work of two angry young reporters, Drew Pearson, a tall, suave diplomatic correspondent for the *Baltimore Sun,* and Robert S. Allen, a short, combative, and unrelenting Washington bureau chief for the *Christian Science Monitor.* Allen wrote the chapter on the press, which singled out Richard Oulahan for strong abuse. He portrayed "the impeccable correspondent for the New York *Times"* as an administration toady, bowing and scraping in return for White House dinner invitations for himself and his publisher, Adolph Ochs, and turning the *Times* into "a willing vehicle for Presidential politics and propaganda." Oulahan's staff of eleven—the largest single newspaper bureau in the capital—Allen dismissed as "typical *Times* men, conservative, hard-working reporters, grinding out the day's grist of news in columns where others turn it out in words." He claimed that Oulahan received a $25,000-a-year salary (three times Allen's own) and explained that such an exalted salary required that the correspondent "never write anything challenging or critical of any one in the White House, high society, big business, and finance." Oulahan's "policy" stories, he charged, were nothing more than "neatly turned editorials printed in the news columns."[43]

Washington Merry-Go-Round went on to assault the press gallery's Standing Committee of Correspondents, which Richard Oulahan had chaired and cherished. Fifty years after adoption of the Standing Committee's rules, Pearson and Allen denounced them as excessively exclusive. Under these rules, only a handful of women had gained membership in the Capitol press galleries—among them Robert Allen's wife, Ruth Finney, a Scripps-Howard reporter. (Oulahan's bureau was among the few to hire a woman political correspondent, Winifred Mallon.) The book further indicted the Standing Committee for denying accreditation to black reporters. For years, black journalists had applied for accreditation but had been rejected on the grounds that they worked for weekly papers. One black reporter filed reams of telegraphic copy to the sole black daily paper to gain admittance but was still turned down. "His claim was legitimate but his color was wrong," concluded Robert Allen. Rather than the formal, quasi-official Standing Committee at the Capitol, Pearson and Allen preferred the "haphazard and informal" White House Press Correspondents' Association, which issued an ornate, gold-embossed press card to any reporter who applied. It was all very "breezy and casual, in the true press manner."[44]

Richard Oulahan defended the Standing Committee's attempts to police the profession. The committee's work was "arduous, thankless, and often unpleasant," since it involved hearing complaints against members, suspension of those who violated the rules, and rejection of applicants who did not meet its requirements. Upon the Standing Committee's good judgment in these matters, he noted, "depends the prestige of the 'Gallery' with Congress and often the reputation of the press." On the whole, the rules, and "the whole process toward an ethical code, written and unwritten," had been progressive. The modern press galleries would no longer tolerate the behavior of old-time correspondents. For instance, as chairman of the Standing Committee during World War I, Oulahan had issued a ruling that barred press gallery members from furnishing advance news to stock brokerage houses, a lucrative practice for many Civil War correspondents. Given the onerous nature of its work, Oulahan seemed surprised at the committee's hotly contested elections, but as correspondent Charles Thompson commented, the committee had "practical absolute control" over the Washington press corps. "It can refuse admission to the gallery to any man, and this carries far more than the mere refusal of a seat," wrote Thompson, for rejection "usually ends by driving him out of the business."[45]

Washington Merry-Go-Round sold widely, earned handsome royalties, and caused a tremendous stir in the capital. Rumors about its authorship cast suspicion on many before Pearson and Allen were exposed. The book's chief target, President Hoover, sent his secretary to Boston to file a protest with the editor of the *Christian Science Monitor.* The editor obliged by firing Robert Allen via the mail. Drew Pearson held his job at the *Sun* until he published an equally outrageous sequel, *More Merry-Go-Round.* The dismissals of Pearson and Allen attracted more public attention to them, enabling the team to launch a popular new syndicated column, the "Merry-Go-Round." [46]

Oulahan had been deeply stung by the best-selling book's charge that he no longer did legwork as a reporter. In fact, Robert Allen had gotten the story wrong. Oulahan's style of reporting had not changed, only his sources had grown more highly placed. He ran the *Times* bureau loosely, deciding each day which story he would cover, and allowing his staff to choose for themselves what other news to follow. As a result, their stories often overlapped, with two or more reporters submitting accounts of the same events. "You and I have a great opportunity here," another new reporter confided to Turner Catledge when he joined the *Times*'s Washington bureau in 1929. "This is a moribund outfit, passing up more stories than they write, and all we have to do is go to it." Oulahan assigned Catledge to cover the House, "the best place to learn about Washington." The bureau chief advised the reporter to spend his first day merely making acquaintances, since Oulahan himself planned to cover the big news of the day, President Hoover's State of the Union message. But the news desk editor had expected Catledge to collect the usual congressional reactions to the president's message. Catledge's predecessor on the House beat rescued him by typing out a story complete with comments from a half dozen congressmen. He knew exactly what they would have said, and felt certain that none would object to his fictitious quotations. [47]

Richard Oulahan literally worked himself to death, both as a result of lifelong work habits and out of determination to prove the *Merry-Go-Round* wrong. While covering some congressional hearings, he contracted pneumonia, which was worsened by his chain-smoking. His last story appeared on the front page of the *New York Times* on 21 December 1931. A week later he died at age sixty-four. Oulahan's unexpected death threw the *Times*'s Washington bureau into despair. His staff collected long pages of eulogies for "one of the best beloved figures in American journalism." House Speaker John Nance Garner called Oulahan "one of the greatest newspaper correspondents this country has produced"; and Senator Claude Swanson confirmed that he had been "implicitly trusted by all members of the Senate" as well as "a confidential and most intelligent adviser to public men." In the rival *New York Herald-Tribune,* Walter Lippmann commended Oulahan's objective style, which had won his bureau "the confidence of readers of all shades of opinion." Conservative columnist David Lawrence celebrated that "Dick Oulahan never felt it was his duty to expose or muck-rake." At Oulahan's home, flowers were delivered with an unsigned note of condolence. His widow recognized the handwriting as Drew Pearson's.[48]

After a brief interregnum, Arthur Krock replaced Oulahan as "The Washington Correspondent" of the *New York Times*. As the new chief, Krock immediately set out to reform the slipshod practices of his bureau's "loosely directed" reporters. He abolished self-determined reporting by appointing a copyeditor to make assignments and set word limits. He also forbade "blacksheeting." The old, freewheeling style that Oulahan embodied no longer had a place in a modern news bureau.[49]

Richard Oulahan died at a time when a new medium was challenging the Washington correspondents. Just as earlier the primacy of newspaper reporting had been challenged by the muck-raking magazines, so by 1930 the print media—both newspapers and periodicals—lost their monopoly on Washington news through competition from radio broadcasting. Newspaper reporters resisted radio correspondents, denying them access to the press galleries. During the 1920s and 1930s the Standing Committee would accredit radio reporters only if they also reported for daily newspapers. Finally, in 1939 Congress established a separate Radio Gallery, becoming the only national legislature to divide its galleries among different forms of media. One Washington correspondent, caught misspeaking on a radio news program, retorted, "What does it matter on radio?" If not with contempt, reporters approached the microphone with trepidation. Richard Oulahan had awaited his first radio address so nervously that announcer Graham McNamee had to calm him down by recommending that he talk into the microphone as if it were a telephone.[50]

Members of Congress also trembled in front of microphones, but many of them set about mastering the new technology. Although experiments to set up microphones in the Senate chamber to broadcast debate were unsuccessful, radio broadcasters generally found Congress a cooperative subject. Senators like William Borah rarely turned down an invitation to speak on the radio. Borah's rich baritone voice and Shakespearean training made him a more attractive radio personality than the flat and dry Herbert Hoover. Not surprisingly, when CBS inaugurated its news service to compete with press associations, it chose an exclusive interview with Senator Borah for its opening feature. The next day's *New York Times* reported the radio interview on its front page.[51]

Less than a year after Oulahan's death, the nation elected a president who understood radio's power of access and turned it to his advantage. With Franklin D. Roosevelt in the White House, the preponderance of press attention shifted irrevocably from Congress to the presidency. The many clashing voices of Congress could never compete with the president's singularly resonant, reassuring tones. Once again, politicians and the press scrambled to adjust their old relationships to the demands of a new medium, to create mutually beneficial rules under which all sides could operate.

Afterword

THE UPHEAVALS of 1932 reversed the political fortunes not only of the Republican and Democratic parties, but also of Congress and the presidency. Over the next dozen years, Franklin D. Roosevelt dramatically expanded the executive branch while fixing press attention firmly on the White House. At the same time, the evolution of media broadcasting further strengthened the president's grip on Washington news. Yet as much as Washington reporting changed over the next half century, it retained many of its traditional elements.

In the press, detached, objective writing and investigative reporting became the rule, although the public's desire for opinion never abated. These counterforces eventually found some reconciliation in bylines and syndicated columns. During the 1920s, David Lawrence, Arthur Brisbane, and Mark Sullivan pioneered the syndicated column of Washington political news. Smaller newspapers soon found that they could buy several columns of syndicated opinion for the cost of sending to Washington a single correspondent, who might not produce more than one column of news a day. As syndicated writers gained license to editorialize, the more constrained "objective" journalists earned their compensation in the form of public identity. For the first time, newspapers began awarding bylines to more than just their most veteran reporters. "In the Depression years the by-line was widely distributed in lieu of money," commented the *Chicago Tribune*'s Washington correspondent, Walter Trohan.[1]

At a time when chain newspapers were transforming once independent newspapers into "a standardized corporate identity," Frederick Lewis Allen observed that syndicated columnists preserved "the old tradition of personal journalism." Whether they read large metropolitan dailies or small-town papers, Americans now had access to the interpretive reporting and conflicting opinions of Drew Pearson and Robert Allen, Walter Lippmann, Paul Mallon, and Frank Kent. Among the regular correspondents, there arose some resentment of the syndicated columnists' freedom to editorialize, while the rules of objective journalism forbade them to express their own views. "Under no circumstances may I add: 'It is my personal opinion that Senator So-and-So doesn't know the budget from a racing form sheet and probably introduced the bill because one of his campaign contributors told him to,'" fumed Kenneth Crawford, before he graduated from correspondent to columnist. Resentment turned to disdain when Washington correspondents complained that "thumb sucking" columnists depended more on inspiration than on hard news.[2]

As bylines and syndicated columns raised the level of identification of the Washington correspondents, intimacy with their sources continued apace with the journalists' elevated status. When Marquis Childs came to Washington as a correspondent for the *St. Louis Post-Dispatch* in the 1930s, he was surprised at how easily he fit into the lofty atmosphere, and "how readily those who had been merely headline names became, if not friends, useful acquaintances." The seductive setting of the embassy party, or the late afternoon drink with the senators gave rise to an irresistible "temptation to be a player, not just an observer."[3]

Childs's colleague at the *Post-Dispatch's* Washington bureau, Paul Y. Anderson, argued that relations between Congress and the press grew "mutually satisfactory in direct ratio to their intimacy." Reporters in direct personal contact with members of Congress enjoyed excellent relations, whereas editors and publishers a distance away had less appreciation for Congress's role in the government. "Here, in other words, is a situation where unfamiliarity breeds contempt." Anderson faulted editors and publishers for their enthrallment with the presidency, treating the president's wishes with deference, publishing whatever he said, and suppressing most of what he wanted kept out of print. Newspapers found it easier to report on the executive than the legislature. "The President is an individual, while Congress is a group," Anderson enumerated. "He is remote and mysterious, while Congress is familiar. His aims are more or less uniform, while the policies of Congress, until formulated in legislation, are confused." Although Herbert Hoover had allowed his press relations to deteriorate to an unprecedented degree of "mutual dislike and distrust," the characteristics that Anderson listed worked in favor of Hoover's media-wise successors.[4]

As late as Hoover's administration, the adjournment of Congress left Washington "a hot and deserted village" that correspondents had trouble getting on the front page. The coming of the New Deal finally made Washington the year-round news capital of the United States. Through bold political initiatives, numerous press conferences, fireside chats, and his magnetic personality, Franklin D. Roosevelt captivated the public and the press. Yet even at the height of the New Deal, Leo Rosten's sociological study of Washington reporting confirmed that Congress remained the primary source of most correspondents' news. With new government programs blossoming all over the capital, correspondents lacked the time to make the rounds of all the agencies and relied on the "excellent shortcuts" of congressional sources. Those who wanted to go beyond the official handouts and press conferences cultivated working relationships with well-informed senators and representatives. "Successful correspondents want friends, flocks of them—in Congress, in the executive departments, and in social life—and try to keep them as friends," wrote correspondent Neil MacNeil, adding, "the lone wolf rarely gets far in Washington."[5]

During the New Deal years, Washington correspondents treasured personal friendships with such powerful congressional leaders as Mississippi Senator Pat Harrison, a reliable news source and "master manipulator" who leaked information to influence public opinion without revealing his own hand. "Many a member of Congress was the making of many a favored reporter by feeding him inside information," wrote Walter Trohan of the *Chicago Tribune*. "Frequently it was far easier to break White House or departmental news from the Hill than from the White House itself or the department concerned." President Roosevelt once complained that anything he told Pat Harrison he could expect to see in the next day's *New York Times*—as indeed Harrison later told Turner Catledge, the *Times* correspondent who benefited most from his confidences.[6]

As the executive branch expanded, Congress turned to the press as an instrument for "controlling the administration." Members leaked news to the press in order to stimulate investigation and shape public opinion. They recognized that reporters at press conferences had the chance to interrogate administration officials more effectively than could Congress. Roland Young, on the staff of the Senate Foreign Relations Committee during World War II, considered it an anomaly that the press could question the president over foreign policy, while his committee could not. Young also watched how the press often forced Congress into the role of critic by soliciting comments from senators and representatives, and how members' responses to reporters' questions often received more publicity than their speeches on the floor.[7]

Despite their mutual dependence, and regardless of party or ideology, many members of Congress felt suspicious of Washington reporters. Walter Trohan estimated that the Washington press corps "was considered to be at least 95 per cent New Deal by its members," and Republican Senator Robert Taft of Ohio was not alone in viewing the press as part of an eastern liberal establishment deeply hostile to midwestern conservatism. The Missouri Democratic Senator Harry Truman loved the movie "Mr. Smith Goes to Washington" for showing Washington correspondents "in their true drunken light." Judging himself as a diligent, hard-working, unsung legislator, Senator Truman complained that the press tried to portray him as a "know-nothing" machine politician. "Most of the senators who really apply themselves never get much headlines," he was still grumbling years later in his presidential memoirs. The liberal Democrat Glen Taylor of Idaho won attention and ridicule for such stunts as strumming his guitar on the Capitol steps and riding a horse across the country to publicize his political stands. "If I play the guitar and croon sitting on a flight of granite steps, that's big news," Senator Taylor complained. "If I work in the Senate to protect Idaho's rivers and pine forests, that's barely worth a one-deck headline."[8]

Yet most congressional correspondents defined themselves as "pro-politician," a term coined by William S. White, dean of Senate reporters during the 1950s. Jack Bell, chief Associated Press correspondent at the Capitol, illustrated this affinity by explaining that the "men and women who trust you as a reporter provide you with the bulk of your news. Most of the time it comes from the well where you have been lowering your bucket for a long time, getting fresh, sweet facts from springs that never seem to run dry."

To *New York Times* correspondent Russell Baker, sent to cover Congress in 1959, the typical Hill reporter grew to resemble the politicians he covered, developing a taste for "garrulity, coarse jokes, and bourbon." Writing about the press in the 1960s, media critic William Rivers reasoned that the more journalists covered the mechanisms of the federal government, the more they came to respect people in public life. "Even the self-proclaimed 'watchdogs' like Drew Pearson, who dig deep into Washington subterranea, confess their admiration for those who make the federal establishment work."[9]

However suspicious Congress felt toward the press, executive branch officials acted even more guardedly. James Reston, who headed the *New York Times* Washington bureau from 1953 through 1964, attributed this phenomena to Congress's operating so much in the open. "They think the good opinion of the press is most important to their re-elections, which dominates much of their thinking; consequently, they see reporters and some of them even read us." Reston regarded the press and congressmen as "natural allies," and pointed out that reporters in the press galleries provided the link between what happened on Capitol Hill and downtown, just as their counterparts in the White House press room were "constantly conveying the views of the President to the members of the Federal legislature."[10]

Television further enhanced the president's ability to speak directly to the nation without press interpretation, yet paradoxically made the White House the choicest assignment for Washington journalists. The high visibility of the White House increased the prestige of its press corps, but for all the glamour disaffected correspondents dismissed the White House press room as "an adult day-care center," and described the White House staff setting out piles of press releases "like dog food" for correspondents to snap up hungrily. One journalist compared the White House press room to "being trapped in the locker room at a football game. You hear the crowd, you know something is going on. When they let you up to see what is going on, you see a lot of activity, but later you find out that was only the half-time show." Working under such restrictions heightened a reporter's urge to build friendships. The most important person in a White House reporter's life quickly became the president's press secretary, as television correspondent Dan Rather recounted his experiences. The temptation was strong to ingratiate oneself, "but for a reporter, especially one covering the White House, that need can be damaging to his work."[11]

When Russell Baker left his assignment at the White House to cover Congress, he felt as if he were climbing out of a closed sewer and into the fresh air. Where before he had been "sitting in this awful lobby waiting for Jim Hagerty to come out with a handout," everyone on Capitol Hill *loved to talk*." But fellow *Times* correspondent Warren Weaver found the talk was hollow because power had shifted elsewhere. The Capitol had become "a hall of illusions, peopled by the myths that the legislative branch remains proudly coequal." Statistical analyses of press coverage of the federal government showed a steady, unrelenting increase in news about the presidency, at Congress's expense.[12]

As the national news coverage of Congress eroded, its members grew to appreciate local and regional coverage as significantly more useful to their reelections. This factor explained the seeming contradiction of the persistently low public opinion of Congress and the high reelection rate of its members. While a few senators and representatives became national figures through leadership posts, seniority, staff, grasp of issues, personality, and presidential ambition, thereby gaining standing in national news-making, most members concerned themselves with the local media in their states and districts. Members continued to campaign for Congress by running against it.[13]

The growth of regional reporting kept the congressional press galleries at the center of Washington journalism. Regional reporters were often "stringers" from news services, who filed stories to a variety of unaffiliated newspapers. Or they represented large chains of newspapers. Regional reporting had a lower standing within the Washington media, but it accounted for the largest number of journalists. By the 1970s, an estimated two-thirds of the reporters on Capitol Hill covered local and regional news.[14]

Lou Cannon, who began as a regional reporter before becoming a correspondent and columnist for the *Washington Post*, observed that regional coverage promoted press relationships with congressmen "based on mutual need and sometimes on mutual laziness." Regional reporters' efforts to give a "local angle" to national news helped the "typically invisible" representative become visible in the home district, where it counted the most. Regional reporters grew to depend on members of Congress from their region for inside information, access to government agencies, and other well-placed tips, all of which improved the reporters' standing with their editors. This "cozy coverage of Congress" too often moved "beyond symbiosis to collusion" when regional reporters tried to avoid criticizing their sources.[15]

In the 1980s, *Wall Street Journal* correspondent Al Hunt judged Congress "the greatest beat in town," where appointments were unnecessary and where reporters could see the most important members every day. Yet some of Hunt's easy access came from the prominence of the paper he represented. "You have to be read in this town," Hunt conceded, noting that the otherwise able *Los Angeles Times* Washington bureau lacked the status of reporters who were "read here every day by sources and colleagues." Correspondents for papers outside Washington and New York became better known by appearing on television talk shows, after which, as the *Boston Globe's* Martin Nolan found, "people return your phone calls quicker."[16]

Television increasingly dominated Washington reporting. Membership in the congressional radio and television galleries tripled during the 1980s, reaching parity with the newspaper reporters' gallery. Newspaper correspondents had never welcomed the new rivalry. Back during the Army-McCarthy hearings in 1954, reporters at the press table had been blinded by powerful floodlights and crowded by crews of television cameramen around the hearing room. *New Republic* writer Michael Strait noted how the old-time reporters "fought grimly to defend the little plots of table on which they scribbled." Politicians found the adjustment equally cumbersome. When the new Senate office building opened in 1958, Senate committees no longer sat around a table with their witnesses, but were now perched "on a circular dais behind a massive paneled bulwark," with witnesses sitting many feet away. At the Senate Commerce Committee, the original sound system installed to cover these distances was so defective that its noise drowned out all deliberation. One senator recalled how the committee, which exercised dominion over television and radio, "had to adjourn its first hearing because it could not control its own squawks."[17]

Members of Congress set about clumsily to master the new media. In the 1950s, Senator Karl Mundt starred in "Your Washington and You on the Air," produced for broadcast in his home state of South Dakota. The show featured the senator answering questions posed by a "Washington correspondent," who turned out to be an employee of the Senate Recording Studio. House members, pointing to the better television coverage that senators received, joked that their colleagues elected to the Senate "get all cleaned up in a Brooks Brothers suit and start combing their hair more neatly because they're going to be on TV." Through television-dominated campaigning, however, members grew increasingly sophisticated in their use of the broadcast media, and by the 1970s both parties in both houses were considering telegenic qualities as criteria for choosing new leadership.[18]

Beyond images and personalities, television reporting had trouble capturing the complexities of legislation. Legislators who worked for months on a complex bill would have only seconds to summarize their case. Press secretaries calculated that no remarks of more than a minute would be carried on a thirty-minute evening news program and began instead to coin catchy phrases. Wisconsin Senator William Proxmire compared television reporting to a sporting event, a vaudeville act, or other forms of mass entertainment, and doubted that it could tolerate the boredom of the legislative process. "Politicians must play the game by the rules of television," lamented Indiana Representative Lee Hamilton, "so they cannot delve into the subtleties and nuances of issues." One solution was to offer television viewers admission to the entire proceedings of Congress. In 1979 the House, and by 1986 the Senate, broke old traditions to permit cameras to film their floor procedures, giving the most direct and uninterpreted access to congressional debates since the days of the *National Intelligencer.*[19]

Television added new dimensions to congressional reporting but did nothing to lessen correspondents' cultivation of personal relationships with their sources. Concern over the ethics of their trade stimulated renewed debate over intimacy between the press and politicians during the 1980s, with Washington columnists David Broder and George F. Will articulating the two poles of the controversy. When Broder began reporting, a veteran correspondent had advised him: "Always set yourself to lean a bit against the people you're covering, and hope whoever is covering the opposition for your paper is doing the same thing." Broder believed that too often Washington correspondents failed to follow that advice. He found reporters on Capitol Hill notably hesitant to document the failings of Congress and its more powerful committee chairmen, for fear of changing an institution in whose "cozy, cliquish environment" they shared a stake. He criticized the journalistic tilt toward all incumbents, reflecting the regional reporters' "powerful motivation to stay on the good side of the congressmen they cover."[20]

George Will viewed intimacy differently. "A journalist once said that the only way for a journalist to look at a politician is down," he noted. "That is unpleasantly self-congratulatory." To write intelligently about politicians, journalists need to see them whole, and to do that "it helps to know a few as friends." Although such friendships offended those who believed a mean edge necessary to write candidly about politicians, Will argued that "relaxation in social settings, reduces the journalist's tendency to regard politicians as mere embodiments of ideas or causes, as simple abstractions rather than complicated human beings."[21]

A century after the Bohemian heyday of Newspaper Row, a network of formal and informal rules and journalistic ethics continue to guide Washington reporting. Standing Committees of Correspondents still judge accreditation to the press, periodical, and radio and television galleries, to prevent journalistic lobbying and protect the reputation of the profession. The Gridiron Club still entertains the high and the mighty, along with those who cover them. "Those of us who dress up in silly costumes and perform in satirical skits," noted Gridiron member David Broder, "have begun to recognize the serious function this annual dinner fulfills, as a tension-breaker and score-settler in the political life of this city." On a daily basis, the mutual responsibilities of such press mechanisms as embargoed news releases and off-the-record and deep-background interviews are respected by politicians and reporters alike. Leaks abound, and journalists vigilantly protect their confidential sources. Considerable improvement has occurred in the representation of women and minorities within the press galleries. Women journalists now cover political news for the major newspapers and broadcast news programs, as well as for local and regional news services. But the persistent influence of "old boy networks" on Capitol Hill has made integration arduous for both congresswomen and reporters. Slowly and reluctantly, the Gridiron and the National Press clubs admitted women and black reporters to their fellowship.[22]

Although wired for computers and advanced telecommunications, the congressional press galleries remain for their inhabitants "the last old-fashioned newsroom." Cluttered and antiquated in appearance, they reflect the nineteenth-century ambience of the chambers below. Their occupants have emerged from behind pseudonyms and have restrained opinion for objectivity. They pride themselves in their work and their durability. "Senators and Representatives, cabinet members and cabinetmakers come and go," correspondent Ernest K. Lindley asserted. "But the Washington press and [media] corps remains, not only as an institution or as a group, but as individuals."[23]

NOTES

BIBLIOGRAPHICAL ESSAY

INDEX

Notes

Introduction

1. Ronald Steel, *Walter Lippmann and the American Century* (Boston, 1980), 388, 418–419, 548–549; Joseph E. Persico, *Edward R. Murrow: An American Original* (New York, 1988), 316; *Washington Post*, 10, 11, 20, 28 July 1983; Jules Witcover, "Revolving-Door Journalists," *Washington Journalism Review* 12 (April 1990): 33–38.
2. Susan Heilman Miller, "Reporters and Congressmen, Living in Symbiosis," *Journalism Monographs* 53 (January 1978): 1–25; William Grieder, "Reporters and Their Sources: Mutual Assured Seduction," *Washington Monthly* 14 (October 1982): 10–19.
3. *Congressional Record*, 72nd Cong., 1st sess, 15622–15624; David S. Broder, *Behind the Front Page: A Candid Look at How the News Is Made* (New York, 1987), 208; Sam Donaldson, *Hold On, Mr. President* (New York, 1987), 123.
4. *Congressional Globe*, 25th Cong., 3rd sess., 93–95.

1. Gales and Seaton

1. *Annals of Congress*, 1st Cong., 1st sess., 917–920; Elizabeth Gregory McPherson, "The History of Reporting the Debates and Proceedings of Congress" (Ph.D. diss., University of North Carolina at Chapel Hill, 1940), 11–16; see also Marion Tinling, "Thomas Lloyd's Reports of the First Federal Congress," *William and Mary Quarterly* 18 (October 1961): 519–545.
2. Prior to the federal Congress, colonial and revolutionary era legislatures had shown similar sensitivity toward press criticism and had called up scores of printers to answer charges of libel. See Leonard W. Levy, *Emergence of a Free Press* (New York, 1985), 19, 75–76, 84; Thomas C. Leonard, *The Power of the Press: The Birth of American Political Reporting* (New York, 1986), 13–59; and Dwight Lee-

land Teeter, "A Legacy of Expression: Philadelphia Newspapers and Congress during the War for Independence, 1775–1783" (Ph.D. diss., University of Wisconsin, 1966). For British parliamentary reporting see Mitchell Stephens, *A History of News: From the Drum to the Satellite* (New York, 1988), 166–171, 235–236.

3. See Noble E. Cunningham, Jr., ed., *The Making of the American Party System, 1789–1809* (Englewood Cliffs, 1965), 25, 87–97; Richard Hofstadter, *The Idea of a Party System: The Rise of Legitimate Opposition in the United States, 1780–1840* (Berkeley, 1969); and Culver H. Smith, *The Press, Politics, and Patronage: The American Government's Use of Newspapers, 1789–1875* (Athens, 1977).

4. McPherson, "History of Reporting Debates," 1–4; F. B. Marbut, *News from the Capital: The Story of Washington Reporting* (Carbondale, 1971), 13–18; Adams quoted in Sol Bloom, *History of the Formation of the Union under the Constitution* (Washington, 1943), 240–242.

5. Reporter Thomas Lloyd could not identify all members and described some speakers as "a baldheaded man" or a "man in blue coat and wig." The doodles that covered his notes suggest that his concentration wandered. James Madison believed that Lloyd "sometimes filled up blanks in his notes from memory or *imagination*." In later years, Madison recalled that Lloyd "became a votary of the bottle and perhaps made too free use of it sometimes at the period of his printed debates." Tinling, "Thomas Lloyd's Reports of the First Federal Congress," 528–533.

6. Roy Swanstrom, *The United States Senate, 1789–1801*, S. Doc. 100–31, 100th Cong., 1st sess. (Washington, 1988), 67–69, 243–244.

7. Frank Luther Mott, *Jefferson and the Press* (Baton Rouge, 1943), 5–10; see also Noble E. Cunningham, Jr., *Circular Letters of Congressmen to Their Constituents, 1789–1829* (Chapel Hill, 1978).

8. Gerald L. Grota, "Philip Freneau's Crusade for Open Sessions of the U.S. Senate," *Journalism Quarterly* 48 (Winter 1971): 667–671; C. L. Grant, "Senator Benjamin Hawkins: Federalist or Republican?" *Journal of the Early Republic* 1 (Fall 1981): 240; Swanstrom, *The United States Senate*, 238–249.

9. Swanstrom, *The United States Senate*, 250; Noble E. Cunningham, Jr., *The Process of Government under Jefferson* (Princeton, 1978), 259–260.

10. Smith, *The Press, Politics, and Patronage*, 2–11; James Morton Smith, *Freedom's Fetters: The Alien and Sedition Laws and American Civil Liberties* (Ithaca, 1956), 94–274.

11. Smith, *Freedom's Fetters*, 277–306; Dumas Malone, *Jefferson and the Ordeal of Liberty* (Boston, 1962), 463–466.

12. *Annals of Congress*, 6th Cong., 1st sess., 78, 87.
13. Ernest J. Eberling, *Congressional Investigation; A Study of the Origin and Development of the Power of Congress to Investigate and Punish Contempt* (New York, 1928), 42–53; Charles R. King, ed., *The Life and Correspondence of Rufus King* (New York, 1896), 284.
14. David Hackett Fisher, *The Revolt of American Conservatism: The Federalist Party in the Era of Jeffersonian Democracy* (New York, 1965), 38; William E. Ames, *A History of the National Intelligencer* (Chapel Hill, 1972), 3–18.
15. Linda K. Kerber, "The Federalist Party," in Arthur M. Schlesinger, Jr., ed., *History of U.S. Political Parties*, vol. 1 (New York, 1973), 100; McPherson, "History of Reporting Debates," 33–34; Ames, *History of the National Intelligencer*, 23–26.
16. *Annals of Congress*, 7th Cong., 1st sess., 406–408; Alex B. Lacy, Jr., "Jefferson and Congress: Congressional Method and Politics, 1801–1809" (Ph.D. diss., University of Virginia, 1963), 44.
17. Ames, *History of the National Intelligencer*, 3–62. On the Republican ideology see Joyce Appleby, *Capitalism and a New Social Order: The Republican Vision of the 1790s* (New York, 1984); Robert E. Shalhope, "Towards a Republican Synthesis," *William and Mary Quarterly* 29 (January 1972): 49–80; and Linda K. Kerber, "The Republican Ideology of the Revolutionary Generation," *American Quarterly* 37 (Fall 1985): 474–495.
18. Smith, *The Press, Politics, and Patronage*, 24–26; Ames, *History of the National Intelligencer*, 61–84; Allen C. Clark, "Joseph Gales, Junior, Editor and Mayor," *Records of the Columbia Historical Society* 23 (Washington, 1920), 93–94; Josephine Seaton, *William Winston Seaton of the National Intelligencer* (New York, 1970 [1871]), 17–19. Joseph Gales, Sr., was working as a printer in Philadelphia when his employer begged him: "You seem able to do everything that is wanted: pray, could you not do these Congressional Reports for us better than this drunken Callender, who gives us so much trouble?" [Charles Lanman], "The *National Intelligencer* and Its Editors," *Atlantic Monthly* 6 (October 1860): 474, 476.
19. Seaton, *William Winston Seaton*, 320.
20. Ames, *History of the National Intelligencer*, 68–69, 80–87; Clark, "Joseph Gales, Junior," 96–97; Seaton, *William Winston Seaton*, 14–16, 76–80; Lanman, "The *National Intelligencer* and Its Editors," 478–479.
21. *Washington Federalist*, 13 January 1802, 17 and 25 March 1802.
22. See "Newspapers Ordered by the Senate," 8 December 1801, and 8th Cong., 1st sess. (1803), Secretary of the Senate, R.G. 46, National Archives; Uriah Tracy to Robert Goodloe Harper, 15 January

1804, Harper to Tracy, 20 January 1804, Miscellaneous Manuscripts, New York Public Library.

23. Marbut, *News from the Capital*, 25–27; Smith, *The Press, Politics, and Patronage*, 21.

24. *National Intelligencer*, 9 June 1818, 3 May 1822; Ames, *History of the National Intelligencer*, 115.

25. Despite the financial success of the *Intelligencer*, Gales and Seaton incurred significant debts, requiring loans from the Bank of the United States that later compromised their independence during Andrew Jackson's "Bank War." See Ames, *History of the National Intelligencer*, 85–116, 176, 192–193, 225–226. Smith, *The Press, Politics, and Patronage*, 32–38.

26. Ames, *History of the National Intelligencer*, 104–113; Seaton, *William Winston Seaton*, 31; McPherson, "History of Reporting Debates," 36–41.

27. McPherson, "History of Reporting Debates," 32, 42–44; *Charleston Courier*, 31 January 1828; Robert Dawidoff, *The Education of John Randolph* (New York, 1979), 254; Clark, "Joseph Gales, Junior," 112.

28. For the origin and definition of party politics during and after the 1820s, see Richard P. McCormick, *The Second American Party System: Party Formation in the Jacksonian Era* (Chapel Hill, 1966), 19–31, 329–356; Richard L. McCormick, *The Party Period and Public Policy: American Politics from the Age of Jackson to the Progressive Era* (New York, 1986), 29–63; and Sean Wilentz, "On Class and Politics in Jacksonian America," *Reviews in American History* 10 (December 1982): 45–63.

29. Jennie W. Scudder, "Historical Sketch of the Unitarian Church of Washington, D.C.," *Records of the Columbia Historical Society* 13 (Washington, 1910), 169; Robert H. Wiebe, *The Opening of American Society: From the Adoption of the Constitution to the Eve of Disunion* (New York, 1984), 194–233; Ames, *The National Intelligencer*, 127–150; James E. Pollard, *The Presidents and the Press* (New York, 1947), 120–126; John Tebbel and Sarah Miles Watts, *The Press and the Presidency: From George Washington to Ronald Reagan* (New York, 1985), 61–62.

30. *National Intelligencer*, 19 April 1823; Merrill D. Peterson, *The Great Triumvirate: Webster, Clay, and Calhoun* (New York, 1988), 113–114.

31. Edward L. Mayo, "Republicanism, Antipartyism, and Jacksonian Party Politics: A View from the Nation's Capital," *American Quarterly* 31 (Spring 1979): 3–20; Robert V. Remini, *Martin Van Buren and the Making of the Democratic Party* (New York, 1959), 139–140. Van Buren had worked with Gales and Seaton to support Crawford's candidacy in 1824, but he had broken with them when he later became

Jackson's "self-appointed congressional manager." See Chase C. Mooney, *William H. Crawford, 1772–1834* (Lexington, 1974), 278, and John Niven, *Martin Van Buren: The Romantic Age of American Politics* (New York, 1983), 191, 266.

32. Charles M. Wiltse, ed., *The Papers of Daniel Webster,* vol. 2 (Hanover, 1976), 399. Gales and Seaton served as printers for Congress for twenty-six years, while Duff Green served for eight years, as did Blair and Rives. Smith, *The Press, Politics, and Patronage,* 90–91, 98, 130–135, 161; also see Pollard, *The Presidents and the Press,* 147–181.

33. *Washington Evening Star,* 1 February 1869; [Ben: Perley Poore] "Washington News," *Harper's Monthly* 48 (January 1874): 227–228. Marbut, *News from the Capital,* 29–36; Joseph T. Buckingham, *Specimens of Newspaper Literature: With Personal Memoirs, Anecdotes, and Reminiscences,* vol. 2 (Boston, 1850), 172; *Providence Journal,* 20 June 1883; J. Frederick Essary, *Covering Washington: Government Reflected to the Public in the Press, 1822–1926* (Boston, 1927), 22–23.

34. Joseph T. Buckingham, *Personal Memoirs and Recollections of Editorial Life,* vol. 2 (Boston, 1852), 3–5, 17, 30, 121–123; Marbut, *News from the Capital,* 34. "We have given but a hasty and extremely imperfect outline of this debate," Buckingham wrote from Washington. "It is not practicable in a daily letter to give the arguments of the gentlemen in full; but we believe that this sketch furnishes a view of the prominent points that were debated." *Boston Courier,* 7 January 1828.

35. Oliver Carlson, *The Man Who Made the News: James Gordon Bennett* (New York, 1942), 74–87; Frederic Hudson, *Journalism in the United States, from 1690 to 1872* (New York, 1873), 286; Isaac C. Pray, *Memoirs of James Gordon Bennett and His Times* (New York, 1855), 78, 87. Ben: Perley Poore, *Perley's Reminiscences of Sixty Years in the National Metropolis,* vol. 1 (Philadelphia, 1886), 58. For Bennett on the Library of Congress, see *New York Enquirer,* 2 February 1828.

36. Charles Francis Adams, ed., *Memoirs of John Quincy Adams,* vols. 8, 9 (Philadelphia, 1876), VIII, 332–333, IX, 56, 441–442; Marbut, *News from the Capital,* 44, 49–50; Poore, *Perley's Reminiscences,* I, 56–57; Poore, "Washington News," 228.

37. *Congressional Globe,* 25th Cong., 2nd sess., 173–176; Adams, ed., *Memoirs of John Quincy Adams,* IX, 493–495.

38. U.S. Congress, House Select Committee of Investigation, *Death of Mr. Cilley—Duel,* H. Rept. 825, 25th Cong., 2nd sess., (Washington, 1838), 9.

39. *Congressional Globe,* 25th Cong., 3rd sess., 59, 93–95. Niles, the founder, editor, and contributor to the *Hartford Times,* was not a candidate for reelection in 1838. He later served as postmaster general in the Van Buren administration and returned to the Senate for another term in 1843. See Niven, *Martin Van Buren,* 210, 468.

40. On the penny press see Dan Schiller, *Objectivity and the News: The Public and the Rise of Commercial Journalism* (Philadelphia, 1981); Michael Schudson, *Discovering the News: A Social History of American Newspapers* (New York, 1978); and John C. Nerone, "The Mythology of the Penny Press," *Critical Studies in Mass Communication* 4 (1987): 376–404.

41. See James Oakes, "From Republicanism to Liberalism: Ideological Change and the Crisis of the Old South," *American Quarterly* 37 (Fall 1985): 551–571; Daniel Walker Howe, *The Political Culture of the American Whigs* (Chicago, 1979); and Peterson, *The Great Triumvirate,* 384–385.

42. McPherson, "History of Reporting Debates," 107–109; Richard Current, *Daniel Webster and the Rise of National Conservatism* (Boston, 1955), 62; Claude M. Feuss, *Daniel Webster,* vol. 1 (Boston, 1930), 383–385; Irving H. Bartlett, *Daniel Webster* (New York, 1978), 4; Leonard, *The Power of the Press,* 79.

43. George F. Hoar, *Autobiography of Seventy Years,* vol. 1 (New York, 1903), 144. James Parton observed of Webster: "People went away from one of his ponderous and empty speeches disappointed, but not ill pleased to boast that they too had 'heard Daniel Webster speak.'" James Parton, *Famous Americans of Recent Times* (Boston, 1867), 105.

44. Baker A. Jamison, *Memories of Great Men, and Events—1840–1861, by a Senate Page* (New York, 1917), 33; Thomas Froncek, ed., *The City of Washington* (New York, 1985), 166. See also Leonard, *The Power of the Press,* 63–96.

45. McPherson, "History of Reporting Debates," 121–125; Thomas Hart Benton, *Thirty Years' View; or, A History of the Working of the American Government for Thirty Years, from 1820 to 1850,* vol. 2 (New York, 1871), 373.

46. McPherson, "History of Reporting Debates," 126–127; *Congressional Globe,* 26th Cong., 1st sess., 297–298, 313. See "From Our Washington Correspondent," *New York Enquirer,* 25 March, 2 February 1828. *Globe* reporters sometimes resorted to flattery to cover their inadequacies. John C. Calhoun, they once noted, "addressed the Senate for nearly an hour and a half in a strain of argument so close and logical that every sentence was in itself an aphorism on that which preceded and that which followed, that no successful attempt

at a synopsis can be made." *Congressional Globe,* 27th Cong., 2nd sess., 266.

47. *Congressional Globe,* 26th Cong., 1st sess., 470; McPherson, "History of Reporting Debates," 127–128.

48. Benton, *Thirty Years' View,* 97–101.

49. Marbut, *News from the Capital,* 60–63; *Senate Journal,* 27th Cong., 1st sess., 78; Select Committee on Reporters, "Sketch of the Plan to Provide for the Reporters' Gallery over the President's Chair in the Senate," 29 July 1841, R.G. 56, National Archives.

50. *Congressional Globe,* 29th Cong., 1st sess., 580–581, 667; Committee to Audit and Control the Contingent Expenses of the Senate, Robert Mills to Senator Sidney Breese, 18 March 1846, 2 April 1846, *Report of the Committee to Audit and Control the Contingent Expenses of the Senate on Certain Proposed Alterations in the Senate Chamber,* 29th Cong., 1st sess., R.G. 46, National Archives.

51. Dow first converted the *Madisonian* into the *United States Journal* before it became the *Daily Times. United States Journal,* 16 December 1845; *Washington Daily Times,* 2, 5 February 1846, 24 March 1846.

52. *Washington Daily Times,* 5, 9, 10, 11 March 1846.

53. U.S. Congress, Senate, *Report of the Select Committee,* S. Doc. 222, 29th Cong., 1st sess.; *Congressional Globe,* 29th Cong., 1st sess., 500–501; *Washington Semi-Weekly Times,* 24 March 1846.

54. *Congressional Globe,* 29th Cong., 2nd sess., 392–400, 406–417; Ernest McPherson Lander, Jr., *Reluctant Imperialists: Calhoun, the South Carolinians, and the Mexican War* (Baton Rouge, 1980), 69–70; Paul H. Bergeron, *The Presidency of James K. Polk* (Lawrence, Kansas, 1987), 171–179. Ritchie did not return to the Senate floor until June 1848; see *New York Tribune,* 3 June 1848.

55. Pollard, *Presidents and the Press,* 250–251; *New York Herald,* 13, 16 March 1848; Bergeron, *James K. Polk,* 181–182.

56. *New York Herald,* 18 April, 3 May 1848; *New York Tribune,* 14 April 1848; Marbut, *News from the Capital,* 86–93.

57. The *Herald* quoted the *Tribune's* Washington correspondent, William Robinson, as reporting in the *Buffalo Express* that Senate secrecy was "the merest farce," for the journal of executive proceedings was made known "at once to the Executive Secretary, to the editor of the government newspaper, and then to every political friend who chooses to seek information of either of these people." *New York Herald,* 6 April 1848.

58. McPherson, "History of Reporting Debates," 136–175; *New York Tribune,* 27 March 1848; Ben: Perley Poore rued the publication of verbatim accounts in the *Congressional Globe,* for their "disastrous

effect upon the eloquence of Congress, which no longer hung upon the accents of its leading members, and rarely read what appeared in the report of its debates." Poore, *Perley's Reminiscences*, I, 302. Thomas C. Leonard found that politicians objected to the "unfeeling accuracy" of the press. Leonard, *The Power of the Press*, 63.

59. Carleton Mabee, *The American Leonardo: A Life of Samuel F.B. Morse* (New York, 1969 [1943]), 206–208, 251–260, 273; Samuel I. Prime, *The Life of Samuel F. B. Morse* (New York, 1974 [1875]), 497; John A. Garraty, *Silas Wright* (New York, 1949), 281–282; *Centennial History of the City of Washington, D.C.* (Dayton, 1892), 466.

60. "The Baltimore American," *Journalist* 12 (8 November 1890): 2; *New York Evening Transcript*, 11, 17 June 1849; Bernard Roshco, *Newsmaking* (Chicago, 1975), 28; *Niles' National Register* 46 (1 June 1844): 211; Richard A. Schwarzlose, "The Nation's First Wire Service: Evidence Supporting a Footnote," *Journalism Quarterly* 48 (Winter 1980): 555–562.

61. Ben: Perley Poore, "Waifs from Washington," *Gleason's Pictoral Drawing-Room Companion* 4 (1 January 1853): 7; Horace Greeley to William E. Robinson, 8 February 1848, Horace Greeley Papers, New York Public Library; *New York Tribune*, 13 March 1848.

62. Greeley to Alfred Vail, 23 March 1848, Greeley Papers, New York Public Library; Oliver Grambling, *A.P.: The Story of News* (New York, 1940), 19–21.

63. *New York Herald*, 11, 17 June 1849.

64. *Congressional Globe*, 31st Cong., 1st sess., 520; Murat Halstead, "Early Editorial Experiences," in Melville Philips, ed., *The Making of a Newspaper* (New York, 1893), 228, 231.

65. Ames, *History of the National Intelligencer*, 309–310; Clark, "Joseph Gales, Junior," 143; Poore, *Perley's Reminiscences*, I, 55; *Chicago Republican*, 8 February 1868. Although Twain wrote after Gales and Seaton's editorships, the paper's style had not changed.

66. Mary Jane Windle, *Life in Washington, and Life Here and There* (Philadelphia, 1859), 152–153, 218–219.

67. Donald B. Cole and John J. McDonough, eds., *Witness to the Young Republic: A Yankee's Journal, 1828–1870, by Benjamin Brown French* (Hanover, N.H., 1989), 331. Seaton, *William Winston Seaton*, 365–366.

2. Horace Greeley's Washington Correspondents

1. Horace Greeley to J. Gallagher, 16 October 1850, Greeley Papers, New York Public Library; Henry Luther Stoddard, *Horace Greeley: Printer, Editor, Crusader* (New York, 1946), 100–101, 183; Ben: Per-

ley Poore, *Perley's Reminiscences of Sixty Years in the National Metropolis*, vol. 1 (Philadelphia, 1886), 310.

2. May D. Russell Young, ed., *Men and Memories: Personal Reminiscences of John Russell Young*, vol. 1 (New York, 1901), 114.

3. Horace Greeley, *Recollections of a Busy Life* (New York, 1868), 106; see John C. Nerone, "The Mythology of the Penny Press," *Critical Studies in Mass Communication* 4 (1987): 376–404.

4. Harriet A. Weed, ed., *Autobiography of Thurlow Weed*, vol. 1 (Boston, 1883), 466–468; Thurlow Weed Barnes, ed., *Memoirs of Thurlow Weed*, vol. 2 (Boston, 1883), 94, 97; Willard Grosvenor Blyer, *Main Currents in the History of American Journalism* (Boston, 1927), 211–212; *New York Tribune*, 1 December 1845; Greeley to Moses A. Cartland, 14 April 1845, Horace Greeley Papers, Library of Congress.

5. Glyndon G. Van Deusen, *Horace Greeley: Nineteenth-Century Crusader* (New York, 1953), 25–32; Barnes, *Memoirs of Thurlow Weed*, 92–93. Between 1849 and 1861, the *Tribune* published 487 pieces by Marx and Engels. See Henry M. Christman, ed., *The American Journals of Marx and Engels* (New York, 1966).

6. S. W. Jackman, ed., *Acton in America: The American Journal of Sir John Acton, 1853* (Shepherdstown, Eng., 1979), 12–13, 24.

7. Greeley's correspondents often advocated issues in advance of him. "I never opened the *Tribune* in those days without a terror as to what they might make me say after 11 o'clock at night," Greeley confided. Young, *Men and Memories*, 115. Greeley to O. A. Bowe, 21 January 1840, and to H. Hubbard, 2 June 1843, Greeley Papers, New York Public Library.

8. Nathan Sergeant, *Public Men and Events from the Commencement of Mr. Monroe's Administration, in 1817, to the Close of Mr. Fillmore's Administration, in 1853*, vol. 2 (Philadelphia, 1875), 288; *New York Tribune*, 12 December 1844.

9. William H. Barnes, *The Fortieth Congress of the United States: Historical and Biographical* (New York, 1869), 311–312; *New York Tribune*, 26 December 1844, 25 March 1845. Robinson became active in Irish-American politics as a student at Yale, where he ingratiated himself with Whig leaders for financial support. See Robinson to William H. Seward, 11 May 1840, Seward Papers, University of Rochester.

10. *New York Tribune*, 27 February 1846. Although he never officially admitted his second identity, "Richelieu" once slipped and wrote: "In the House today, Mr. Sawyer got himself into a scrape. Though I have helped him get into notoriety, he doesn't always consult me."

New York Tribune, 22 March 1848. See also F. B. Marbut, *News from the Capital: The Story of Washington Reporting* (Carbondale, 1971), 71−73.

11. *Congressional Globe*, 29th Cong., 1st sess., 457, and 29th Cong., 2nd sess., 224; *New York Tribune*, 14 June, 6 July 1846.

12. Louis A. Gobright, *Recollections of Men and Things at Washington, during the Third of a Century* (Philadelphia, 1869), 76−77; *New York Tribune*, 6, 11 March 1846; see also Robinson's after-dinner toast, reported in the *New York Tribune*, 4 January 1848.

13. *New York Tribune*, 5, 6 June 1846, 3, 8, 14 July 1846; Allan Nevins, ed., *Polk: The Diary of a President, 1845−1849* (New York, 1968), 109.

14. *Philadelphia North American*, 22 July 1846; *New York Tribune*, 25 July 1846; *Washington Union*, 23 July 1846.

15. Testimony of James Wallace, editor of the *North American*, in "A Select Committee to Inquire into the Means by which the Proceedings and Documents of Secret Sessions Have Become Public," 29th Cong., 1st sess., R.G. 46, National Archives. Harvey regularly signed letters as "A Friend," most notably his telegram in 1861 alerting the governor of South Carolina of federal plans to reinforce Fort Sumter. See John G. Nicolay and John Hay, *Abraham Lincoln, A History*, vol. 4 (New York, 1904), 31−32.

16. Testimony of James E. Harvey, William E. Robinson, and George A. Dwight to the Select Committee, R.G. 46, National Archives; *New York Tribune*, 1, 12 August 1846. Horace Greeley wondered how George Dwight could afford so fine a parlor at the best Washington hotel and could entertain so generously on a correspondent's salary. "Very easily," a friend explained, "he is the agent of the British wool interest, well salaried to look after the welfare of his employers." James Parton, "Log-Rolling at Washington," *Atlantic Monthly*, 141 (July 1869): 368.

17. Greeley to Robinson, 2 January 1848 [incorrectly dated 1847], and Greeley to Robinson and T. D. Reilley, 11 November 1849, Greeley Papers, New York Public Library; *New York Tribune*, c. January 1848; Barnes, *Fortieth Congress*, 311−316.

18. *New York Times*, 6 March 1864; *Appleton's Cyclopedia*, vol. 4 (New York, 1888), 200; *National Era*, 4 February 1847. The *New York Herald* identified March as the *Tribune's* correspondent on 3 May 1848. William A. Cole of the Papers of Daniel Webster, at Dartmouth College, provided information on Charles March's family and career.

19. Van Deusen, *Horace Greeley*, 126−128; Greeley, *Recollections*, 216−224; James Parton, *The Life of Horace Greeley: Editor of the New York Tribune* (New York, 1855), 290; Henry Luther Stoddard, *Horace*

Greeley: Printer, Editor, Crusader (New York, 1946), 57–58; *New York Tribune*, 5, 8, 20, 29 December 1848, 29 January 1849; Willard H. Smith, *Schuyler Colfax: The Changing Fortunes of a Political Idol* (Indianapolis, 1952), 52.

20. *New York Tribune*, 13 December 1847, 13 March 1850.
21. *New York Tribune*, 12, 15 April 1850; Jane Grey Swisshelm, *Half a Century* (Chicago, 1880), 125; Lester B. Shippee, "Jane Grey Swisshelm: Agitator," *Mississippi Valley Historical Review* 7 (December 1920): 212.
22. Maurine Hoffman Beasley, "The First Women Washington Correspondents," *George Washington University Washington Studies* 4 (Washington, 1976): 7; Swisshelm, *Half a Century*, 130; *Congressional Globe*, 31st Cong., 1st sess., 762; *New York Tribune*, 15, 19 April 1850.
23. Swisshelm, *Half a Century*, 131–134; *New York Tribune*, 15, 29 April, 13 May 1850; Swisshelm to Greeley, 25 July 1858, Greeley Papers, New York Public Library.
24. Horace Greeley to A. E. Bovey, 6 May 1850, Greeley Papers, Library of Congress; Robert Franklin Durden, *James Shepherd Pike: Republicanism and the American Negro, 1850–1882* (Durham, 1957), 3–13; James S. Pike, *First Blows of the Civil War* (New York, 1879), 7, 17, 26, 32, 40–41.
25. *New York Tribune*, 29 April 1850; Pike, *First Blows of the Civil War*, 43–48.
26. Pike, *First Blows of the Civil War*, 89, 97–98; Stoddard, *Horace Greeley*, 139.
27. Barnes, *Memoirs of Thurlow Weed*, 220; Greeley to Seward, 12 March 1852, Greeley Papers, Library of Congress; Greeley to Seward, 6 February 1853, Greeley Papers, New York Public Library; see also Frances Brown, *Raymond of the Times* (New York, 1951).
28. Jeter A. Isely, *Horace Greeley and the Republican Party, 1853–1861* (Princeton, 1947), 53–55; Pike, *First Blows of the Civil War*, 203–205.
29. James S. Pike to William Pitt Fessenden, 10 February, 15 May 1854, James S. Pike Papers, Library of Congress; Pike, *First Blows of the Civil War*, 219; Charles A. Jellison, *Fessenden of Maine: Civil War Senator* (Syracuse, 1962), 73–78; *New York Tribune*, 6 March 1854.
30. *New York Tribune*, 6 March 1854; Paul Revere Frothingham, *Edward Everett, Orator and Statesman* (Boston, 1925), 353.
31. Pike, *First Blows of the Civil War*, 49–50, 112–113.
32. Charles Lanman, *Biographical Annals of the Civil Government of the United States during Its First Century* (Detroit, 1976 [1876]), 191; U.S. Congress, House of Representatives, Select Committee,

Reports on Alleged Corrupt Combinations of Members of Congress,
H. Rept. 243, 34th Cong., 3rd sess. (Washington, 1857), 115; for
examples of Harvey's political relations, see James E. Harvey to John
McLean, 12 April 1846, McLean Papers, Library of Congress; and
Harvey to Willie P. Mangum, 25 August 1846, Mangum Papers, Library of Congress.

33. Greeley, *Recollections,* 345; *New York Tribune,* 1 December 1855;
Van Deusen, *Horace Greeley,* 200–203; William E. Gienapp, *The
Origins of the Republican Party, 1852–1856* (New York, 1987), 239–
248.

34. Greeley to Charles A. Dana, 8 January 1856, Greeley Papers, New
York Public Library.

35. Isely, *Horace Greeley and the Republican Party,* 147; Greeley, *Recollections of a Busy Life,* 347–352; *New York Tribune,* 28, 31 January
1856.

36. Greeley to Dana, 1 February 1856, Greeley Papers, Library of Congress; *New York Tribune,* 4–6 February 1856; Pike, *First Blows of
the Civil War,* 305; see also Isely, *Horace Greeley and the Republican
Party,* 142–164.

37. Pike, *First Blows of the Civil War,* 339–340.

38. *New York Tribune,* 16 December 1856, 3 January, 24 February 1857;
Select Committee, *Alleged Corrupt Combinations,* 115. See also
Mark W. Summers, *The Plundering Generation: Corruption and the
Crisis of Union, 1849–1861* (Oxford, 1987).

39. *New York Times,* 6 January 1857; *Congressional Globe,* 34th Cong.,
3rd sess., 274–277; Ben: Perley Poore, "Washington News," *Harper's
Monthly* 48 (January 1874): 229–230; Marbut, *News from the Capital,* 97–103.

40. Neil MacNeil, *Forge of Democracy: The House of Representatives*
(New York, 1963), 188–189; Select Committee, *Alleged Corrupt
Combinations,* 1–39, 66. As a result of the Simonton case, Congress
enacted legislation providing that recalcitrant witnesses could be
held in contempt and tried by federal courts.

41. *New York Tribune,* 19, 24 April 1848, 19 January, 21 February 1857.
An anonymous letter to William Seward warned him that "unfavorable comment is excited in political circles, by your supposed connection with that little scamp Simonton, whose notorious venality,
and shameless system of blackmailing, caused him to be expelled
from Congress as a reporter, and has also caused all of the heads of
Departments and the President to refuse him any recognition whatsoever. He uses your name and reputation." A Friend to William E.
Seward, January 1857, Seward Papers, University of Rochester.

42. Durden, *James Shepherd Pike*, 19–27; *New York Tribune*, 20 December 1856, 3, 21, 30 January 1857.

43. Don E. Fehrenbacher, *The Dred Scott Case: Its Significance in American Law and Politics* (New York, 1978), 288–290, 666.

44. *New York Tribune*, 8 May 1858; Pike, *First Blows of the Civil War*, 431–432. Pike deleted Hanscom's name from his published correspondence, but the name appears in Pike's personal papers. See Charles A. Dana to Pike, 4 and 11 February 1859, Pike Papers, Calais Free Library, Calais, Maine. Harvey's poor opinion of Hanscom is cited in Marbut, *News from the Capital*, 70.

45. Van Deusen, *Thurlow Weed*, 231–254; Van Deusen, *William Henry Seward* (New York, 1967), 221–226; *New York Tribune*, 10 April 1861.

46. Barnes, *The Fortieth Congress*, 313; Durden, *James Shepherd Pike*, 45–51; James E. Harvey to William E. Seward, 13, 14 March 1861, Seward Papers, University of Rochester. See also Harry J. Carman and Reinhard H. Luthin, *Lincoln and Patronage* (New York, 1943), for Lincoln's rewards to the press.

47. Lurton D. Ingersoll, *The Life of Horace Greeley* (Chicago, 1873), 394–395; *New York Tribune*, 25 June 1861.

48. Ingersoll, *The Life of Horace Greeley*, 394–395; *New York Tribune*, 25 June 1861. The "picnic battle" is vividly described in Margaret Leech, *Reveille in Washington, 1860–1865* (New York 1962 [1941]), 121–125; and in J. Cutler Andrews, *The North Reports the Civil War* (Pittsburgh, 1955), 85–101.

49. *Washington Evening Star*, 24 July 1861; *New York Tribune*, 24 July 1861; *New York Sun*, 5 December 1872; Charles A. Dana, *Recollections of the Civil War* (New York, 1898), 1–2.

3. Horace White Speculates on the War

1. Henry Van Ness Boynton, "The Press and Public Men," *Century Magazine* 42 (October 1891): 854.

2. See Allan G. Bogue, *The Earnest Men: Republicans of the Civil War Senate* (Ithaca, 1981); and Leonard P. Curry, *Blueprint for Modern America: Non-Military Legislation of the First Civil War Congress* (Nashville, 1968).

3. *Washington Evening Star*, 24 July 1861, 1 February 1883; *New York Tribune*, 24 July 1861; *New York Sun*, 5 December 1872; *Providence Journal*, 20 June 1883.

4. Ben: Perley Poore, *Perley's Reminiscences of Sixty Years in the National Metropolis*, vol. 2 (Philadelphia, 1887), 126. James S. Pike, *First Blows of the Civil War* (New York, 1879), 439. The rich litera-

ture on Civil War correspondents in Washington includes J. Cutler Andrews, *The North Reports the Civil War* (Pittsburgh, 1955); Louis M. Starr, *Bohemian Brigade, Civil War Newsmen in Action* (Wisconsin, 1987 [1954]); and Bernard A. Weisberger, *Reporters for the Union* (Westport, 1977 [1953]).

5. Joseph Logsdon, *Horace White, Nineteenth-Century Liberal* (Westport, 1971), 3–41; Lloyd Wendt, *Chicago Tribune: The Rise of a Great American Newspaper* (Chicago, 1979), 207; Oswald Garrison Villard, "Horace White," *Dictionary of American Biography,* vol. 19 (New York, 1946), 104–105; *New York Evening Post,* 18 September 1916.

6. Logsdon, *Horace White,* 41–61; Horace White, *The Lincoln and Douglas Debates* (Chicago, 1914); James E. Pollard, *The Presidents and the Press* (New York, 1947), 326–328; Philip Kinsley, *The Chicago Tribune: Its First Hundred Years, 1847–1865,* vol. 1 (Chicago, 1943), 71–90.

7. Horace White, *The Life of Lyman Trumbull* (Boston, 1913), 168–169; Logsdon, *Horace White,* 78; for the significance of boardinghouse life in Washington, see James Sterling Young, *The Washington Community, 1800–1828* (New York, 1966).

8. Albert G. Riddle, *Recollections of War Times, Reminiscences of Men and Events in Washington, 1860–1865* (New York, 1895), 223. On wartime Washington, see Margaret Leach, *Reveille in Washington, 1860–1865* (New York, 1941).

9. *New York Times,* 5 January 1859; *Congressional Globe,* 35th Cong., 1st sess., 32, 641, 756.

10. *Congressional Record,* 98th Cong., 1st sess., S11209; see also Lauros G. McConachie, *Congressional Committees: A Study of the Origins and Development of Our National and Local Legislative Methods* (New York, 1898).

11. Washburne's patronage for White cost him nothing, by comparison to the cash payments he had to make to win the support of the *Chicago Tribune* and other papers. George H. Mayer, *The Republican Party, 1854–1966* (New York, 1967), 20; Logsdon, *Horace White,* 78–80, 89, 102; *Congressional Globe,* 37th Cong., 2nd sess., Appendix 94.

12. Information on correspondents serving as committee clerks can be obtained in the *Congressional Directories* and the annual reports of the Secretary of the Senate and Clerk of the House.

13. E. B. Wight to W. W. Clapp, 5 January 1877, W. W. Clapp Papers, Library of Congress.

14. If money failed, Hanscom used intimidation. He once threatened Senator Ben Wade, chairman of the Joint Committee on the Conduct

of the War, with unfavorable publicity unless he released information from closed-door sessions. When Wade refused, Hanscom made good his threat by repeatedly denouncing the senator in the *Herald*. Simon Hanscom to James Gordon Bennett, 4 February 1862, Malcom Ives to Bennett, 8 February 1862, James Gordon Bennett Papers, Library of Congress; E. B. Wight to W. W. Clapp, 24 January 1876, W. W. Clapp Papers, Library of Congress.

15. Brooks's lifestyle can be measured by his room rate of $75 a month, compared to Henry Villard's $45 for room and board. By the war's end, a California senator arranged for Brooks to return west as director of the Customs House in San Francisco. Brooks's plumb earned him a sneer from correspondent James Simonton, who asked if it could be called a success to take a man "out of an honorable and influential profession and [make] him the agent and instrument of an unscrupulous politician, who tolerates nothing less than slavish obedience in those who lick official crumbs of favor from his table." Wayne C. Temple and Justice G. Turner, "Lincoln's 'Castine,' Noah Brooks," *Lincoln Herald* 72 (Fall 1970): 81, 85, 95–96.

16. Temple and Turner, "Lincoln's 'Castine,'" 78; Starr, *Bohemian Brigade*, 78; see also Stephen W. Sears, "The First News Blackout," *American Heritage* (June/July 1985): 24–31.

17. George W. Adams to Manton Marble, 10 November 1862, Manton Marble Papers, Library of Congress; U.S. Congress, House of Representatives, Committee on the Judiciary, *Telegraph Censorship*, H. Rept. 64, 37th Cong., 2nd sess. (Washington, 1862), 5; see also Weisberger, *Reporters for the Union*, 74–124.

18. House Judiciary Committee, *Telegraph Censorship*, 3, 8–9.

19. Ibid., 14; Andrews, *The North Reports the Civil War*, 193.

20. *Washington Evening Star*, 4, 11 October 1886.

21. Andrews, *The North Reports the Civil War*, 194; Henry M. Flint to James Gordon Bennett, 10 September 1862, Bennett Papers, Library of Congress.

22. Information on occupations of members was drawn from biographies in William H. Barnes, *History of the Thirty-Ninth Congress of the United States* (New York, 1868), 577–624.

23. O. J. Hollister, *Life of Schuyler Colfax* (New York, 1886), 219–221. Examples of Colfax's wooing of the press can be found in various collections of papers: those of Horace Greeley, New York Public Library; John Russell Young, Library of Congress; and Uriah Hunt Painter, Pennsylvania Historical Society.

24. "Washington is a great school to me," John Russell Young wrote to his sister. "I see men and manners, and learn the ways and means of government." John Russell Young, correspondence and notes com-

piled by Young for his biography, I, 98–99, 107, G. B. Ringwalt to
Young, 18 October 1861, Young to May Young, 2 February 1862,
John Russell Young Papers, Library of Congress; May D. Russell
Young, ed., *Men and Memories: Personal Reminiscences of John Rus-
sell Young*, vol. 1 (New York, 1901), 2–6; Henry Watterson, *'Marse
Henry': An Autobiography*, vol. 2 (New York 1974 [1919]), 235–237.

25. Harry J. Carman and Reinhard H. Luthin, *Lincoln and the Patron-
age* (New York, 1943), 119–129; John Tebbel and Sarah Miles Watts,
*The Press and the Presidency: From George Washington to Ronald
Reagan* (New York, 1985), 179–194.

26. Starr, *Bohemian Brigade*, 154; Pollard, *The Presidents and the Press*,
373.

27. U.S. Congress, Joint Committee on the Conduct of the War, *Report
of the Joint Committee on the Conduct of the War*, vol. 1, S. Rept.
108, 37th Cong., 3rd sess. (Washington, 1863), 283–294; T. Harry
Williams, *Lincoln and the Radicals* (Madison, 1941), 247–248; Elizabeth Joan Doyle, "The Conduct of the War, 1861," in Arthur M.
Schlesinger, Jr., and Roger Bruns, eds., *Congress Investigates: A
Documented History, 1792–1974*, vol. 2 (New York, 1975), 1228–
1229.

28. H. D. Cooke to Uriah Painter, 7 March 1863, Thomas P. Akers to
Painter, 25 March 1865, Cherry, Davis & Co., to Painter, 4 May
1865, Painter Papers, Pennsylvania Historical Society; Katherine H.
Amend, "Henry D. Cooke," *Dictionary of American Biography*, vol.
4 (New York, 1946), 382–383.

29. Logsdon, *Horace White*, 79–80; *Chicago Tribune*, 1 April 1862. For
the significance of corruption as a Republican issue in the 1850s, see
Mark W. Summers, *The Plundering Generation: Corruption and the
Crisis of the Union, 1849–1861* (New York, 1987).

30. Regis de Trobriand, *Four Years with the Army of the Potomac* (Bos-
ton, 1889), 134–135; Francis A. Richardson, "Recollections of a
Washington Newspaper Correspondent," *Records of the Columbia
Historical Society*, vol. 6 (Washington, 1903), 24.

31. Richardson, "Recollections of a Washington Correspondent," 24;
Logsdon, *Horace White*, 97, 104; see also "The Businessman's War,"
in Robert Cruden, *The War That Never Ended: The American Civil
War* (Englewood Cliffs, 1973), 169–192.

32. David Donald, *Charles Sumner and the Rights of Man* (New York,
1970), 146; Herbert Mitgang, ed., *Washington, D.C., in Lincoln's
Times, by Noah Brooks* (Chicago, 1971), 97.

33. Starr, *Bohemian Brigade*, 317; Logsdon, *Horace White*, 96–98;
Wendt, *Chicago Tribune*, 218; Kinsley, *The Chicago Tribune*, 227–
228, 323; *New York Evening Post*, 18 September 1916.

34. John Sherman to Horace Greeley, 5 February 1865, Horace Greeley Papers, Library of Congress.
35. Logsdon, *Horace White*, 196–201.
36. *New York Times*, 22, 29 September 1916; see also *Chicago Tribune*, 19 September 1916.

4. Ben: Perley Poore and the Bohemian Brigade

1. Julian Wilcox, "Journalism as a Profession," *Galaxy* 4 (November 1867): 798–799; *Boston Journal*, 20 November 1863; *Harper's Weekly*, 7 March 1868, 146.
2. Accredited members of the House and Senate press galleries have been listed in the *Congressional Directory* since 1860. Biographical information on the prewar correspondents may be found in Ralph McKenzie, *Washington Correspondents, Past and Present* (New York, 1903). See also Joseph Patrick McKerns, "Benjamin Perley Poore of the Boston *Journal:* His Life and Times as a Washington Correspondent, 1850–1887" (Ph.D. diss., University of Minnesota, 1979); Lawrence A. Gobright, *Recollections of Men and Things at Washington* (Philadelphia, 1869); and David Bartlett's obituary, *Washington Evening Star*, 4 October 1886.
3. Orrin Chalfant Painter, *Genealogy and Biographical Sketches of the Family of Samuel Painter* (Baltimore, 1903), 23; Royal Cortissoz, *The Life of Whitelaw Reid* (New York, 1921); Charles C. Clayton, *Little Mack, Joseph B. McCullagh of the St. Louis Globe-Democrat* (Carbondale, 1969); *Washington Evening Star*, 11 October 1886; *Washington Post*, 4 June 1905; *New York Times*, 4 June 1905.
4. *Washington Post*, 29 May 1887; McKerns, "Benjamin Perley Poore," 1–3.
5. McKerns, "Benjamin Perley Poore," 3–60. "Biographical Sketch of Ben: Perley Poore, Contributed by His Wife," in Ben: Perley Poore, *Perley's Reminiscences of Sixty Years in the National Metropolis*, vol. 2 (Philadelphia, 1887), 533–543; Ben: Perley Poore, "Waifs from Washington," *Gleason's Pictorial Drawing-Room Companion* 4 (1 January 1853): 7.
6. *New York Times*, 29 May 1887; *Washington Evening Star*, 30 May 1887; *Washington Post*, 29 May 1887; *Journalist* 5 (4 June 1887): 1; Mary Jane Windle, *Life in Washington, and Here and There* (Philadelphia, 1859), 270; Elizabeth Stillinger, *The Antiquers* (New York, 1980), 27–34; Poore to W. W. Clapp, 28 August 1868, W. W. Clapp Papers, Houghton Library, Harvard University.
7. Poore, "Waifs from Washington," *Gleason's Pictorial Drawing-Room Companion* 4 (19 March 1853): 190; Lyon Gardiner Tyler, *The Letters and Times of the Tylers* (Williamsburg, 1896), 201; Charles F. Libbie

& Co., *Catalogue of the Valuable and Extensive Collection of Autographs and Historical Manuscripts Collected by the Late Major Ben: Perley Poore of Newburyport, Mass.* (Boston, 1888), in the collection of the Essex Institute, Salem, Mass.; see also Ben: Perley Poore to William W. Clapp, 28 August 1868, Clapp Papers, Houghton Library, Harvard University.

8. Charles Lanman, *The Story of a Book* (Washington, n.d.), 22. Lanman was a writer and artist, director of the Copyright Bureau and odd-jobs patronage man. See Poore, "Waifs from Washington," *Gleason's Pictorial Drawing-Room Companion* 4 (5 February 1853): 87.

9. William F. G. Hanks, "How We Get Our News," *Harper's Monthly* 34 (May 1867): 517.

10. Edward Winslow Martin [James Dabney McCabe], *Behind the Scenes in Washington* (New York, 1873), 65; Poore, *Perley's Reminiscences*, II, 234–235.

11. Edward L. Carter, "The Revolution in Journalism during the Civil War," *Lincoln Herald* 73 (Winter 1971): 235; Louis M. Starr, *Bohemian Brigade: Civil War Newsmen in Action* (Wisconsin, 1987 [1954]), 1954, 4–5, 62–63; Charles Paul Freund, "Newspaper Row," *Washington Journalism Review* 1 (January/February 1978): 62–65.

12. Henry Villard, *Memoirs of Henry Villard, Journalist and Financier, 1835–1900*, vol. 1 (New York, 1969 [1904]), 339; Carter, "Revolution in Journalism," 235; Franc Wilkie, *Pen and Powder* (Boston, 1888), 181–182, 190–191.

13. O. O. Stealey, *Twenty Years in the Press Gallery* (New York, 1906), 1–2. A similar situation existed in the Ottawa Press Gallery; see Paul Rutherford, *A Victorian Authority: The Daily Press in Late Nineteenth-Century Canada* (Toronto, 1982), 82.

14. [Ben: Perley Poore], "Washington News," *Harper's Monthly* 48 (January 1874): 234–235.

15. Poore to Major Charles O. Rogers, 24 November 1868, and Poore to W. W. Clapp, 30 November 1868, W. W. Clapp Papers, Library of Congress.

16. Michael Les Benedict, *A Compromise of Principle: Congressional Republicans and Reconstruction, 1863–1869* (New York, 1974), 109; *Washington Sunday Morning Chronicle*, 4, 18 June 1865. It was Colonel Forney who gave Vice President–elect Johnson the brandy that intoxicated him at his inauguration in 1865. See Clayton, *Little Mack*, 42–43.

17. Benedict, *A Compromise of Principle*, 147–156; W. R. Brock, *An American Crisis: Congress and Reconstruction, 1865–1867* (New York, 1963), 104–106; *Washington Sunday Morning Chronicle*, 11, 18, 25 February 1866; see also Eric Foner, *Reconstruction, America's Second Revolution* (New York, 1988).

18. James M. McPherson, *Ordeal by Fire: The Civil War and Reconstruction* (New York, 1982), 575; D. F. Drinkwater, *Letters to the Connecticut Courant . . .* (Washington, 1867), 20; Joseph Logsdon, *Horace White, Nineteenth-Century Liberal* (Westport, 1971), 120; *New York Tribune,* 17 September 1866.

19. *Washington Evening Star,* 3 December 1867. See also Warden's obituary in *Journalist* 11 (12 April 1890): 6–7.

20. *Washington National Republican,* 26 April 1867; James E. Pollard, *The Presidents and the Press,* 369–376, 413–429. Buffington also signed his name "Buffinton." Clerks around Washington knew that the congressman endorsed every constituent request for patronage and other favors but changed the spelling of his name on the endorsement to indicate whether he wanted the individual rewarded or ignored.

21. Clayton, *Little Mack,* 45–46; Pollard, *The Presidents and the Press,* 369–376, 413–429; Poore, "Washington News," 232–234.

22. Francis Richardson identified Representative Benjamin F. Butler as the "author of interviewing one's self." Francis Richardson, "Recollections of a Washington Newspaper Correspondent," *Records of the Columbia Historical Society,* vol. 6 (Washington, 1903), 32; Poore, "Washington News," 231–234; Poore, *Perley's Reminiscences,* II, 525.

23. "Mark Twain in Washington," *Daily Alta California,* 15 January 1868.

24. "Reminiscences of James M. Dalzell," *Records of the Columbia Historical Society,* vol. 27 (Washington, 1925), 279; William H. Barnes, *History of the Thirty-Ninth Congress of the United States* (New York, 1868), 15–18; Richardson, "Recollections of a Washington Newspaper Correspondent," 24; Henry Van Ness Boynton, "The Press and Public Men," *Century Magazine* 42 (October 1891): 853–862.

25. Elmer Davis, *History of the New York Times, 1851–1921* (New York, 1921), 67–69; *New York Tribune,* 28 November 1867.

26. May D. Russell Young, ed., *Men and Memories: Personal Reminiscences by John Russell Young,* vol. 1 (New York, 1901), 115–117; *New York Tribune,* 24 February 1868.

27. Richardson, "Recollections of a Washington Newspaper Correspondent," 36–37.

28. Poore to W. W. Clapp, 6 March 1868, Clapp Papers, Library of Congress; Richardson, "Recollections of a Washington Newspaper Correspondent," 37.

29. Albert Bigelow Paine, ed., *Mark Twain's Letters,* vol. 1 (New York, 1917), 151; *Chicago Republican,* 19 February 1868.

30. "Reminiscences of James M. Dalzell," 95.

31. Emily Edson Briggs, *The Olivia Letters* (New York, 1906), 60–61; Emily E. Briggs to Benjamin Wade, 7 April 1868, Benjamin Wade Papers, Library of Congress.

32. Logsdon, *Horace White*, 149-151; George Alfred Townsend, *Washington, Outside and Inside* (Hartford, 1873), 506-508, 674.

33. Poore to W. W. Clapp, 31 January, 24 April, 7, 27 May 1868, Clapp Papers, Library of Congress; Henry Boynton to Whitelaw Reid, 23 October 1869, Whitelaw Reid Papers, Library of Congress.

34. Clayton, *Little Mack*, 62; Richardson, "Recollections of a Washington Newspaper Correspondent," 38; Charles A. Dana to Uriah Painter, 1 February, 31 March, 5, 23 June 1868, Uriah Painter Papers, Pennsylvania Historical Society.

35. Robert W. Winston, *Andrew Johnson, Plebeian and Patriot* (New York, 1928), 440-441; *New York Tribune*, 10 March 1868.

36. *New York Tribune*, 2 March 1868; Richardson, "Recollections of a Washington Newspaper Correspondent," 38.

37. Proceedings of the dinner were published in the *Washington Evening Star*, 13 January 1868.

38. Poore to W. W. Clapp, 6 March 1868, Clapp Papers, Library of Congress; Zebulon L. White to Reid, 26 November 1870, 15 December 1875, Reid Papers, Library of Congress.

39. H. V. Boynton to Whitelaw Reid, 9 February 1869, Sidney Andrews to Whitelaw Reid, 11 November 1869, Reid Papers, Library of Congress; Poore to Charles O. Rogers, 17 November 1868, and Poore to W. W. Clapp, 30 November 1868, Clapp Papers, Library of Congress.

40. Zebulon White's private correspondence with the editor of the *New York Tribune* makes it clear that Ramsdell did the bidding for the treaty. See Z. L. White to Whitelaw Reid, 11 May 1871, Reid Papers, Library of Congress.

41. *Congressional Globe*, 42nd Cong., special sess., 874, 908; Z. L. White to Whitelaw Reid, 11 May 1871, Reid Papers, Library of Congress; F. B. Marbut, *News from the Capital: The Story of Washington Reporting* (Carbondale, 1971), 141-145.

42. J. R. G. H. [John Rose Greene Hassard] to Whitelaw Reid, 22 May 1871, Reid Papers, Library of Congress; U.S. Senate, Select Committee, *Publication of the Treaty of Washington*, 42nd Cong., special sess., S. Rept. 5 (Washington, 1871), 15.

43. Poore to W. W. Clapp, 23 February 1871, Clapp Papers, Houghton Library; Poore to Major Charles O. Rogers, 17 November 1868, W. W. Clapp Papers, Library of Congress.

44. Poore to W. W. Clapp, 13, 17 April 1883, Clapp to Poore, 15 April 1833, E. B. Wight to Clapp, 15 April 1883, Clapp Papers, Library of Congress; Poore to [Ainsworth Rand] Spofford, 23 January 1886, Ben: Perley Poore Papers, Essex Institute, Salem, Mass.; *Washington Evening Star*, 18, 30 May 1887; "Biographical Sketch of Ben: Perley Poore, Contributed by His Wife," 542-543.

5. Uriah Hunt Painter, Lobbyist

1. Ben: Perley Poore, *Perley's Reminiscences of Sixty Years in the National Metropolis*, vol. 2 (Philadelphia, 1887), 513–515; George Alfred Townsend, *Washington, Outside and Inside* (Hartford, 1873), 738; Paul S. Holbo, *Tarnished Expansion: The Alaska Scandal, the Press, and Congress, 1867–1871* (Knoxville, 1983), 30; see also Samuel P. Huntington, "Modernization and Corruption," in Arnold J. Heidenheimer, ed., *Political Corruption: Readings in Comparative Analysis* (New Brunswick, 1978), 492–500.

2. David Donald, *Charles Sumner and the Rights of Man* (New York, 1970), 304–310; *Philadelphia Inquirer*, 1–10 April 1867; see also Ronald J. Jensen, *The Alaska Purchase and Russian-American Relations* (Seattle, 1975).

3. U.S. Congress, House of Representatives, Committee on Public Expenditures, *Alaska Investigation*, H. Rept. 25, 40th Cong., 3rd sess. (Washington, 1869), 23, 32–35, 38–41; Holbo, *Tarnished Expansion*, 51. Walker, a former U.S. Senator and Treasury secretary, and Stanton, a former U.S. Representative, were active lobbyists in Washington and proprietors of a Democratic pro-Union paper, the *Continental Monthly*, from 1862 to 1864.

4. *Alaska Investigation*, 25–30.

5. Ibid., 11–16. The Russian minister, Baron Edouard de Stoeckl, also gave $1,000 to M. M. Noah for favorable editorials in the *San Francisco Alta California*. Paul S. Holbo, in his careful study of the Alaska scandal, concluded that the Russian minister most likely pocketed the largest share of any funds provided for lobbying on behalf of the treaty. Holbo, *Tarnished Expansion*, 34, 46, 49–50, 71–73.

6. *Alaska Investigation*, 16–19, 22–25, 35–38.

7. Ibid., 38–41; *New York Times*, 6 February 1869.

8. Townsend, *Washington, Outside and Inside*, 515–520.

9. *New York Tribune*, 6 February 1869; Holbo, *Tarnished Expansion*, 75–76.

10. *New York Tribune*, 6 February 1869. The *Chester Republican*, 12 February 1869, had this to say of the congressman's outburst: "Mr. Broomall but repeats his opinion of the press, as expressed over and over again, in years past. He always affected to despise newspapers and those connected with them, and yet but few public men in our country have received more newspaper support. With the declaration before us that 'he would not believe any Washington correspondent under oath,' we cannot reconcile his well known attachment to Mr. Uriah H. Painter, the Washington correspondent of the Philadelphia *Inquirer* and other newspapers, who is just now in some difficulty . . . Can it be that Mr. B. judges *other* newspaper correspondents by his intimate friend, Mr. Painter?"

11. Henry V. N. Boynton to Whitelaw Reid, 9 February 1869, Whitelaw Reid Papers, Library of Congress.

12. *Alaska Investigation*, 1–5; Paul Holbo argues that the Alaska scandal left Americans skeptical of expansionists' motives and helped retard the acquisition of overseas territory for the next thirty years. See *Tarnished Expansion*, xvi-xix.

13. Orrin Chalfant Painter, *Genealogy and Biographical Sketches of the Family of Samuel Painter* (Baltimore, 1903), 43–45; *West Chester Daily Local News*, 29 July 1884, clipping in Painter Papers, Historical Society of Pennsylvania.

14. *Philadelphia Evening Bulletin*, 23 October 1900; "History of the Philadelphia Inquirer," supplement, *Philadelphia Inquirer*, 16 September 1962.

15. Newspaper clippings on Painter, Chester County Historical Society; *Philadelphia Inquirer*, 23 July 1861; Henry Villard, *Memoirs of Henry Villard, Journalist and Financier, 1835–1900*, vol. 1 (Boston, 1904), 194–197. See also Edmund Stedman's recollections of escaping the battlefield with Painter, in Laura Stedman and George M. Gould, *Life and Letters of Edmund Clarence Stedman* (New York, 1910), 233–234.

16. *Philadelphia Inquirer*, 22, 23 July 1861; E. P. Oberholtzer, *Jay Cooke, Financier of the Civil War*, vol. 1 (Philadelphia, 1907), 146–147.

17. Painter to W. W. Harding, 24 February 1866, Harding to Painter, 2 January 1867, Painter Papers, Historical Society of Pennsylvania.

18. Jay Cooke to Painter, 17 December 1867, Henry D. Cooke to Painter, 19 February 1867, W. W. Harding to Painter, 21 February, 9 March 1867, Painter Papers.

19. Emily Edson Briggs, *The Olivia Letters* (New York, 1906), 29; James Parton, "Falsehood in the Daily Press," *Harper's Monthly* 49 (July 1874): 279.

20. James Parton, "Log-Rolling at Washington," *Atlantic Monthly* 145 (July 1869): 361, 372–378; Parton, "The Small Sins of Congress," *Atlantic Monthly* 145 (November 1869): 524; Briggs, *The Olivia Letters*, 91–94.

21. Townsend, *Washington, Outside and Inside*, 257–260, 285–287.

22. See Margaret Susan Thompson, *The "Spider Web": Congress and Lobbying in the Age of Grant* (Ithaca, 1985); and David Rothman, *Politics and Power: The United States Senate, 1869–1901* (Cambridge, 1966), 191–220.

23. James Fisk, Jr., to Painter, 25 January 1870, Tom Scott to Painter, 14 May 1866, 9 March 1867, 23 November 1867, 2, 5 April 1869, Painter Papers, Historical Society of Pennsylvania.

24. *New York Commercial,* 25 October 1900; newspaper clippings, 17 July 1866, in files of Chester County Historical Society; Ben Wade to Painter, 26 April 1869, Painter Papers.
25. James Wilson to Painter, 9 April 1872, Painter Papers.
26. F. C. Grey to Benjamin Butler, 28 March 1870, Benjamin Butler Papers, Library of Congress. Grey identified Painter's lobbying partners as W. B. Shaw, Joseph Macfarland, L. L. Crounse, Sam Wilkeson, and E. P. Brooks. *Philadelphia Evening Journal,* 27 April 1863; *Philadelphia Evening Bulletin,* 23 October 1900; *New York World,* 5 April 1898.
27. Clipping, 22 February 1893, Chester County Historical Society; Painter, *Genealogy,* 45.
28. Painter, *Genealogy,* 43–44; clipping, 26 October 1873, Chester County Historical Society.
29. *Congressional Globe,* 41st Cong., 1st sess., 538; see also W. Allan Wilbur, "The Credit Mobilier Scandal, 1873," in Arthur M. Schlesinger, Jr., and Roger Bruns, eds., *Congress Investigates: A Documented History, 1792–1974,* vol. 3 (New York, 1975), 1849–1863; for an alternative view see Robert William Fogel, *The Union Pacific Railroad: A Case of Premature Enterprise* (Baltimore, 1960), 74–90.
30. U.S. Congress, House Select Committee, *Credit Mobilier Investigation,* H. Rept. 77, 42nd Cong., 3rd sess. (Washington, 1873), 31–32.
31. Hans L. Trefousse, *Carl Schurz: A Biography* (Knoxville, 1982), 197–215.
32. *New York Sun,* 4, 10 September 1872; Willard H. Smith, *Schuyler Colfax: The Changing Fortunes of a Political Idol* (Indianapolis, 1952), 369–374; *New York Tribune,* 8 January 1873.
33. Townsend, *Washington, Outside and Inside,* 400–421.
34. *Philadelphia Inquirer,* 30 September, 7 October 1872.
35. David Seville Muzzey, *James G. Blaine, A Political Idol of Other Days* (Port Washington, 1963 [1934]), 64–69.
36. *New York Times,* 6–8, 10 January 1873; *New York Tribune,* 8 January 1873.
37. *Credit Mobilier Investigation,* 319–320.
38. U.S. Congress, Senate Select Committee, *Credit Mobilier,* S. Rept. 519, 43rd Cong., 3rd sess. (Washington, 1873), v, 32–33, 39.
39. Townsend, *Washington, Outside and Inside,* 423; *New York Tribune,* 19 February 1873.
40. O. J. Hollister, *Life of Schuyler Colfax* (New York, 1886), 418–419; see also Smith, *Schuyler Colfax,* 374–416.
41. *New York Tribune,* 25 February, 4, 6 March 1873; *Philadelphia Inquirer,* 5 March 1873.

42. Henry V. N. Boynton, "The Press and Public Men," *Century Magazine* 42 (October 1891): 855.

43. Frank G. Carpenter, *Carp's Washington* (New York, 1960), 269.

44. See Leonard Alexander Swann, Jr., *John Roach, Maritime Engineer: The Years as a Naval Contractor, 1862–1886* (Annapolis, 1965), and Maury Klein, *The Life and Legend of Jay Gould* (Baltimore, 1986), for the background of the Pacific Mail fight and its chief protagonists.

45. John Roach to Painter, 24 February, 19 April, 20, 22, 23 May 1874, 28 January, 6 February 1875, Albert B. Chandler to Painter, 16 August 1876, Painter to Jay Gould, 8 April 1877, Painter Papers, Historical Society of Pennsylvania.

46. U.S. Congress, House Committee on Ways and Means, *China Mail Service,* H. Rept. 268, 43rd Cong., 2nd sess. (Washington, 1875), v, xviii, xix, 370–375; *Congressional Record,* 43rd Cong., 2nd sess, 2282; F. B. Marbut, *News from the Capital: The Story of Washington Reporting* (Carbondale, 1971), 147.

47. U.S. Congress, Joint Select Committee Appointed to Inquire into the Affairs of the Government of the District of Columbia, *Report,* Rept. 453, part 3, 43rd Cong., 1st sess. (Washington, 1874), 1232–1233, 1260–1261; see also *Journalist* 11 (12 April 1890): 6–7; and William M. Maury, *Alexander "Boss" Shepherd and the Board of Public Works* (Washington, 1975).

48. *New York World,* undated clipping, Chester County Historical Society; Marbut, *News From the Capital,* 154–156.

49. *Journalist* 1 (29 March 1884): 10; 1 (15 November 1884), 7.

50. *New York World,* undated clipping, Chester County Historical Society; Robert Conot, *A Streak of Luck* (New York, 1979), 56, 84, 89, 109–110, 265.

51. Unidentified newspaper clipping, 13 November 1926, Chester Historical Society; *New York World,* 5 April 1898; *Washington Post,* 21 October 1900; Painter to Gardner G. Hubbard, 30 December 1872, Painter Papers, Historical Society of Pennsylvania.

52. Eileen Taddonio Groce, "Lafayette Square Opera House: End of Act I in Washington, D.C., Theatre History," paper delivered at the Conference on Washington, D.C., Historical Studies, 5 February 1982; Ralph McKenzie, *Washington Correspondents, Past and Present* (New York, 1903), 23. See obituaries in *Washington Evening Star,* 20 October 1900; *Washington Post,* 21 October 1900; *Philadelphia Press,* 22 October 1900.

6. General Boynton Makes Peace

1. *New York Times,* 14 August 1883; Ralph McKenzie, *Washington Correspondents, Past and Present* (New York, 1903), 18; Theron C.

Crawford, "The Special Correspondents at Washington," *Cosmopolitan* 12 (January 1892): 357; *Washington Post,* 4 June 1905.

2. *Cincinnati Commercial-Gazette,* 28 April 1883; George Henry Haynes, "Charles Brandon Boynton," *Dictionary of American Biography,* vol. 1 (New York, 1946), 536–537.

3. *Washington Post,* 4 June 1905; *Washington Evening Star,* 4 October 1890, 4 June 1905.

4. Crawford, "The Special Correspondents at Washington," 357; *Cincinnati Commercial-Gazette,* 2 March 1883; *Congressional Globe,* 40th Cong,, 3rd sess., 408 (article reprinted from *New York Tribune*).

5. *Washington Post,* 4 June 1905; O. O. Stealey, *Twenty Years in the Press Gallery* (New York, 1906), 2; Richard V. Oulahan, book draft, "Presidents and Publicity," Herbert Hoover Library, West Branch, Iowa.

6. Stealey, *Twenty Years in the Press Gallery,* 2. The functioning of Boynton's office on Newspaper Row emerges in testimony given in U.S. Congress, House of Representatives, Select Committee, *Charges against H. V. Boynton,* H. Rept. 1112, 48th Cong., 1st sess. (Washington, 1884).

7. Henry V. N. Boynton, "The Press and Public Men," *Century Magazine* 42 (October 1891): 853, 856–858.

8. Alan G. Bogue, *The Earnest Men: Republicans of the Civil War Senate* (Ithaca, 1981), 42; Earle Dudley Ross, "James Harlan," *Dictionary of American Biography,* vol. 7 (New York, 1946), 268–269.

9. Jonathan Brigham, *James Harlan* (Iowa City, 1913), 205–209; *Congressional Globe,* 40th Cong., 3rd sess., 408–409.

10. Henry V. Boynton to Whitelaw Reid, 24 January 1869, Whitelaw Reid Papers, Library of Congress; *Congressional Globe,* 40th Cong., 3rd sess., 408–411.

11. Brigham, *James Harlan,* 242–251, 260–269, 275–282.

12. James Bryce, *The American Commonwealth,* vol. 2 (London, 1888), 233–235.

13. Boynton to Whitelaw Reid, 9 February 1869, Reid Papers; Boynton, "The Press and Public Men," 855, 862.

14. *Washington Evening Star,* 7 December 1889; F. B. Marbut, *News from the Capital: The Story of Washington Reporting* (Carbondale, 1971), 154–156.

15. *Washington Evening Star,* 7 December 1869; Marbut, *News from the Capital,* 154–156.

16. Marbut, *News from the Capital,* 162–164; I have drawn material on women and black press gallery members from various issues of the *Congressional Directory;* see also Chapter 8.

17. *Charges against H. V. Boynton,* 131–132, 152, 182; see also Ada C.

McCown, *The Congressional Conference Committee* (New York, 1967 [1927]), 12, concerning Democratic sources inside the conference committee.

18. J. Warren Keifer, *Slavery and Four Years of War: A Political History of Slavery in the United States*, vol. 2 (New York, 1900), 251–255, 267–268, 272–273; Arthur C. Cole, "J. Warren Keifer," *Dictionary of American Biography*, supp. 1 (New York, 1946), 460–461.

19. *Charges against H. V. Boynton*, 17, 155; *Cincinnati Commercial-Gazette*, 2–4 March 1883.

20. *Washington Evening Star*, 5 March 1883; *Congressional Globe*, 40th Cong., 3rd sess., 3744, 3747; *Charges against H. V. Boynton*, 215–216; *Cincinnati Commercial-Gazette*, 4 March 1883.

21. *Charges against H. V. Boynton*, 183–186.

22. *Washington Evening Star*, 7 December 1889.

23. *Charges against H. V. Boynton*, 215–219; Keifer, *Slavery and Four Years of War*, 273.

24. *Charges against H. V. Boynton*, 17, 19–21. On McGarrahan's claim, see also [Rollin H. Kirk], *Many Secrets Revealed; or, Ten Years behind the Scenes in Washington City* (Washington, 1885), 18–19.

25. *Charges against H. V. Boynton*, iv, 19.

26. Ibid., 97–124, 266–269.

27. *Washington Evening Star*, 2 April 1884; *Cincinnati Commercial-Gazette*, 3 April 1884.

28. Boynton, "The Press and Public Men," 855.

29. O. O. Stealey, *The Birth of the Gridiron Club* (Washington, 1927), copy in the Gridiron Club Papers, Library of Congress. See also James Free, *The First One Hundred Years: A Casual Chronicle of the Gridiron Club* (Washington, 1985).

30. *The Gridiron Club Annals, 1885–1905, Twentieth Anniversary Dinner, January 28, 1905* (Washington, 1905), 7–10; Arthur Wallace Dunn, *Gridiron Nights* (New York, 1915), 2–3; Stealey, *Birth of the Gridiron Club*; *Washington Evening Star*, 14 January 1889.

31. Dunn, *Gridiron Nights*, 6; "The Gridiron Club Records," 8 February 1896, Gridiron Club Papers; GATH's offending article appeared in the *New York Sun*, 2 February 1896.

32. Menus, entertainment, and guest lists are available in the scrapbooks of the Gridiron Club Papers, Library of Congress; Boynton, "The Press and Public Men," 855; *Journalist* 11 (3 May 1890): 4.

33. *Philadelphia Press*, 19 November 1886; *Journalist* 1 (15 November 1884): 7.

34. Excerpts from a family history by Charles Everett Kern (Boynton's assistant at the Washington bureau of the *Commercial-Gazette*), 56–58, in the possession of Charles E. Kern II, Alexandria, Virginia;

Washington Post, 4 June 1905. See also Carl J. Becker, "National News Spinners," *Brooklyn Times*, 22 January 1887.

7. James G. Blaine, Journalist and Politician

1. John James Ingalls, *The Writings of John James Ingalls: Essays, Addresses, and Orations* (Kansas City, 1902), 415–442.
2. *Washington Evening Star*, 2 February 1889.
3. "Opinion-Molding," *Nation* 9 (12 August 1869): 126–127; *Journalist* 1 (19 April 1884): 9; "Journalists in Politics," *Journalist* 5 (3 September 1887): 12.
4. "Journalists in Congress," *American* 1 (23 October 1880): 25–27.
5. Henry J. Davis, *Half a Century with the Providence Journal* (Providence, 1904), 16–17, 20, 125–126, 231–235; John Baird McNulty, *Older Than the Nation: The Story of the Hartford Courant* (Stonington, Conn., 1964), 88–143; Edward P. Mitchell, *Memoirs of an Editor: Fifty Years of American Journalism* (New York, 1924), 373–374; *Washington Evening Star*, 22 December 1888.
6. William E. Connelley, *The Life of Preston B. Plumb* (Chicago, 1913), 381–385.
7. Chauncey Depew, *My Memories of Eighty Years* (New York, 1924), 141; Noah Brooks, *Statesmen: Men of Achievement* (New York, 1893), 310–311. Warren Sussman noted the dichotomy between the nineteenth-century concern over character and the twentieth-century obsession with personality in *Culture as History: The Transformation of American Society in the Twentieth Century* (New York, 1894), 273–274.
8. William C. Hudson, *Random Recollections of an Old Political Reporter* (New York, 1893), 128; Henry L. Stoddard, *As I Knew Them: Presidents and Politics from Grant to Coolidge* (New York, 1927), 94; Ben: Perley Poore, *Perley's Reminiscences of Sixty Years in the National Metropolis*, vol. 2 (Philadelphia, 1887), 211; Poore to W. W. Clapp, 15 January 1876, William W. Clapp Papers, Library of Congress.
9. David Saville Muzzey, *James G. Blaine: A Political Idol of Other Days* (New York, 1934), 12–41; Gail Hamilton [Mary Abigail Dodge], *Biography of James G. Blaine* (Norwich, Conn., 1895), 99–103; Edward Stanwood *James Gillespie Blaine* (Boston, 1905), 35, 42–43; Brooks, *Statesmen*, 284; H. J. Ramsdell and Ben: Perley Poore, *Life and Times of James G. Blaine and Gen. John A. Logan* (Philadelphia, 1884), 37–39; Theron Clark Crawford, *James G. Blaine: A Study of His Life and Career from the Standpoint of a Personal Witness of the Principal Events in His History* (Philadelphia, 1893), 61.
10. *Boston Journal*, 27 March 1876; Hamilton, *James G. Blaine*, 107–

108; James G. Blaine, *Twenty Years of Congress: From Lincoln to Garfield,* vol. 2 (Norwich, Conn., 1886), 508.

11. *Boston Journal,* 27 March 1876; Hamilton, *James G. Blaine,* 121-124.

12. Depew, *My Memories of Eighty Years,* 121; Brooks, *Statesmen,* 311; Ingalls, *Writings,* 428. See also Hans Trefouse, *Carl Schurz: A Biography* (Knoxville, 1982), 159-160.

13. David S. Barry, *Forty Years in Washington* (New York, 1924), 69.

14. *Congressional Globe,* 39th Cong., 1st sess., 2298-2299.

15. David M. Jordan, *Roscoe Conkling of New York: Voice in the Senate* (Ithaca, 1971), 61-84, 420-421; Hamilton, *James G. Blaine,* 157-181.

16. David S. Barry, "News-Gathering at the Capital," *Chautauqua* 22 (December 1897): 284; "Blaine as a Newspaper Man," *Journalist* 19 (17 March 1894): 2-3.

17. Henry Adams, *Democracy* (New York, 1961 [1880]), 83; Brooks, *Statesmen,* 294.

18. "James G. Blaine at Hot Springs, Ark.," *Journalist* 18 (20 January 1894): 3; Barry, "News-Gathering at the Capital," 284.

19. James G. Smart, "Information Control, Thought Control: Whitelaw Reid and the Nation's News Services," *Public Historian* 3 (Spring 1981): 25; Blaine to Reid, 10 May 1870, 28 November 1871, 6 January 1876, 20 July 1876, 21 July 1879, Whitelaw Reid Papers, Library of Congress. Blaine worked so diligently for Gould's interests in Congress that his opponents tagged him "Jay Gould's errand boy." See Maury Klein, *The Life and Legend of Jay Gould* (Baltimore, 1986), 135, 174.

20. Blaine to W. W. Clapp, 25 November 1875, W. W. Clapp Papers, Houghton Library, Harvard University; Poore to Clapp, 15 January 1876, Clapp Papers, Library of Congress.

21. Blaine, *Twenty Years of Congress,* 553-554; *Congressional Record,* 44th Cong., 1st sess., 323-330; *Boston Journal,* 17, 18 January 1876; *New York Tribune,* 11 January 1876.

22. *New York Times,* 14 January 1876; Ingalls, *Writings,* 419; Charles E. Smith to Blaine, 18 January 1876, James Watson Webb to Blaine, 1876, Blaine Papers, Library of Congress; Hamilton, *James G. Blaine,* 380-381.

23. E. B. Wight to Clapp, 28, 29 February 1876, Clapp Papers, Library of Congress. On Blaine's finances, see James Talcott Kitson, "The Congressional Career of James G. Blaine," (Ph.D. diss., Case Western Reserve, 1971), 229-250.

24. *New York Times,* 14, 16 April, 2 May 1876; Muzzey, *James G. Blaine,* 302-304; *Congressional Record,* 44th Cong., 1st sess., 2724-2725;

Washington Evening Star, 15, 27 April 1876; *Cincinnati Gazette*, 25, 27 April 1876; *Boston Journal*, 2 June 1876. See also Keith Ian Polakoff, *The Politics of Inertia: The Election of 1876 and the End of Reconstruction* (Baton Rouge, 1976), 16–69; and Margaret Leach and Harry J. Brown, *The Garfield Orbit: The Life of President James A. Garfield* (New York, 1978), 281–282.

25. *New York Times*, 28, 29 May, 2, 6 June 1876; *Boston Journal*, 2 June 1876; *New York Tribune*, 6 June 1876; *Cincinnati Gazette*, 7 June 1876; *Congressional Record*, 44th Cong., 1st sess., 3602–3617.

26. *New York Tribune*, 6 June 1876; *Philadelphia Inquirer*, 6 June 1876; Crawford, *James G. Blaine*, 18–24.

27. Blaine quoted in H. Wayne Morgan, *From Hayes to McKinley: National Party Politics, 1877–1896* (Syracuse, 1969), 69; Harriet S. Blaine Beale, ed., *Letters of Mrs. James G. Blaine*, vol. 2 (New York, 1908), 269; James Bryce, *The American Commonwealth*, vol. 2 (London, 1888), 204, 234.

28. Hamilton, *James G. Blaine*, 242; Blaine to Reid, 10 December 1875, Reid Papers, Library of Congress; James Watson Webb to Blaine, 1876, Blaine Papers, Library of Congress. On the independence of the press, see Michael E. McGerr, *The Decline of Popular Politics: The American North, 1865–1928* (New York, 1986), 107–137; and Michael Schudson, *Discovering the News: A Social History of American Newspapers* (New York, 1978), 61–87.

29. George F. Hoar, *Autobiography of Seventy Years*, vol. 2 (New York, 1903), 269–270.

30. Richard E. Welch, Jr., *The Presidencies of Grover Cleveland* (Lawrence, Kans., 1988), 18, 104, 121, 222; Allan Nevins, *Grover Cleveland: A Study in Courage* (New York, 1932), 307–310; see also Horace Samuel Merrill, *Bourbon Leader: Grover Cleveland and the Democratic Party* (Boston, 1957); Richard V. Oulahan, "Presidents and Publicity," book draft, Oulahan Papers, Herbert Hoover Library, West Branch, Iowa; W. W. Price, "How the Work of Gathering White House News Has Changed," *Washington Evening Star*, 16 December 1902.

31. Barry, *Forty Years in Washington*, 166–217; Nevins, *Grover Cleveland*, 529–533.

32. C. C. Buel, "Our Fellow Citizen at the White House," *Century Magazine* 53 (March 1897): 646–647, 662–663.

33. Oulahan, "Presidents and Publicity." See George Juergens, *News from the White House: The Presidential-Press Relationship in the Progressive Era* (Chicago, 1981), 1–40; and Robert C. Hilderbrand, *Power and the People: Executive Management of Public Opinion in Foreign Affairs, 1897–1921* (Chapel Hill, 1981), 8–71.

8. Emily Briggs and the Women Correspondents

1. Charles Murray, *Sub Rosa* (New York, 1880), 62.
2. Accredited women journalists in 1879 included: Mrs. Emily Briggs, Mrs. S. F. Crocker, Mary Fields *(Chicago Journal)*, Miss Emma James *(Sacramento Record Union)*, Mrs. A. D. Johnston *(Rochester Democrat)*, Mrs. M. D. Lincoln *(Cleveland Plain Dealer)*, Miss M. E. Mann, Miss J. V. McCann *(Norristown Daily Herald)*, Lura McNall *(Lockport Journal)*, Mrs. J. A. Roberts *(Washington Gazette)*, Mary Gay Robinson *(New York Witness)*, Mrs. Mary Shannon *(New Orleans Picayune)*, Miss Austine Snead *(Boston Herald)*, Mrs. F. C. Snead *(Louisville Courier-Journal)*, Mrs. Sarah J. A. Spencer *(New North West)*, Emily R. Steineslet *(St. Louis Republican)*, Mrs. Nellie S. Stowell *(Washington Post)*, Mrs. G. W. Thomson *(Syracuse Journal)*, Fannie B. Ward *(Washington Chronicle)*, and Miss Sallie Woodbury *(National Republican)*.
3. Henry Adams, *Democracy: An American Novel* (New York, 1961 [1880]), 17, 22; Henry Loomis Nelson, "Washington Women," *Harper's Weekly* 34 (25 October 1890): 834; see also Eleanor Flexner, *Century of Struggle: The Woman's Rights Movement in the United States* (Cambridge, 1975).
4. *Washington Evening Star,* 19 May 1888; Isabel C. Barrows, "Chopped Straw; or, The Memories of Threescore Years," manuscript memoir, New York Public Library.
5. *Washington Evening Star,* 30 August 1890.
6. Mark Twain and Charles Dudley Warner, *The Gilded Age* (Seattle, 1968 [1873]); *Washington Evening Star,* 31 January 1891; see also Margaret Susan Thompson, *The "Spider Web": Congress and Lobbying in the Age of Grant* (Ithaca, 1985).
7. Maurine Beasley, "The Curious Career of Anne Royall," *Journalism History* 3/4 (Winter 1976–77): 98–102; Beasley, *The First Women Washington Correspondents* (Washington, 1976), 3–5; Diary of Isaac Bassett, Senate Commission on Art, Washington, D.C. See also Sarah H. Porter, *The Life and Times of Anne Royall* (Cedar Rapids, 1909); George Stuyvesant Jackson, *Uncommon Scold* (Boston, 1937); Bessie Rowland Jones, *Anne Royall's U.S.A.* (New Brunswick, 1972); and Alice S. Maxwell and Marion B. Dunlevy, *Virago! The Story of Anne Newport Royall (1769–1854)* (Jefferson, N.C., 1985).
8. Beasley, *First Women Washington Correspondents,* 4.
9. Ibid., 6–9; Ishbel Ross, *Ladies of the Press: The Story of Women in Journalism by an Insider* (New York, 1936), 323–327; see also Jane Grey Swisshelm, *Half a Century* (Chicago, 1880).
10. *Cincinnati Gazette,* 15 April 1876; Beasley, *First Women Washington Correspondents,* 15–19; Ross, *Ladies of the Press,* 327–331; Grace

Greenwood, *Greenwood Leaves* (Boston, 1850); see also Stanley Harrold, *Gamaliel Bailey and Antislavery Union* (Kent, 1986). The London fishmongers at Billingsgate won fame for their coarse and abusive language.

11. Emily Edson Briggs, *The Olivia Letters: Being Some History of Washington City for Forty Years as Told by the Letters of a Newspaper Correspondent* (New York, 1906), 87. See also Gail Hamilton, *Gail Hamilton's Life in Letters* (Boston, 1901).

12. Ross, *Ladies of the Press*, 332; Beasley, "Mary Clemmer Ames: A Victorian Woman Journalist," *Hayes Historical Journal* 2 (Spring 1978): 57–63; Beasley, *First Women Washington Correspondents*, 10–12; Edmund Hudson, *An American Woman's Life and Work: A Memorial of Mary Clemmer* (Boston, 1886); Briggs, *The Olivia Letters*, 59–61.

13. J. Cutler Andrews, "Mary E. Clemmer Ames," in Barbara Sicherman and Carol Hurd Green, eds., *Notable American Women* (Cambridge, 1978), 40–42; Beasley, *First Women Washington Correspondents*, 11.

14. Fannie Aymer Mathews, "Men, Women, and Pens," *Journalist* 19 (31 March 1894): 2–3; see also Joan Jacobs Brumberg and Nancy Tomes, "Woman in the Professions: A Research Agenda for American Historians," *Reviews in American History* 10 (June 1982): 275–296.

15. Edith Sessions Tupper, "Women in Journalism," *Journalist* 19 (28 April 1894): 6–7.

16. J. L. H., "A Woman's Experience of Newspaper Work," *Harper's Weekly* 34 (25 January 1890): 74–75; Foster Coates, "Women's Chances as Journalists," *Ladies' Home Journal* 7 (September 1890): 13.

17. J. L. H., "A Woman's Experience," 13.

18. Henry James, *Novels, 1881–1886* (New York, 1986), 274–279; Frances Hodgson Burnett, *Through One Administration* (New York, 1969 [1883]), 38–39.

19. Beasley, *First Women Washington Correspondents*, 12–14; Ishbel Ross, "Emily Pomona Edson Briggs," in Barbara Sicherman and Carol Hurd Green, eds., *Notable American Women* (Cambridge, 1978), 242; *Washington Post*, 10 July 1904.

20. *Washington Post*, 10 July 1904.

21. Briggs, *The Olivia Letters*, 10–13.

22. Ibid., 30–36, 66–68.

23. Ibid., 91–94. Widely contrasting views on the lobbying tactics of Gould, Huntington, and Dillon can be found in John Tipple, "Big Businessmen and a New Economy," in H. Wayne Morgan, ed., *The Gilded Age* (Syracuse, 1970), 13–30; Matthew Josephson, *The Robber Barons: The Great American Capitalists, 1861–1901* (New York, 1934); and Maury Klein, *The Life and Legend of Jay Gould* (Baltimore, 1986), 160–175.

24. Briggs, *The Olivia Letters*, 105–111.
25. Ibid., 130–135.
26. Ibid., 196–197.
27. [Rollin H. Kirk], *Many Secrets Revealed; or, Ten Years behind the Scenes in Washington City* (Washington, 1885).
28. *Chicago Republican*, 8 February 1868.
29. Kathryn Allamong Jacob, "High Society in Washington during the Gilded Age, 1865–1900: 'Three Distinct Aristocracies,'" (Ph.D. diss., Johns Hopkins University, 1986), 58–69; Henry Adams, *The Education of Henry Adams* (Boston, 1917), 256–257.
30. Jacob, "High Society in Washington," 69–91; Florence Howe Hall, *Social Usages at Washington* (New York, 1909), v, 127.
31. Jacob, "High Society in Washington," 92–156; F. B. Marbut, *News from the Capital: The Story of Washington Reporting* (Carbondale, 1971), 153–158, 250–251.
32. *Washington Post*, 10 July 1904. In retirement, Briggs continued to follow the political scene. In 1894 she put up bail money to release the leaders of Coxey's Army—those involved in an unemployment march on Washington. See Carlos A. Schwantes, *Coxey's Army: An American Odyssey* (Lincoln, 1985), 181.
33. Laura Jones's letter to the editor, quoted in M. S. Burke, "Women and the Reporters' Gallery," *Journalist* 11 (24 May 1890): 13.
34. Burke, "Women and the Reporters' Gallery," 13.
35. F. A. G. Handy to M. S. Burke, quoted in Burke, "Women and the Reporters' Gallery," 13. Burke later published *The Son of Hercules; or, The Truth about the Financial Legislation of the Republican Party* (Washington, 1894), a defense of Republican policies against the criticisms of another woman writer. Missing Margaret Burke, Ishbel Ross notes that Isabel Worrell Ball was accredited to the press galleries in 1891, *Ladies of the Press*, 331.
36. O. O. Stealey, *The Birth of the Gridiron Club* (Washington, 1927); Gridiron Scrapbooks, Gridiron Club Papers, Library of Congress. The National Women's Press Association was an outgrowth of the Ladies' Press Club; Beasley, *First Women Washington Correspondents*, 14.
37. Julian Ralph, "Our National Capital," *Harper's New Monthly Magazine* 539 (April 1895).

9. *The Senate Fires James Rankin Young*

1. *Congressional Record*, 49th Cong., 1st sess., 3427.
2. David J. Rothman, *Power and Politics: The United States Senate, 1869–1901* (Cambridge, 1966), 43–72; Hay quoted in George H. Haynes, *The Senate of the United States*, vol. 2 (New York, 1938),

570; see also Woodrow Wilson, *Congressional Government: A Study in American Politics* (New York, 1967 [1885]).

3. *Washington Evening Star,* 7 December 1889; see also R. Earl Mc-Clendon, "Violations of Secrecy *In Re* Senate Executive Sessions, 1789–1929," *American Historical Review* 51 (October 1945): 35–54.

4. Edmund Alton, *Among the Law-Makers* (New York, 1892), 78; *Congressional Globe,* 42nd Cong., special sess., 857; *New York Evening Post,* 18 March 1905.

5. Ben: Perley Poore, "The Capitol at Washington," *Century Magazine* 3 (April 1883): 818.

6. *New York Times,* 7 February 1892.

7. Arthur M. Schlesinger, Jr., *The Imperial Presidency* (New York, 1974), 87–88; W. Stull Holt, *Treaties Defeated by the Senate: A Study of the Struggle between President and the Senate over the Conduct of Foreign Relations* (Baltimore, 1933), 121–164; Roy Swanstrom, *The United States Senate, 1787–1801: A Dissertation on the First Fourteen Years of the Upper Legislative Body,* S. Doc 100–31, 100th Cong., 1st sess. (Washington, 1988), 113–127.

8. *New York Tribune,* 14, 26 January 1859; diary of Isaac Bassett, Senate Commission on Art, Washington, D.C.

9. *Washington Evening Star,* 11 February 1888; *Journalist* 1 (10 May 1884): 8.

10. *Congressional Record,* 49th Cong., 1st sess., 3427; Louis A. Coolidge, *An Old-Fashioned Senator: Orville H. Platt of Connecticut* (New York, 1910), 395–400.

11. *New York Times,* 3, 7 March 1890; *Journalist* 2 (28 March 1885): 6.

12. U.S. Senate, *Journal of the Executive Proceedings of the Senate, 1889–1891,* vol. 27 (Washington, 1901), 487–488; *New York Times,* 5 March 1890.

13. *New York Times,* 4 March 1890; *New York Tribune,* 19 February 1890; *New York Evening Post,* 18 March 1905.

14. *New York Times,* 5, 12 March 1890.

15. *New York Times,* 5–8 March 1890.

16. *New York Times,* 12–14 March 1890; David Barry, "News-Gathering at the Capital," *Chautauquan* 22 (December 1897): 282.

17. George Gantham Bain, "Washington," *Journalist* 11 (10 May 1890): 6.

18. John Russell Young, correspondence and notes for his biography, I, 6, and John Russell Young to Rose Fitzpatrick, 21 June 1863, John Russell Young Papers, Library of Congress.

19. Bingham Duncan, *Whitelaw Reid: Journalist, Politician, Diplomat* (Athens, 1975), 38–39. John Russell Young biography, IV, Young Papers, Library of Congress; Z. L. White to Whitelaw Reid, 19 November 1870, Whitelaw Reid Papers, Library of Congress.

20. Gridiron Scrapbooks, vol. A, Gridiron Papers, Library of Congress.
21. *Washington Evening Star,* 7 March 1891.
22. *Journalist* 1 (19 April 1884): 9; 1 (26 April 1884): 9.
23. "Positions of Trust, The Secretary and Executive Clerk of the Senate," newspaper clipping, c. 1891, Anson McCook Papers, Library of Congress.
24. Ibid.; not until 1903 were stenographers allowed to record executive sessions, according to correspondent Charles Thompson; *New York Times,* 15 March 1903, clipping in Thompson Papers, Princeton University.
25. *New York Times,* 31 March 1892.
26. *New York Times,* 28 March 1892.
27. *New York Tribune,* 26, 28 March 1892; *Washington Post,* 11 March, 19 April 1892.
28. *New York Times,* 28 March 1892, 6 February 1905.
29. Gridiron Club Records, part 2, vol. l., and Young to P. V. DeGraw, 11 August 1892, Gridiron Club Papers, Library of Congress. The Standing Committee of Correspondents considered holding its own investigation but concluded that it lacked jurisdiction in the dispute. *New York Times,* 3 June 1892; O. O. Stealey, *Twenty Years in the Press Gallery* (New York, 1906), 7.
30. O. O. Stealey, "Birth of the Gridiron Club," Gridiron Club Records, part 2, vol. 1, Gridiron Club Papers, Library of Congress; *Washington Evening Star,* 18 December 1924.
31. *Washington Post,* 21 May 1929; *Congressional Record,* 71st Cong., 1st sess., 1598, 1624; the correct vote can be found in the *Senate Journal of Executive Proceedings,* vol. 68, part 1 (Washington, 1931), 88.
32. Herbert F. Magulies, *Senator Lenroot of Wisconsin: A Political Biography, 1900–1929* (Columbia, 1977), 403–405; *New York Herald Tribune,* 23 April 1929; *New York World,* 23 May 1929; George W. Norris, "Secrecy in the Senate," *Nation* (5 May 1936), and "Public Business Transacted in Secret," press release, 24 January 1929, George Norris Papers, Library of Congress.
33. *Congressional Record,* 71st Cong., 1st sess., 1617–1624; George H. Manning, "Secret Vote Arouses Senate," *Editor and Publisher* 62 (25 May 1929): 64.
34. *New York Times,* 23 May 1929, 31 July 1950; *Washington Post,* 24 May 1929; Patrick J. Maney, *"Young Bob" La Follette: A Biography of Robert M. La Follette, Jr., 1895–1953* (Columbia, 1978), 63–65; F. B. Marbut, *News from the Capital: The Story of Washington Reporting* (Carbondale, 1971), 159–161; see also G. Gould Lincoln (chairman, Standing Committee of Correspondents) to Senator

George H. Moses, c. May 1929, Robert M. La Follette, Jr., Papers, Library of Congress.

35. *Congressional Record*, 71st Cong., 1st sess., 1814–1815; *New York World*, 24 May 1929; *Baltimore Sun*, 23 May 1929.
36. *New York Times*, 24 May 1929; La Follette, "Radio Forum" speech, 1 June 1929, La Follette Papers, Library of Congress.
37. George H. Manning, "Press Triumph over Secret Vote in Senate Doubly Emphasized," *Editor and Publisher* 62 (22 June 1929): 32; *Milwaukee Journal*, 24 May 1929, clipping in La Follette Papers, Library of Congress; *Congressional Record*, 71st Cong., 1st sess., 3048–3055.

10. David Barry and the Loyalty of the Senate

1. David S. Barry, "The Loyalty of the Senate," *New England Magazine* 35 (October 1906): 137–148, and 35 (November 1906): 265–276.
2. George H. Haynes, *The Election of Senators* (New York, 1906), vii; "Unworthy Senators," *Independent* 30 (30 November 1905): 1291–1292; Oswald Garrison Villard, "The Senate's Role of Dishonor," *Nation* 81 (7 December 1905): 456; "Is the United States Senate the Corrupt Tool of the Standard Oil Company?" *Arena* 35 (January 1906): 72–74; Barry, "The Loyalty of the Senate," 141.
3. See "The Newspaper versus the Magazine," *Newspaperdom* 18 (12 April 1906): 1; and Louis Filler, *The Muckrakers: Crusaders for American Liberalism* (Chicago, 1968).
4. H. V. N. Boynton, "The Press and Public Men," *Century Magazine* 42 (October 1891): 853–855.
5. David S. Barry, *Forty Years in Washington* (Boston, 1924); and Ralph M. McKenzie, *Washington Correspondents, Past and Present* (New York, 1903), 39.
6. Crosby S. Noyes, "Washington Journalism, Past and Present," *Washington Evening Star*, 16 December 1902.
7. Richard S. Howland to David S. Barry, 26 February 1904, Nelson W. Aldrich Papers, Library of Congress. See also Barry's biographical statement in the *Congressional Directory*, 66th Cong., 1st sess. (Washington, 1919), 235.
8. Nathaniel Wright Stephenson, *Nelson W. Aldrich, A Leader in American Politics* (New York, 1930), 240; *Congressional Directory*, 59th Cong., 2nd sess. (Washington, 1906). Members of Congress submit their own biographical statements to the *Directory*, including and omitting information as they see fit.
9. Stephenson, *Nelson W. Aldrich*, 198, 459; Horace Samuel Merrill and Marion Galbraith Merrill, *The Republican Command, 1897–1913* (Lexington, 1971), 26; Will Irvin, "The American Newspaper," *Col-*

lier's 47 (1 July 1911): 18, and 47 (8 July 1911): 116; George H. Mayer, *The Republican Party* (New York, 1964), 26.

10. Bob Charles Holcomb, "Senator Joe Bailey: Two Decades of Controversy," (Ph.D. diss., Texas Technological College, 1968), 426; John Braeman, *Albert J. Beveridge, American Nationalist* (Chicago, 1971), 73, 77, 142. Indiana's other senator, Albert J. Beveridge, wanted papers in the hands of his friends, to counter Fairbanks's influence. "If I could have a paper out here that was owned by a single man and not known as my friend so that it could say the just and true things about me . . . it would, of course, be a great help to me," Beveridge wrote Albert Shaw, editor of *Review of Reviews*, 26 December 1906, Albert J. Beveridge Papers, Library of Congress.

11. David Barry, "Over the Hill to Demagoguery," *New Outlook* 161 (February 1933): 40–42.

12. O. O. Stealey to Bruce Haldeman, c. February 1909, Henry Watterson Papers, Library of Congress. Writing an increase in salary, Stealey noted that "the average pay of the heads of [Washington news] bureaus I find is about $65 per week. Nearly all of those correspondents are allowed to purchase news and good stories." For a study of the impact of salaries on reporters outside Washington, see Ted Curtis Smythe, "The Reporter, 1880–1900: Working Conditions and Their Influence on the News," *Journalism History* 6 (Spring 1980): 1–10.

13. Charles W. Thompson, "Biographical Sketch, 1935," Charles W. Thompson Papers, Seeley G. Mudd Manuscript Library, Princeton University; T. T. Williams, "Temptations of a Young Journalist," *Cosmopolitan* 40 (April 1906): 679–682.

14. E. B. Wight to W. W. Clapp, 5 January 1877, Ben: Perley Poore to Clapp, 28 March 1877, W. W. Clapp Papers, Library of Congress; McKenzie, *Washington Correspondents*, 23, 53–54.

15. "Noted Newspaperman Is Dead," *Newspaperdom* 17 (23 August 1906): 3; McKenzie, *Washington Correspondents*, 99–100.

16. Henry Watterson, introduction to Stealey, *Twenty Years in the Press Gallery*, vii-ix; T. C. Crawford, "The Special Correspondent at Washington," *Cosmopolitan* 12 (January 1892): 355; Louis Ludlow, *From Cornfield to Press Gallery: Adventures and Reminiscences of a Veteran Washington Correspondent* (Washington, 1924), 186.

17. Will Irvin, "The American Newspaper," *Collier's* 47 (1 July 1911): 18.

18. Stealey, *Twenty Years in the Press Gallery*, 3.

19. Stephenson, *Nelson W. Aldrich*, 94; Richard V. Oulahan, "Presidents and Publicity," book draft, Oulahan Papers, Herbert Hoover Library, West Branch, Iowa; Barry, *Forty Years in Washington*, 152–153; Louis Arthur Coolidge and James Burton Reynolds, *The Show at*

Washington (Washington, 1894), 77; Crawford, "The Special Correspondent," 352.

20. Ludlow, *From Cornfield to Press Gallery*, 258, 268; Francis A. Richardson, "Recollections of a Washington Newspaper Correspondent," *Records of the Columbia Historical Society*, vol. 6 (Washington, 1903), 27; Charles Willis Thompson, *Party Leaders of the Time* (New York, 1906), 351–358.

21. Ludlow, *From Cornfield to Press Gallery*, 236–238, 259–260; "Between the Quotes," *Editor and Publisher* 5 (31 March 1906): 3.

22. *Journalist* 2 (3 October 1885): 2; Chalmers Roberts, *The Washington Post: The First One Hundred Years* (Boston, 1977), 53. Lincoln Steffens, *The Autobiography of Lincoln Steffens* (New York, 1931), 503–510, 577, 581.

23. "The Treason of the Senate," *Cosmopolitan* 40 (February 1906): 477–480; Abe C. Ravitz, *David Graham Phillips* (New York, 1966), 83–91; see also Richard L. McCormick, "The Discovery that Business Corrupts Politics: A Reappraisal of the Origins of Progressivism," *American Historical Review* 86 (April 1981): 247–274. The series was later edited and published by George E. Mowry and Judson Grenier, *The Treason of the Senate* (Chicago, 1964), although their book omitted the photographs that accompanied the magazine articles. See also Thomas C. Leonard, *The Power of the Press: The Birth of American Political Reporting* (New York, 1986), 204–210.

24. Mowry and Grenier, eds., *The Treason of the Senate*, 16; "The Men Who Make the News," *Journalist* 38 (30 December 1905): 168. An earlier article noted that Depew was regarded "with something akin to affection by almost all the newspaper reporters who have ever met him, for he invariably tried to help." W. Blackstone Hopson, "Rail, River, and Ocean," *Journalist* 18 (21 October 1893): 12–13. See also Chauncey Depew, *My Memories of Eighty Years* (New York, 1922), 347–348.

25. Theodore Roosevelt to George Otto Trevelyan, 22 January 1906, to George V. L. Meyer, 1 February 1906, to Lincoln Steffens, 6 February 1906, and to John St. Low Stachey, 12 February 1906, Theodore Roosevelt Papers, Library of Congress. Merrill and Merrill, *The Republican Command*, 204–221. On Roosevelt and the press see George Juergens, *News from the White House: The Presidential-Press Relationship in the Progressive Era* (Chicago, 1981), 14–90; and Robert C. Hilderbrand, *Power and the People: Executive Management of Public Opinion in Foreign Affairs, 1897–1921* (Chapel Hill, 1981), 52–71.

26. Roosevelt to Frank S. Black, 9 January 1906, and to William Howard Taft, 15 March 1906, Roosevelt Papers.

27. "Uncle Joe's Dinner," *Editor and Publisher* 5 (24 March 1906): 1–3; Barry, "The Loyalty of the Senate," 275; *New York Times*, 28 January 1906; Harold Brayman, *The President Speaks off the Record . . . Historic Evenings with America's Leaders, the Press, the Other Men of Power at Washington's Exclusive Gridiron Club* (Princeton, 1976), 58.

28. "'Muck-Rake' in Journalism," *Editor and Publisher* 5 (14 April 1906): 2; Samuel E. Moffett, "'The Man with the Muck-Rake': Some Aspects of a Premeditated Sermon," *Collier's* 37 (28 April 1906): 19; *Review of Reviews* 33 (May 1906): 522; Albert J. Beveridge to David Graham Phillips, 18 April 1906, Beveridge Papers, Library of Congress.

29. *Cosmopolitan*, 40 (November 1906), advertisement giving circulation statistics for the series; Merrill and Merrill, *The Republican Command*, 218; William Henry Harbaugh, *The Life and Times of Theodore Roosevelt* (New York, 1963), 255–259.

30. John C. Spooner to J. Aikens, *Milwaukee Evening Wisconsin*, 14 June 1906, John C. Spooner Papers, Library of Congress; *New York Times*, 21 May 1906 (unsigned, but in Thompson's scrapbooks, Thompson Papers, Seeley G. Mudd Manuscript Library, Princeton University).

31. See Michael E. McGerr, *The Decline of Popular Politics: The American North, 1865–1928* (New York, 1986), 107–137, 184–210; Leonard, *The Power of the Press*, 193–221; and Paul Kleppner, *Who Voted? The Dynamics of Electoral Turnout, 1870–1980* (New York, 1982).

32. *New York Times*, 14 October 1906 (clipping in the Thompson Papers, Mudd Manuscript Library, Princeton University).

33. Rollo Ogden, "Some Aspects of Journalism," *Atlantic Monthly* 98 (July 1906): 12–20; Samuel Bowles, "The Independent Press," *North American Review* 183 (July 1906): 40–46.

34. Barry, "Over the Hill to Demagoguery," 40–42.

35. *Congressional Record*, 72nd Cong., 2nd sess., 3269–3282, 3511–3530; *New York Times*, 4 February 1933; Senate Judiciary Committee, *David S. Barry, Sergeant-at-Arms, United States Senate*, 72nd Cong., 2nd sess. (Washington, 1933), 2.

11. Richard V. Oulahan, Bureau Chief

1. *New York Times*, 1 January 1932. Oulahan was also briefly the publisher of the *New York Sun*.

2. Richard V. Oulahan, "Presidents and Publicity," book draft [not paged consecutively], and remarks at the meeting of the Society of Newspaper Editors, 17 April 1931, Richard Oulahan Papers, Herbert Hoover Library, West Branch, Iowa. Oulahan's papers, including

draft chapters for books on Washington, provide a rich source of information and anecdotes.

3. Delbert Clark, *Washington Dateline* (New York, 1941), 22–23.

4. Oulahan, "Presidents and Publicity."

5. Edward G. Lowry, *Washington Close-Ups: Intimate Views of Some Public Figures* (Boston, 1921), 143.

6. [Drew Pearson and Robert S. Allen], *Washington Merry-Go-Round* (New York, 1931), 337; As late as the 1960 presidential campaign, David Broder was introduced to the ritual of "saving the blacks." "If one of the brethren were too drunk to write a coherent story of his own, some senior reporter would come through the bus collecting 'blacks' from the rest of us. He would borrow a paragraph from this story and another from that and quickly piece together a passable composition under the byline of the besotted journalist." *Washington Post*, 15 November 1987.

7. Oulahan, "Presidents and Publicity."

8. Robert Simpson to the Standing Committee of Correspondents, 2 December 1911, Minutes of the Standing Committee of Correspondents, Senate Press Gallery; excerpts from a family history by Charles Everett Kern, in the possession of Charles E. Kern II, Alexandria, Virginia; O. O. Stealey remarks, May 1911, Gridiron Club Records, Library of Congress.

9. "Vale, Bohemia!" *Journalist* 19 (5 May 1894): 8; "The Decay of the Bohemian," *Journalist* 21 (29 May 1897); Allan Forman, "A Somewhat Personal Chat," *Journalist* 39 (16 June 1906): 108; *Washington Post*, 4 June 1905. Charles M. Pepper, *Everyday Life in Washington . . . with Pen and Camera* (New York, 1900), 403. See Michael Schudson, *Discovering the News: A Social History of American Newspapers* (New York, 1978), 121–159.

10. Ashmun N. Brown, "Richard Victor Oulahan," in *1932* [National Press Club Yearbook] (Washington, 1932), 23–26; Joe Mitchell Chappel, "Affairs at Washington," *National Magazine* 28 (September 1908): 608; "Reminiscences of Sevellon Brown," 9, and "Reminiscences of James T. Wilson, Jr.," 42, Oral History Research Office, Columbia University.

11. Chappel, "Affairs in Washington," 609; *New York Times*, 31 December 1931; *Evening Missourian*, 13 August 1921, and "Sketch of Richard V. Oulahan," Oulahan Papers, Herbert Hoover Library, West Branch, Iowa. The manuscripts for two unpublished memoirs of Washington journalism are in the Oulahan Papers.

12. Oulahan, "Presidents and Publicity"; Robert C. Hilderbrand, *Power and the People: Executive Management of Public Opinion in Foreign Affairs, 1897–1921* (Chapel Hill, 1981), 8–11; James E. Pollard, *The*

Presidents and the Press (New York, 1947), 557; Woodrow Wilson, *Congressional Government: A Study in American Politics* (Cleveland, 1956 [1885]). 22.

13. Clifford P. Westermeier, *Who Rush to Glory: The Cowboy Volunteers of 1898* (Caldwell, Idaho, 1958), 32–34; W. M. Kiplinger, *Washington Is Like That* (New York, 1942), 424; *New York Times*, 31 December 1931.

14. Oulahan, "Presidents and Publicity"; Oulahan, "What the President Can and Cannot Do," *Ladies Home Journal* (October 1908), clipping in Oulahan Papers, Herbert Hoover Library, West Branch, Iowa; George Juergens, *News from the White House: The Presidential-Press Relationship in the Progressive Era* (Chicago, 1981), 1–40; Oscar King Davis, *Released for Publication: Some Inside Political History of Theodore Roosevelt and His Times, 1898–1918* (Boston, 1925), 61; J. Frederick Essary, *Covering Washington: Government Reflected to the Public in the Press, 1822–1926* (Boston, 1927), 88; W. W. Price, "How the Work of Gathering White House News Has Changed," *Washington Evening Star*, 16 December 1902; "Press Room at the White House," *Journalist* 32 (22 November 1902): 54.

15. See Albert Shaw's *Cartoon History of Roosevelt's Career* (New York, 1910); Oulahan, "Presidents and Publicity."

16. Isaac Marcasson to Richard Oulahan, 4 November 1908, and Oulahan to Marcasson, 7 November 1908, William Howard Taft to Richard V. Oulahan, 21 November 1908, Oulahan Papers, Herbert Hoover Library, West Branch, Iowa; Juergens, *News from the White House*, 122; "Reminiscences of Sevellon Brown," 11–13.

17. *New York Times*, 26 June 1910; Juergens, *News from the White House*, 91–125; Hilderbrand, *Power and the People*, 72–92.

18. Charles W. Thompson to Reuben Adiel Bull, 8 March 1913, in Arthur Link et al., eds., *The Papers of Woodrow Wilson*, vol. 27 (Princeton, 1978), 164–166; Richard Oulahan to Charles Thompson, 28 April 1913, Thompson Papers, Princeton University; Gay Talese, *The Kingdom and the Power* (New York, 1969), 359; Lippmann quoted in Douglass Cater, *The Fourth Branch of Government* (Boston, 1959), 47.

19. Oulahan, "Presidents and Publicity"; Robert C. Hilderbrand, ed., *The Complete Press Conferences, 1913–1919: The Papers of Woodrow Wilson* (Princeton, 1981), xi.

20. Oulahan, "Presidents and Publicity"; Juergens, *News from the White House*, 141–145; Hilderbrand, *Power and the People*, 93–108; Louis Ludlow, *From Corn Field to Press Gallery: Adventures and Reminiscences of a Veteran Washington Correspondent* (Washington, 1924), 352.

21. Juergens, *News from the White House*, 159–160; Oulahan to Woodrow Wilson, 18 April 1916, Wilson to Oulahan, 20 April 1916, in Arthur S. Link et al., eds., *The Papers of Woodrow Wilson*, vol. 36 (Princeton, 1981), xxx, 516. Oulahan was later married to Sue Courts, whom he first met at his son's wedding. They met again in Paris in 1919, on a "blind date" arranged by President Wilson's physician, Lt. Cary Grayson, and were married soon after.

22. Stephen E. Ponder, "Executive Publicity and Congressional Resistance, 1905–1913: Congress and the Roosevelt Administration's PR Men," *Congress and the Presidency* 13 (Autumn 1986): 177–186; F. B. Marbut, *News from the Capital: The Story of Washington Reporting* (Carbondale, 1971), 192–196; William L. Rivers, *The Opinion Makers: The Washington Press Corps* (Boston, 1967), 138; Schudson, *Discovering the News*, 134–144.

23. "Reminiscences of Sevellon Brown," 6; Lindsay Rogers complained that "Washington correspondents are no longer interpreters or even news gatherers; were they to use all the 'handouts' given them, their papers would have space for nothing else." Lindsay Rogers, *The American Senate* (New York, 1926).

24. After the representative lost his seat, St. Clair returned to journalism and in 1919 began the first syndicated Washington column, "Folks and Things around Washington," which lasted two years and appeared in some twenty-five newspapers. Lambert St. Clair, *I've Met the Folks You Read About* (New York, 1940), 113–114, 179–180.

25. Franc Roberts Havenner Reminiscences (1 September 1953), 57, Regional Oral History Office, University of California, Berkeley. Havenner himself later won election to the U.S. House of Representatives.

26. Juergens, *News from the White House*, 182–185; Hilderbrand, *Power and the People*, 142–197; Schudson, *Discovering the News*, 142; Minutes, 18 July 1918, Standing Committee of Correspondents, Senate Press Gallery.

27. *New York Times*, 16 January 1919; Juergens, *News from the White House*, 209, 242–244; Hilderbrand, *Power and the People*, 183; Arthur Krock, *Memoirs: Sixty Years on the Firing Line* (New York, 1968), 108–109.

28. *New York Times*, 11 July 1919; Oulahan, "Presidents and Publicity."

29. *Washington Evening Star*, 13 August 1919; Oulahan, "Presidents and Publicity."

30. LeRoy Ashby, *The Spearless Leader: Senator Borah and the Progressive Movement in the 1920's* (Urbana, 1972), 17–20.

31. Ibid.; Clark, *Washington Dateline*, 168–169; Robert James Maddox, *William E. Borah and American Foreign Policy* (Baton Rouge, 1969),

87; Mary Louise Perrine, *Elephants and Donkeys: The Memoirs of Mary Borah* (Moscow, Idaho, 1976), 149; Claudius O. Johnson, *Borah of Idaho* (Seattle, 1967 [1936]), 326; Robert E. Burke, "Hiram Johnson's Impressions of William E. Borah," *Idaho Yesterday* 17 (Spring, 1973): 6–10.

32. Thomas L. Stokes, *Chip off My Shoulder* (Princeton, 1940), 216–217, 292; and [Pearson and Allen], *Washington Merry-Go-Round*, 343.

33. Cabell Phillips, ed., *Dateline: Washington, The Story of National Affairs Journalism in the Life and Times of the National Press Club* (Garden City, 1949), 68–69; Cater, *Fourth Branch of Government*, 93; Essary, *Covering Washington*, 212–213.

34. St. Clair, *I've Met the Folks You Read About*, 139; Lowry, *Washington Close-Ups*, 61–64.

35. Rogers, *The American Senate*, 217–219, 226–227, 231; Frank R. Kent, "Mr. Coolidge," *American Mercury* 2 (August 1924): 389–390.

36. Oulahan, "Presidents and Publicity."

37. Oulahan Radio Address, National Broadcasting Company, 19 February 1929; Oulahan, "Gathering the News at Washington," *Quill* 9 (April 1921): 5; "Remarks of Richard V. Oulahan at the Meeting of the American Society of Newspaper Editors," Washington, D.C., 17 April 1931, Oulahan Papers, Herbert Hoover Library, West Branch, Iowa.

38. As one example, Oulahan cited the leaked story he received in 1919, from President Wilson's advisers, that the president had grown perturbed over disagreements among the Allies at the Paris Peace Conference and had ordered the steamship *George Washington* readied for a return to Washington. Oulahan declined to declare this simply a shrewd ploy to pressure the French government but noted that the story had its affect: the French modified their position, and Wilson signed the treaty. "Remarks of Richard V. Oulahan," 17 April 1931, Oulahan Papers.

39. Arthur Krock, *The Consent of the Governed, and Other Deceits* (Boston, 1971), 224–225.

40. J. J. Marrinan to Christian A. Herter, 6 November 1923, Hoover Papers (Commerce), Hoover Library, West Branch, Iowa; *New York Herald-Tribune*, 31 December 1931; Craig Lloyd, *Aggressive Introvert: A Study of Herbert Hoover and Public Relations Management, 1912–1932* (Columbus, 1972), 6, 60–61, 164–168; Charles Michelson, *The Ghost Talks* (New York, 1944), 17, 28.

41. [Pearson and Allen], *Washington Merry-Go-Round*, 329–331; Clark, *Washington Dateline*, 17; David Burner, *Herbert Hoover: A Public Life* (New York, 1979), 235; George H. Manning, "'Tightening' of

Press Relations Irks Washington Correspondents," *Editor and Publisher* 62 (6 July 1929): 25.

42. [Pearson and Allen], *Washington Merry-Go-Round*, 321–322; Arthur Krock, in a *New York Times* review of *Washington Merry-Go-Round*, 25 July 1931, labeled the book a collection of "whispered anecdotes," "anonymous gossip," and "cruel banter" from Washington social gatherings.

43. [Pearson and Allen], *Washington Merry-Go-Round*, 323, 344–346.

44. Ibid., 328, 331–333. Ishbel Ross, *Ladies of the Press: The Story of Women in Journalism by an Insider* (New York, 1936), 342–345. Not until 1947 did the Senate finally order the Standing Committee to admit a black reporter. Marbut, *News from the Capital*, 162–165.

45. Statement by Richard Oulahan, chairman, Standing Committee of Correspondents, 64th Cong., December 1915, Minutes, 5 February 1917, Standing Committee of Correspondents, Senate Press Gallery; Oulahan, "White House and the Press," book draft, Hoover Library; Charles Thompson, *Party Leaders of the Time* (New York, 1906), 352–353.

46. Charles Fischer, *The Columnists* (New York, 1944), 218–240; see also "Pearson, Drew (Andrew Russell), and Allen, Robert (Sharon)," *Current Biography, 1941* (New York, 1941), 658–661; *New York Times*, 13 September 1931. In an earlier incident, Richard Oulahan concluded that Drew Pearson had violated the rule of confidentiality. When Oulahan arranged for Pearson to interview a government official, Pearson reported the contents of a document on the official's desk, not meant for disclosure. As a result, an angry Oulahan never again spoke to Pearson. Courts Oulahan to author, 18 June 1990.

47. Turner Catledge, *My Life and the Times* (New York, 1971), 59–60.

48. Ibid., 77; *New York Times*, 21, 31 December 1931, 1, 3 January 1932; *New York Herald-Tribune*, 31 December 1931; Courts Oulahan to author, 18 June 1990. See also eulogies by John Callan O'Laughlin, J. Fred Essary, and Arthur S. Henning, April 1932, Gridiron Club Records, Library of Congress. Characteristically, during the last hearings he covered, Oulahan offered his notes to a young reporter who arrived late. *Washington Post*, 2 January 1932.

49. Krock, *Sixty Years on the Firing Line*, 80–81; James Hagerty had been the *Times*'s first choice to replace Oulahan, but he disliked living in Washington. See Catledge, *My Life and the Times*, 60, 77; also James Sayler, "Window on an Age: Arthur Krock and the New Deal Era, 1929–1941" (Ph.D. diss., Rutgers University, 1978); and Talese, *The Kingdom and the Power*, 299.

50. Theodore F. Koop, "We Interrupt This Program . . ." in Phillips, *Dateline: Washington*, 82; *Washington Post*, 2 January 1932.

51. Cater, *Fourth Branch of Government*, 92; *New York Times*, 2 March 1929, 2 March 1930, 28 December 1930. Robert Sobel, *The Manipulators: America in the Media Age* (Garden City, 1976), 117–178.

Afterword

1. Walter Trohan, *Political Animals: Memoirs of a Sentimental Cynic* (Garden City, 1975), 359.
2. Frederick Lewis Allen, *Since Yesterday: The Nineteen-Thirties in America* (New York, 1961 [1939]), 219; Robert S. Lynd and Helen Merrell Lynd, *Middletown in Transition: A Study in Cultural Conflicts* (New York, 1937), 375–376; Kenneth G. Crawford, *The Pressure Boys: The Inside Story of Lobbying in America* (New York, 1939), vii-viii; Thomas L. Stokes, *Chip off My Shoulder* (Princeton, 1940), 253.
3. Marquis Childs, *Witness to Power* (New York, 1975), 5.
4. Paul Anderson, "Address before the Oklahoma Press Association," 27 May 1932, reprinted in the *Congressional Record*, 72nd Cong., 1st sess., 15622–15623.
5. Stokes, *Chip off My Shoulder*, 217; "Washington, D.C.," *Fortune* 9 (March 1934): 59; Leo C. Rosten, *The Washington Correspondent* (New York, 1937), 78–79; Neil MacNeil, *Without Fear or Favor* (New York, 1940), 163–164. See also Graham J. White, *FDR and the Press* (Chicago, 1979).
6. Trohan, *Political Animals*, 57, 164; Turner Catledge, *My Life and the Times* (New York, 1971), 71–73.
7. Roland Young, *This Is Congress* (New York, 1943), 196–197.
8. Trohan, *Political Animals*, 35; *New York Times*, 25 November 1959; Robert H. Ferrell, ed., *Dear Bess: The Letters from Harry to Bess Truman, 1910–1959* (New York, 1983), 397, 426; Harry S. Truman, *Memoirs: Year of Decisions*, vol. 1 (New York, 1955), 146; F. Ross Peterson, *Prophet without Honor: Glen H. Taylor and the Fight for American Liberalism* (Lexington, 1974), 92–94, 185.
9. Jack Bell, "Covering Congress" in Ray Eldon Hiebert, ed., *The Press in Washington* (New York, 1966), 147; Russell Baker, "An American in Washington," *Columbia Journalism Review* 1 (Spring 1962): 10; William L. Rivers, *The Opinion Makers: The Washington Press Corps* (Boston, 1967), 186.
10. James Reston, *The Artillery of the Press, Its Influence on American Foreign Policy* (New York, 1967), 72.
11. Robert E. Gilbert, "President versus Congress: The Struggle for Public Attention," *Congress and the Presidency* 16 (Autumn 1989): 83–102; *Washington Post*, 25 January 1983; *New York Times*, 31 January 1983; "Washington's Press Corps," *Newsweek*, 25 May 1981, 92;

Dan Rather, *The Camera Never Blinks: Adventures of a TV Journalist* (New York, 1977), 216–217. See also Stephen Hess, *The Washington Reporters* (Washington, 1981), 51–52.

12. Eleanor Randolph, "The Secret Pleasures of the White House Press," *Washington Monthly* 10 (March 1978): 30; Timothy Crouse, *The Boys on the Bus* (New York, 1973), 195; "Russell Baker," in Nora Ephron, *Scribble, Scribble: Notes on the Media* (New York, 1978), 81–86; Russell Baker, *An American in Washington* (New York, 1961), 75–84, 140–171; Warren Weaver, *Both Your Houses* (New York, 1978), 3; Elmer E. Cornwell, Jr., "Presidential News: The Expanding Public Image," *Journalism Quarterly* 36 (Summer 1959): 275–283; Alan P. Balutis, "Congress, the President, and the Press," *Journalism Quarterly* 53 (August 1976): 513.

13. Stephanie Greco Larson, "The Presidents and Congress in the Media," *Annals* 499 (September 1988): 64–74; Robert O. Blanchard, "Journalists, Social Scientists, and Public Affairs," *Congress and the Presidency* 9 (Autumn 1982): 111–112; Hess, *The Washington Reporters*, 48–49; Michael J. Robinson, "Three Faces of Congressional Media," in Thomas E. Mann and Norman J. Ornstein, eds., *The New Congress* (Washington, 1981), 55–96.

14. Hess, *The Washington Reporters*, 38–40; "Press Work from the Other Side," [Congressional] *Staff Journal*, March/April 1981, 8; Len Allen, "Makeup of the Senate Press," in Commission on the Operation of the Senate, *Senate Communications with the Public*, Committee Print, 94th Cong., 2nd sess. (Washington, 1977), 26; Bill Hogan, "The Congressional Correspondent," *Washington Journalism Review*, June 1981, 35.

15. Lou Cannon, *Reporting: An Inside View* (Sacramento, 1977), 181–193.

16. "Editor's Notes," *Washingtonian* 17 (September 1982): 6; Raymond M. Lane, "The Wall Street Journal: Washington's Top Bureau?" *Washington Journalism Review* 1 (January/February 1978): 54–59; "Washington's Press Corps," *Newsweek*, 25 May 1981, 91–92.

17. Carol Matlack, "Live from Capitol Hill," *National Journal* 21 (18 February 1989): 390–394; Michael Straight, *Trial by Television* (Boston, 1954), 4–5; Norris Cotton, *In the Senate, amidst the Conflict and Turmoil* (New York, 1978), 56.

18. George Dixon, *Leaning on a Column* . . . (Philadelphia, 1961), 109–111; *Congressional Record*, 95th Cong., 1st sess., E5353; Michael J. Malbin, "The Senate Republican Leaders—Life without a President," *National Journal* 9 (21 May 1977): 777.

19. *Congressional Record*, 97th Cong, 1st sess, E2468; 99th Cong., 1st sess., S16846; *Washington Post*, 19 February 1979, 3 June 1986; Ann

Cooper, "Curtain Rising on House TV amid Aid-to-Incumbent Fears," *Congressional Quarterly,* 10 February 1979, 252–254; George F. Will, "TV, or Not TV?" *Newsweek,* 25 April 1983, 100.

20. Martin F. Nolan, "High Priest of Politics," *Washingtonian* 15 (November 1979): 133–136; *Washington Post,* 20 July 1983; David Broder, *Behind the Front Page: A Candid Look at How the News Is Made* (New York, 1987), 209, 214–237.

21. George F. Will, "Journalists and Politicians," *Newsweek,* 19 January 1981, 92.

22. Stephen Hess, "Policing the Washington Press Corps: The Role of the Standing Committee of Correspondents," Brookings Institution Discussion Papers in Governmental Studies (Washington, 1986); *Washington Post,* 1 April 1987. For a discussion of women in Congress, see Representative Martha Griffith, oral history interview, 47–48, 88–89, 149–150, Former Members of Congress Oral History Project, Library of Congress.

23. Stephen Hess, "A Look inside the Hill Press Galleries: Reporters at Work," *Roll Call* (24 July 1986): 9; Ernest K. Lindley, "The Years of Danger," in Warren K. Agee, *The Press and the Public Interest* (Washington, 1968), 12–13.

Bibliographical Essay

As WRITERS who daily scribbled notes on the back of envelopes and in pocket notebooks, few newspaper correspondents left manuscript collections. Fortunately, editors and publishers tended to save their records, which contain correspondence from Washington reporters—dealing in large part with their working conditions. Valuable editorial collections for this book were the papers of James Gordon Bennett, Horace Greeley, Manton Marble, Whitelaw Reid, and Henry Watterson, at the Library of Congress, and Greeley's papers at the New York Public Library. The papers of W. W. Clapp at the Library of Congress and at the Houghton Library, Harvard University, consist largely of his correspondence with Ben: Perley Poore.

Among the correspondents' collections, other Poore papers are located at the Essex Institute, Salem, Massachusetts. Uriah Hunt Painter, most likely because he saved his papers as evidence to use in his various law suits, left a rich manuscript collection at the Pennsylvania Historical Society, Philadelphia; newspaper clippings on his career are available at the Chester County Historical Society, Chester, Pennsylvania. John Russell Young's papers at the Library of Congress were more revealing than the memoirs that his widow edited. The Charles W. Thompson papers at Seeley G. Mudd Manuscript Library, Princeton University, and Richard V. Oulahan's unpublished memoirs at the Herbert Hoover Library, West Branch, Iowa, are important for twentieth-century Washington correspondence. A manuscript of the memoirs of Charles Everett Kern is in the possession of his grandson, Charles E. Kern II, a member of the House Judiciary Committee staff.

The Gridiron Club Records, at the Library of Congress, offer a cache of minutes, menus, skits, and obituaries. For research on the twentieth century, the minutes of the Standing Committee of Correspondents are available at the Senate Press Gallery. Although brief, these minutes offer a glimpse into the Standing Committee's self-policing of the press galleries.

Political collections that shed light on politicians' relations with the press include Nelson W. Aldrich, Chester A. Arthur, Albert J. Beveridge, James G. Blaine, Benjamin F. Butler, Robert M. LaFollette, Jr., Anson McCook, John McLean, Willie P. Magnum, George Norris, Theodore Roosevelt, John C. Spooner, and Thomas Walsh, at the Library of Congress; the William E. Seward Papers at the University of Rochester, and the Herbert Hoover Papers, Herbert Hoover Library, West Branch, Iowa. Much information on the congressional correspondents can also be gleaned from the records of the United States Senate and House of Representatives, at the Center for Legislative Archives at the National Archives.

Given the time-span of this study, only a few oral histories were relevant. Most useful were those of Sevellon Brown, Arthur Krock, and James T. Wilson at the Columbia University Oral History Office, and Franc Roberts Havenner, at the Regional Oral History Office, University of California, Berkeley.

A wide variety of government documents provided information, including the *Annals of Congress, Congressional Globe, Congressional Record,* and *Senate Executive Journals,* as well as the *Congressional Directories,* which list both all correspondents accredited to the press galleries and all committee clerks.

Committee hearings of various Senate and House investigations revealed much about newspaper correspondents of the time. Among these were: U.S. House of Representatives, Select Committee, *Reports on Alleged Corrupt Combinations of Members of Congress,* H. Rept. 243, 34th Cong., 3rd sess., 1857. Committee on the Judiciary, *Telegraph Censorship,* H. Rept. 64, 37th Cong., 2nd sess., 1862. Committee on Public Expenditures, *Alaska Investigation,* H. Rept. 25, 40th Cong., 3rd sess., 1869. Committee on Ways and Means, *China Mail Service,* H. Rept. 268, 43rd Cong., 2nd sess., 1875. Select Committee, *Credit Mobilier Investigation,* H. Rept. 77, 42nd Cong., 3rd sess., 1877. Select Committee, *Charges against H. V. Boynton,* H. Rept. 1112. 48th Cong., 1st sess., 1884.

United States Senate, *Report of the Select Committee,* S. Doc.

222, 29th Cong., 1st sess., 1846. Joint Committee on the Conduct of the War, *Report of the Joint Committee on the Conduct of the War*, S. Rept. 108, 37th Cong., 3rd sess., 1863. Select Committee, *Publication of the Treaty of Washington*, S. Rept. 5, 42nd Cong., special sess., 1871. Select Committee, *Credit Mobilier*, S. Rept. 9, 43rd Cong., 3rd sess., 1873. Joint Select Committee Appointed to Inquire into the Affairs of the District of Columbia, *Report*, Rept. 453, part 3, 43rd Cong., 1st sess., 1874. Committee on the Judiciary, *David S. Barry, Sergeant-at-Arms, United States Senate*, 72nd Cong., 2nd sess., 1933.

The necessary starting place among secondary studies is F. B. Marbut's *News from the Capital: The Story of Washington Reporting* (Carbondale, 1971). As an Associated Press reporter in the 1930s, Marbut was himself a member of the press gallery, before he wrote this study as his doctoral dissertation. Also important are Robert O. Blanchard, ed., *Congress and the News Media* (New York, 1974); Stephen Hess, *The Washington Reporters* (Washington, 1981); Vincent Howard, "The Two Congresses: A Study of the Changing Roles and Relationships of the National Legislature and the Washington Reporters, as Revealed Particularly in Press Accounts of Legislative Activity, 1860–1913." (Ph.D. diss, University of Chicago, 1976); Elizabeth Gregory McPherson, "The History of Reporting the Debates and Proceedings of Congress" (Ph.D. diss., University of North Carolina, Chapel Hill, 1940); Ted Curtis Smythe, "The Reporter, 1880–1900: Working Conditions and Their Influence on the News," *Journalism History* 6 (Spring 1980); and Roy Swanstrom, *The United States Senate, 1789–1801*, S. Doc. 100–31, 100th Cong., 1st sess. (Washington, 1988).

Other useful studies relating to Washington journalism include William Ames, *A History of the National Intelligencer* (Chapel Hill, 1972); J. Cutler Andrews, *The North Reports the Civil War* (Pittsburgh, 1955); Maurine Beasley, *The First Women Washington Correspondents* (Washington, 1976); James Free, *The First One Hundred Years: A Casual Chronicle of the Gridiron Club* (Washington, 1985); Robert C. Hilderbrand, *Power and the People: Executive Management of Public Opinion in Foreign Affairs, 1897–1921* (Chapel Hill, 1981); Paul S. Holbo, *Tarnished Expansion: The Alaska Scandal, the Press, and Congress, 1867–1871* (Knoxville, 1983); George Juergens, *News from the White House: The Presidential-Press Relationship in the Progressive Era* (Chicago,

1981); Thomas C. Leonard, *The Power of the Press: The Birth of American Political Reporting* (New York, 1986); Cabell Phillips, ed., *Dateline: Washington, The Story of National Affairs Journalism in the Life and Times of the National Press Club* (Garden City, 1949); James E. Pollard, *The Presidents and the Press* (New York, 1947); Stephen E. Ponder, "Executive Publicity and Congressional Resistance, 1905–1913: Congress and the Roosevelt Administration's PR Men," *Congress and the Presidency* 13 (Autumn 1986); Dan Schiller, *Objectivity and the News: The Public and the Rise of Commercial Journalism* (Philadelphia, 1981); Michael Schudson, *Discovering the News: A Social History of American Newspapers* (New York, 1978); Richard A. Schwarzlose, "The Nation's First Wire Service: Evidence Supporting a Footnote," *Journalism Quarterly* 48 (Winter 1980); Culver H. Smith, *The Press, Politics, and Patronage: The American Government's Use of Newspapers, 1789–1875* (Athens, 1977); Louis M. Starr, *Bohemian Brigade: Civil War Newsmen in Action* (Madison, 1987 [1954]); John Tebbel and Sarah Miles Watts, *The Press and the Presidency: From George Washington to Ronald Reagan* (New York, 1985); and Bernard Weisberger, *The American Newspaperman* (Chicago, 1961), and *Reporters for the Union* (Westport, 1977 [1953]).

A comparative example of correspondents at the Canadian parliament can be found in Paul Rutherford, *A Victorian Authority: The Daily Press in Late Nineteenth Century Toronto* (Toronto, 1982). And a broad world-survey is available in Mitchell Stephens, *A History of News: From the Drum to the Satellite* (New York, 1988).

For placing the correspondents within their Washington setting, the best studies are Constance McLaughlin Green, *Washington, Village and Capital* (Princeton, 1962); Kathryn Allamong Jacob, "High Society in Washington during the Gilded Age, 1865–1900: 'Three Distinct Aristocracies'" (Ph.D. diss., Johns Hopkins University, 1986); Margaret Leech, *Reveille in Washington, 1860–1865* (New York, 1962 [1941]); and *The WPA Guide to Washington, D.C.* (New York, 1983 [1942]).

Among journalists' biographies, those I found most helpful are "The National Intelligencer and Its Editors," *Atlantic Monthly* 6 (October 1860); Charles C. Clayton, *Little Mack, Joseph B. McCullagh of the St. Louis Globe-Democrat* (Carbondale, 1969); Bingham Duncan, *Whitelaw Reid: Journalist, Politician, Diplomat*

(Athens, 1975); Robert Franklin Durden, *James Shepherd Pike: Republicanism and the American Negro, 1850–1882* (Durham, 1957); Joseph Logsdon, *Horace White, Nineteenth Century Liberal* (Westport, 1971); Joseph P. McKerns, "Benjamin Perley Poore of the *Boston Journal:* His Life and Times as a Washington Correspondent, 1850–1887" (Ph.D. diss., University of Minnesota, 1979); James Sayler, "Window on an Age: Arthur Krock and the New Deal Era, 1929–1941 (Ph.D. diss., Rutgers University, 1978); Josephine Seaton, *William Winston Seaton and the National Intelligencer* (New York, 1970 [1871]); Wayne C. Temple and Justine G. Turner, "Lincoln's 'Castine,' Noah Brooks," *Lincoln Herald* 72 (Fall 1970); Marion Tinling, "Thomas Lloyd's Reports of the First Federal Congress," *William and Mary Quarterly* 18 (October 1961).

The Washington correspondents offered their own commentary through their essays. In addition to occasion pieces in newspapers, I drew particularly on the following journal articles: "Reminiscences of James M. Dalzell," *Records of the Columbia Historical Society* (Washington, 1925); David S. Barry, "The Loyalty of the Senate," *New England Magazine* 35 (October 1906) and 35 (November 1906), "News-Gathering at the Capital," *Chautauqua* 22 (December 1897), and "Over the Hill to Demagoguery," *New Outlook* 161 (February 1933); Henry Van Ness Boynton, "The Press and Public Men," *Century Magazine* 42 (October 1891); Theron C. Crawford, "The Special Correspondents at Washington," *Cosmopolitan* 12 (January 1892); J. L. H., "A Woman's Experience of Newspaper Work," *Harper's Weekly* 34 (25 January 1890); Newbold Noyes, "Crosby Stuart Noyes: His Life and Times," *Records of the Columbia Historical Society* (Washington, 1940); Richard V. Oulahan, "Gathering the News at Washington," *Quill* 9 (April 1921), and "What the President Can and Cannot Do," *Ladies Home Journal*, October 1908; James Parton, "Falsehoods in the Daily Press," *Harper's Monthly* 49 (July 1874), "Log-Rolling at Washington," *Atlantic Monthly* 141 (July 1869), and "The Small Sins of Congress," *Atlantic Monthly* 145 (November 1869); Ben: Perley Poore, "The Capital at Washington," *Century Magazine* 3 (April 1883), and "Washington News," *Harper's Magazine* 48 (January 1874); Francis A. Richardson, "Recollections of a Washington Newspaper Correspondent," *Records of the Columbia Historical Society* (Washington, 1903); George Alfred Townsend, "Recollections and Reflections," *Lippincott's Monthly Magazine* 38 (November 1886); Julian Wilcox,

"Journalism as a Profession," *Galaxy* 4 (November 1867); T. T. Williams, "Temptations of a Young Journalist," *Cosmopolitan* 40 (April 1906).

Correspondents' memoirs, collected letters, and other related publications include David S. Barry, *Forty Years in Washington* (New York, 1924); Emily Edson Briggs, *The Olivia Letters* (New York, 1906); Noah Brooks, *Statesmen: Men of Achievement* (New York, 1883); Joseph T. Buckingham, *Personal Memoirs and Recollections of Editorial Life* (Boston, 1852), and *Specimens of Newspaper Literature: With Personal Memoirs, Anecdotes, and Reminiscences* (Boston, 1850); Frank Carpenter, *Carp's Washington* (New York, 1960); Turner Catledge, *My Life and the Times* (New York, 1971); Delbert Clark, *Washington Dateline* (New York, 1941); Louis A. Coolidge and James Burton Reynolds, *The Show at Washington* (Washington, 1894); Theron Clark Crawford, *James G. Blaine: A Study of His Life and Career* (Philadelphia, 1893); Charles A. Dana, *Recollections of the Civil War* (New York, 1898); Oscar King Davis, *Released for Publication: Some Inside Political History of Theodore Roosevelt and His Times, 1898–1918* (Boston, 1925); D. F. Drinkwater, *Letters to the Connecticut Courant. . .* (Washington, 1867); J. Frederick Essary, *Covering Washington: Government Reflected to the Public in the Press, 1822–1926* (Boston, 1927); Lawrence A. Gobright, *Recollections of Men and Things at Washington, during the Third of a Century* (Philadelphia, 1869); Horace Greeley, *Recollections of a Busy Life* (New York, 1868); Gail Hamilton [Abigail Dodge], *Biography of James G. Blaine* (Norwich, 1895), and *Gail Hamilton's Life in Letters* (Boston, 1901); [Rollin H. Kirk], *Many Secrets Revealed; or, Ten Years behind the Scenes in Washington City* (Washington, 1885); Arthur Krock, *The Consent of the Governed, and Other Deceits* (Boston, 1971), and *Memoirs: Sixty Years on the Firing Line* (New York, 1968); Edward G. Lowry, *Washington Close-Ups: Intimate Views of Some Public Figures* (Boston, 1921); Louis Ludlow, *From Cornfield to Press Gallery: Adventures and Reminiscences of a Veteran Washington Correspondent* (Washington, 1924); Edward Winslow Martin [James Dabney McCabe], *Behind the Scenes in Washington* (New York, 1873); Ralph McKenzie, *Washington Correspondents, Past and Present* (New York, 1903); [Drew Pearson and Robert S. Allen], *Washington Merry-Go-Round* (New York, 1931); James S. Pike, *First Blows of the Civil War* (New York,

1879); Ben: Perley Poore, *Perley's Reminiscences of Sixty Years in the National Metropolis*, 2 vols. (Philadelphia, 1886–1887); Ishbel Ross, *Ladies of the Press: The Story of Women in Journalism by an Insider* (New York, 1936); Lambert St. Clair, *I've Met the Folks You Read About* (New York, 1940); Nathan Sergeant, *Public Men and Events from the Commencement of Mr. Monroe's Administration, in 1817, to the Close of Mr. Filmore's Administration, in 1853* (Philadelphia, 1875); O. O. Stealey, *The Birth of the Gridiron Club* (Washington, 1927), and *Twenty Years in the Press Gallery* (New York, 1906); Thomas L. Stokes, *Chip off My Shoulder* (Princeton, 1940); Jane Grey Swisshelm, *Half a Century* (Chicago, 1880); Charles Thompson, *Party Leaders of the Time* (New York, 1906); George Alfred Townsend, *Rustics in Rebellion: A Yankee Reporter on the Road to Richmond, 1861–65* (Chapel Hill, 1950), and *Washington, Outside and Inside* (Hartford, 1873); Henry Villard, *Memoirs of Henry Villard, Journalist and Financier, 1835–1900* (Boston, 1904); Henry Watterson, *"Marse Henry": An Autobiography* (New York, 1974 [1919]); Horace White, *The Life of Lyman Trumbull* (Boston, 1913), and *The Lincoln and Douglas Debates* (Chicago, 1914); Franc Wilkie, *Pen and Powder* (Boston, 1888); Mary Jane Windle, *Life in Washington, and Life Here and There* (Philadelphia, 1859); May D. Russell Young, ed., *Men and Memories: Personal Reminiscences by John Russell Young* (New York, 1901).

Correspondents often harbored literary ambitions and used their observations of Washington politics and journalism as the basis for their novels. Revealing fictional depictions of life on Newspaper Row include Frances Hodgson Burnett, *Through One Administration* (New York, 1969 [1883]); Theron Clark Crawford, *A Man and His Soul: An Occult Romance of Washington Life* (New York, 1894); Charles T. Murray, *Sub Rosa* (New York, 1880); and Mark Twain and Charles Dudley Warner, *The Gilded Age* (Seattle, 1968 [1873]).

Index